Luton Sixth Form College
Bradgers Hill Road, Luton Beds. LU2 7EW

Return on or before the last date stamped below

The
Radio Times
Story

by
Tony Currie

Foreword by
John Peel

KELLY PUBLICATIONS
2001

Illustrations in this book are from
Radio Times
unless otherwise indicated,
and are
BBC copyright

Cover design

by
George Mackie

The publishers wish to thank
Radio Times
for their kind permission to reproduce text and illustrations,
and offer our appreciation to all those artists whose work enhances this volume

First published by
KELLY PUBLICATIONS
6 Redlands, Tiverton, Devon EX16 4DH UK
2001

ISBN 1-903053-09-9

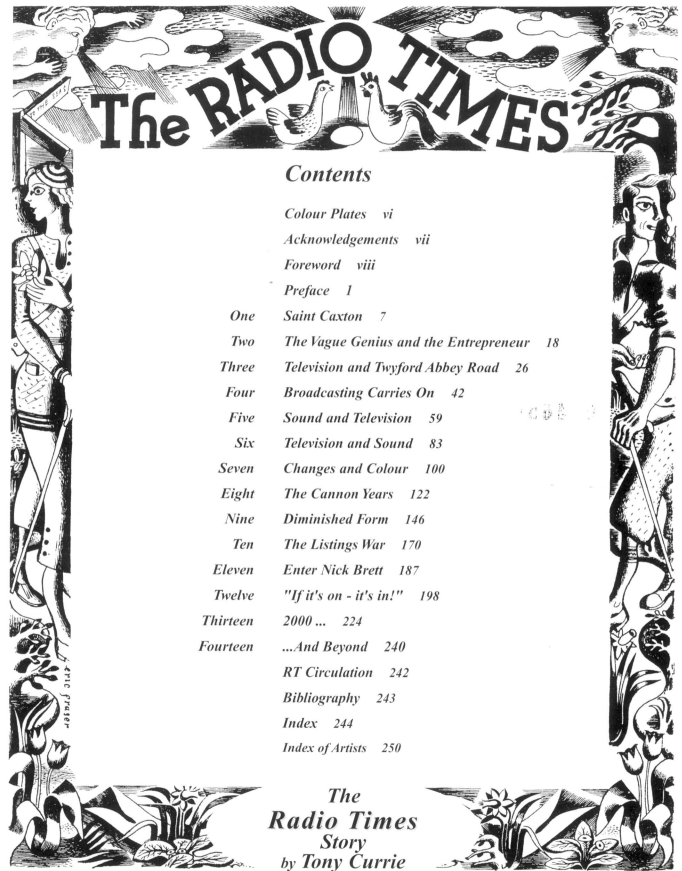

The RADIO TIMES

Contents

The
Radio Times
Story
by Tony Currie

Border by Eric Fraser   April 1928

Colour Plates

This book is dedicated to
Geoff Thompson, Peter Lord, Wallace Grevatt
and everyone else who has treasured even a single issue of
the *Radio Times*
beyond its cover date!

Acknowledgements

19.23 **THE RADIO TIMES**
(to 20.00)   **STORY**
by Tony Currie
Foreword by John Peel
and help from

Managing Editor	Roger Hughes
Past Editor	Nick Brett
Past Editor	Sue Robinson
Former Art Editor	David Driver
Former Billings Editor	Grace Harbinson MBE
Former Billings Editor	Hilary Cope Morgan
Artist	Elizabeth Odling
Son of Artist Eric Fraser	Geoffrey Fraser
Publisher, *Radio Times*	Ashley Munday
Knight in Shining Armour	Paul Taylor
Fairy Godmother	Gillian Reynolds
Granny	Jessie H. Walker

Technical assistance from Leo Currie
The proofs were read by Karin Spalter
Cover design by George Mackie
Book Design and Layout by Lynda Kelly
Executive Producer: Len Kelly
(All reproductions of *Radio Times* in this book are
BBC copyright)

Foreword

by Jonathan Cusick

We probably had one of those embroidery covers for our *Radio Times*. Not one that matched the curtains though - that would have been just a little bit vulgar, wouldn't it? And, in common with most decent folk, I don't suppose we ever actually kept the *Radio Times* in the embroidery cover anyway. I'd like to pretend that I remember my brothers and I rushing, wild-eyed with excitement, to read the latest issue when it was brought up from the village, but I don't. The *Radio Times*, way back in the days before we had television, was just sort of there in the sitting-room; dependable and necessary, but hardly exciting in the way that the *Eagle* or *Film Fun* were exciting or in a way that the comics the American servicemen gave us were exciting. These even *smelled* exciting. I don't remember that the Radio Times smelled at all. But it did tell you what was on *Children's Hour,* and I do remember reading the listings for the Third Programme and believing that when I grew up I would, through processes I couldn't even imagine, listen to and understand talks on 14th Century Flemish poetry. I even imagined settling back of an evening, with a wife and and a few attractive children, to listen to something lively about Ibsen. Or have I just imagined that I imagined that? In the event, none of these things happened. Radio changed, the *Radio Times* changed and I changed. But hardly a day passes without someone in the house shouting, "Anyone seen the *Radio Times*?" That hasn't changed.

John Peel
December 2000

Preface

This is the story of a love affair.

It began in the most unlikely of ways. At the tender age of four I discovered, by experiment, that my Granny's living room carpet rested on a layer of old newspapers, there having been little underfelt around in the bleak days immediately following the Second World War when Granny moved in to her little cottage.

In one particularly accessible corner, just under the standard lamp, I discovered pages of the Christmas *Radio Times* from 1952.

It was now 1956, and already the magazine looked rather different. Whether its festive page decorations, or the significant differences in style attracted my youthful eye I know not. But I can tell you that its discovery signalled open season on floor coverings.

Before long, I had unconsciously become a collector. Not for me the bubble-gum cards, conkers or stamps of my contemporaries. I was the proud possessor of a pile of smelly, tattered, incomplete issues of *The Radio Times* from 1951 to 1954. Of course it was still necessary to acquire the ability to read - a skill gained in no small part by my constant perusal of precious newsprint.

I can still recall running excitedly into my Primary 1 classroom on Thursdays to tell Miss Miller, "Today's the day we get the *Radio Times*!"

As with all true loves, the initial passion has never dimmed, and over the years I have come to know every nuance of my love's life and times. A cellarful of paper and memorabilia, an indulgent wife and family, and successive editors of that fine paper will all testify to that! But why *Radio Times* rather than *The Dandy* or *Superman* or *New Musical Express*?

Magazines may come and go, but for the past 77 years *Radio Times* has occupied a unique position in millions of households throughout the British Isles.

To turn the yellowing pages of its 300+ volumes is to tap into a social history of Britain from genteel Edwardian times to the in-yer-face age of the internet. A chronicle of how the vast majority of citizens of these islands has been spending leisure time - from fiddling with cat's whiskers in 1923 in an effort to capture the tinny sounds of the Savoy Orpheans band on a pair of headphones laid in a biscuit tin, to hanging on the latest digital widescreen colour NICAM stereo goings-on in Albert Square in 2000.

As a leading patron of modern graphic art from its inception, the *Radio Times* pages are scattered with a rich blend of contemporary drawings, sketches, decorations and cartoons - not to mention photographs of the century's (however fleeting) famous.

CHRISTMAS DAY morning and afternoon

me Service

(809 kc/s)

1.0 Greenwich Time Signal
NEWS

1.10 ITMA
Scapa Flow
Ted Kavanagh introduces a re-
broadcast of the programme
recorded during a visit to the
Home Fleet on January 11, 1944
Tommy Handley
Horace Percival, Bryan Herbert
Bill Stephens, Dorothy Summers
Dino Galvani, Jean Capra
Paula Green, Sydney Keith
Fred Yule
Musicians of the Home Fleet
Conducted by Charles Shadwell
Script and lyrics by Ted Kavanagh
Produced by Francis Worsley
(BBC recording)

1.40 RAWICZ and LANDAUER
on two pianos
in a programme of unbroken
melody especially for you
(BBC recording)

2.0 THE
QUEEN'S INHERITANCE
See foot of page and page 6

3.0 H.M. THE QUEEN

3.15 DENIS MATTHEWS
(piano)
Sonata No. 30, in A............Haydn
Three Fantasies, Op. 16...Mendelssohn
Ballade in G minor, Op. 23......Chopin

3.45 TWENTY QUESTIONS
Challenge Match
The resident team:
Anona Winn, Joy Adamson
Jack Train, Richard Dimbleby
versus
Radio personalities
Audrey Russell, Margot Holden
Robert MacDermot, John Ellison
In the chair, Gilbert Harding
(BBC recording)
(' Twenty Questions' is broadcast by
arrangement with Maurice Winnick; Mar-
got Holden is appearing at the Windmill
Theatre, London)

4.30 IN ALL DIRECTIONS
with
Peter Ustinov, Peter Jones
and the Aeolian Players
Written by
Peter Ustinov and Peter Jones
Edited by
Frank Muir and Denis Norden
Produced by Pat Dixon
(Yesterday's recorded broadcast)

Programmes from 5.0 overleaf

In Other Home Services

LONDON (330 m.; 908 kc/s)
9.30-10.15 Service from Timbercombe
Parish Church, near Minehead,
Somerset: the Rev. Canon S. E.
Swann.

N. IRELAND (261 m.; 1,151 kc/s)
9.30-10.15 As Scottish.

WELSH (341 m.; 881 kc/s)
9.30-9.45 Christmas Greetings in
Welsh from people abroad.
9.45-10.15 Gwasanaeth Nadolig.

'O come, all ye faithful'

9.0 a.m. Big Ben
NEWS

9.10 CHILDREN'S CHOICE
...s introduces
request records for the
younger generation

9.55 FIVE TO TEN
A story, a hymn, and a prayer

10.0 Greenwich Time Signal
SOLDIERS
OF THE QUEEN
A Christmas Ceremonial
with
The State Trumpeters
of the Household Cavalry;
The Life Guards
and The Royal Horse Guards
(The Blues)
The Massed Bands of the
Brigade of Guards:
Band of the Grenadier Guards
Band of the Coldstream Guards
Band of the Scots Guards
Band of the Irish Guards
Band of the Welsh Guards
Corps of Drums of the
3rd Btn. Coldstream Guards
Pipes and Drums of the
2nd Btn. The Scots Guards
Introduced by Peter Madden
Produced by Harry Mortimer
(BBC recording)

10.30 THE BILLY COTTON
BAND SHOW
presenting the
Tunes of the Year
with Alan Breeze
and Doreen Stephens
Script by Clem Bernard
Produced by Glyn Jones
(BBC recording)

Light Pro
1,500 m. (200 kc/s)

11.0 CHRISTMAS AT SANDY'S
Sandy Macpherson invites you to
the theatre-organ studio for half
an hour
His guests include:
Ada Alsop, Scott Joynt
Gerald Shaw and Charles Smart

11.30 CHRISTMAS
SERVICE
Good Christian men, rejoice
With heart and soul and voice
Give ye heed to what we say:
Jesus Christ is born today
From the Parish Church of
Menston - in - Wharfedale, York-
shire, Conducted by the Vicar,
the Rev. T. C. Hammond
Organist, Hugh F. Gadsby

12.0 FAMILY
FAVOURITES
From the Forces
Gramophone records chosen by
Servicemen in Hong Kong,
Malaya, Korea, and the Middle
East, with each tune introduced
by the man who chose it, in re-
cordings made on the spot
In London, Jean Metcalfe
Another programme tomorrow at 12.0

1.0 WELSH RAREBIT
with Gladys Morgan
Harry Secombe, Dorothy Squires
Ossie Morris, Ann Walters
The Cardiff Snowflakes Choir
(Continued in next column)

AT TWO O'CLOCK
'The Queen's Inheritance'
A WORLD-WIDE SEQUENCE
OF CHRISTMAS GREETINGS AND GOODWILL
Narrator: Robert Donat
Music composed by William Alwyn
London Symphony Orchestra conducted by John Hollingsworth
PRODUCTION BY LAURENCE GILLIAM AND ALAN BURGESS
★
AT THREE O'CLOCK
A CHRISTMAS MESSAGE
TO THE COMMONWEALTH BY
Her Majesty
THE QUEEN

THIS Christmas Day Queen Elizabeth the Second
inherits and renews the tradition of royal broadcasts at Christmas to the peoples of the Commonwealth. For the first time since, when broadcasting from
South Africa on her twenty-first birthday, Her Majesty
as it was ... her life to their service, her peoples have their
(Recorded) to pledge themselves in their turn. From
To be ... nent in the world, from Dominions, Colonies,
... ome country, from Servicemen in Korea, from
ships ... sea and airmen in flight, the voices of men,
women, and children of the Commonwealth are linked
together by radio in one great family of peoples, to
exchange Christmas greetings and to send pledges of their
love and loyalty to their young Queen
★
Laurence Gilliam describes the scope of the broadcast in
an illustrated article on pages 6 and 7

Rescued from under the carpet   ***Issue 1519   19 Dec 1952***

By no means immune to the whims of fashion, its style and content reflect prevailing tastes in literary and artistic makeup, as its pages transmute from grey regimented blocks of type, screen printed on rough pulp to fine colour on forest-friendly glossy art paper.

It is one of the greatest successes in publishing history. At an educated estimate, some ten billion copies have been circulated - one issue alone selling over eleven million in 1988, enough to earn it a place in the *Guinness Book of Records* as the biggest-selling edition of any publication in British history. Yet the tale of this unique periodical has hitherto remained untold.

And it all started because of an ultimatum........

The British Broadcasting Company was born out of necessity.

A number of British manufacturers had begun to sell sets of parts from which the purchaser could construct a wireless receiver. Indeed, a few even supplied this new-fangled device ready made.

But the proud owners of these shiny new toys were to be disappointed once the thrill of joining all the bits together had subsided. There was almost nothing to be heard, save a few bits of Morse code and the occasional test transmission. The ether was far from alive with the sound of music.

What was needed to boost this fledgling industry was a supply of broadcasts: a national chain of radio transmitters putting out noises that potential purchasers might consider worth the effort of obtaining a set in order to hear. Accordingly, the manufacturers got together and united under the banner of the BBC. It was a commercial necessity. And the BBC was a commercial organisation.

Its first general manager, a dour and complex Scotsman with impossibly high ideals, was John Reith. He ran the BBC as if it had received its mandate to broadcast to the peoples of these islands from none lower than The Almighty. Indeed, he often convinced those with whom he came into contact of the BBC's Divine Commission.

He did not, however, have much success with the Newspaper Proprietors' Association.

This trade body - which, ironically, existed to serve the collective commercial interests of its members in exactly the same way as the BBC did for the radio manufacturers - took umbrage at Reith's expectation that the BBC's daily programme schedules be printed, as a matter of right, in their members' publications.

In fact, since the BBC had begun its daily broadcast programmes in 1922 some newspapers had indeed devoted space to the printing of the daily programmes, without charge, starting with *The Times* which, from New Year's Day 1923, devoted a mere two inches of type to the BBC's daily listings. This of course was all the space that was required, since the London station merely broadcast Children's Hour from 5.00 to 5.45pm, and then after a break of three-quarters of an hour just fifty-five minutes' worth of orchestral music!

But on 13th January 1923 the NPA gave notice to the BBC, that in future it would have to pay normal advertising rates if it desired to see its schedules in print. Not unreasonably, the NPA took the view that, as a commercial broadcasting company with excellent prospects, it should pay its way like anybody else.

Unsurprisingly, Reith took an altogether contrary view. From the lofty heights of his office - in the BBC's first home on the Thames embankment at Savoy Hill - he could readily see that including his programme information in a newspaper was very likely to increase its readership. And so he refused to negotiate with the NPA.

Luckily for Reith the millionaire proprietor of *Selfridge's*, Gordon Selfridge, was a wireless enthusiast with considerably more vision than the NPA: he offered to include programme listings for the BBC's London station, 2LO, as part of Selfridge's regular advertisements in the London evening paper, the *Pall Mall Gazette*.

The studio at 2LO

The result of this unexpected outlet was that circulation of the *Pall Mall Gazette* took a spectacular upturn; the NPA capitulated, and the radio listings returned to the daily press. Reith was jubilant. "They have made proper fools of themselves," he wrote of the NPA in his diary entry for 21st February 1923.

During this forty-day storm in a teacup Reith had hatched the idea of printing and publishing the programme details for all of the BBC's broadcasting stations throughout the British Isles in one organ of its own.

By 10th May Reith had persuaded his Board of Directors to adopt a resolution that

> The General Manager makes the appointment of an individual to deal with propaganda publicity and the production of a magazine.

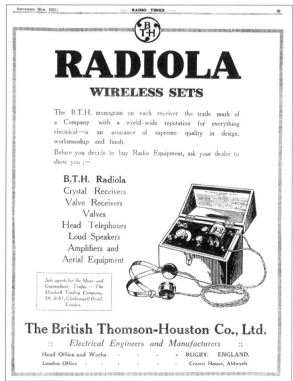

Advertisement from the first issue

With hindsight, it is ironic to discover that when Reith sought a publisher willing to undertake production of his wireless paper on the basis of a share of profits and a minimum annual sum guaranteed to the BBC, only one was immediately willing to take the risk. That firm was George Newnes Ltd, best known as publishers of the frivolous popular weekly *Tit-Bits*.

The deal they agreed gave them two-thirds of the profits up to a certain point and half thereafter, with a guarantee of £1,000 a year to the BBC in any event.

Somewhat surprisingly - in view of Reith's tendency to want everything to do with the BBC under his complete and personal control - editorial control was left entirely in the hands of Newnes, with the BBC merely supplying programme listings and information.

With a relatively short lead time for the production of the first edition, Newnes opted not to advertise for an editor, but seconded one of its most reliable men, Leonard Crocombe, who had edited *Tit-Bits* since 1918 (which he continued to do until 1945) as well as the first paper aimed at filmgoers, launched in 1913.

Crocombe's knowledge and experience of the popular press were crucial in allowing him to get the format for *The Radio Times* right first time without recourse to Audience Profiles, Focus Groups or Branding Consultants.

In the matter of advertising sales though, *The Radio Times* did not receive an easy passage. Vested interests were to see to that.

The radio industry - chiefly the BBC's own shareholders - insisted that *The Radio Times* must not carry advertisements which encouraged wireless enthusiasts to purchase separate components with which to construct their own sets. The publishers of other wireless magazines and papers had to be reassured that the *The Radio Times* didn't set out to compete with them, and would not contain detailed technical articles.

Fortunately this left the door open for the founding companies of the BBC to push their wireless wares - alongside cigarette manufacturers, book publishers, and the manufacturers who suggested that *The Radio Times* readers could make their wireless set...

...as ornamental as it is amusing and instructive if the woodwork is treated regularly with RONUK SANITARY FLOOR POLISH. (It is equally good for all exposed vulcanite parts).

Doubtless aided by a case or two of RONUK, the first issue was a *tour de force*.

Radio Times
Editors

Leonard Crocombe	1923	–	1926
Walter Fuller	1926	–	1927
Eric Maschwitz	1927	–	1933
Maurice Gorham	1933	–	1941
Gordon Stowell	1941	–	1944
Tom Henn	1944	–	1954
Douglas Williams	1954	–	1968
C. J. Campbell Nairne	1968	–	1969
Geoffrey Cannon	1969	–	1979
Brian Gearing	1979	–	1988
Nicholas Brett	1988	–	1996
Sue Robinson	1996	–	2000
Nicholas Brett	2000	–	

Border by Victor Reinganum   From cover of issue 1858   19 June 1959

CHAPTER ONE
Saint Caxton

Leonard Crocombe had long been fascinated by the wireless.

Drop capitals by T. C. Derrick 1927/28

Before the radio manufacturers formed their broadcasting alliance, there had been assorted experiments in using wireless telephony (hitherto considered only to be of major use in one-to-one communications) as a means of broadcasting information and entertainment to an audience of *more* than one.

The first of these experiments had been from the Marconi Company's station 2MT, based in a rather unremarkable wooden hut at Writtle near Chelmsford in Essex. It began broadcasting a weekly half-hour of what we might today recognise as 'programmes' on 14th February 1922.

Running the show, as it were, was a team of bright young men that included Peter Eckersley who was the head of Marconi's experimental section. His task in developing the material they transmitted involved overcoming such impossible obstacles as the Post Office licence requirement that the station should shut down for a three-minute break after every three minutes of transmission. This was apparently so that they could listen out for official orders to stop broadcasting if they were interfering with 'more important services'. (Many painstaking hours of listening failed to discern any such a request).

Eckersley applied his born sense of showmanship (a skill not often found in a radio engineer) and, one day, instead of just playing gramophone records, he approached the crude microphone and began to talk to it. (He later confessed to having been assisted by a visit to 'the local' en route to the hut.)

> A certain ebullience, which often overcomes me when I have an audience, prompted a less formal attitude towards the microphone than was customary.

The delighted looks on the faces of his colleagues made him

Peter Eckersley

> ...more exuberantly informal than I had perhaps intended. I failed to play all the records, even though we never shut down for the regulation three minutes, and I went on talking and talking, convincing myself that I was being very funny.

In the sober and less than ebullient light of the following day, Eckersley was less convinced and began to worry about the responses he might receive in the mail.

> There was to my relief, only one protest and that could hardly be counted against me because it came from Head Office and was signed by Arthur Burrows, head of the Publicity Department, who had been shocked by my frivolity. Fifty or more postcards from ordinary listeners testified that 'a good time was had by all'. The theme of the fan mail was 'Do it again, we like it'.

As the broadcasting progressed, Eckersley and his pals became more outrageous, even writing their own theme song to the tune of Tosti's *Goodbye*:

> Dearest, the concert's ended, sad wails the heterodyne.
> You must soon switch off your valves, I must soon switch off mine.
> Write back and say you heard me, your 'hook up' and where and how,
> Quick! for the engine's failing, goodbye you old low-brow.

One of Eckersley's fans was Crocombe who had written enthusiastically about the pioneering broadcasts in *Tit-Bits*. Subsequently, fired by the idea that *Tit-Bits* should sponsor some programmes of its own, Crocombe variously worried the folk at 2MT, the Chief Engineer of the Post Office and even the Postmaster-General himself to get permission to contribute a programme under the auspices of his own paper.

Leonard Crocombe

> They refused. It was an advertisement. (I knew that!) I kept on worrying, however, until at last, probably to get rid of me as a pest, I was invited by the British Broadcasting Company to broadcast from 2LO.
>
> That turn was given on March 14th, 1923, from the top of Marconi House; I contributed a talk, alleged to be funny, month by month from each of the six stations of those days.

Crocombe's aspirations to become a broadcaster fulfilled, his enthusiasm waxed. He went on to make further broadcasts in North America, and continued to feature articles about broadcasting in *Tit-Bits* at every opportunity.

As Reith concluded his arrangements with Newnes, Crocombe was being primed to take charge. Ten years later Crocombe himself wrote:

> *Radio Times* began, for me, with the tinkle of my 'phone bell one summer morning in 1923. The mellifluent tones of my friend, Arthur R. Burrows, then Director of Programmes, [who had been shocked by Eckersley's frivolity] spoke to me: would I lunch with him that day? He had something important to discuss. We met at Simpson's.
>
> The important matter that Burrows wished to discuss was the scheme by which my employers were to publish *The Radio Times* in collaboration with the B.B.C. I was then, as now, the editor of *Tit-Bits*.
>
> So I hurried back to the office, sought the ear of Big Business [in the human form of his Managing Director, Lord Riddell] and registered my own enthusiasm.
>
> A few weeks later, I returned from a month's holiday in Belgium, with my mind full of my own job, to be told that I was also the Editor of *The Radio Times* - with a colleague, Herbert Parker, a nephew of the Right Hon. J. R. Clynes M.P., to look after the policy end for the B.B.C.; moreover it had been decided by the B.B.C. that the first number of *The Radio Times* must be ready for press in seven days.
>
> And, by Saint Caxton, we did it!

Why Newnes had not wired for Crocombe to return from his holiday earlier, he never discovered. But he had little time to ponder such questions:

> ...it was not many hours before our excellent Master Printer, Mr. Bauser, was 'phoning to ask for 'make-up' and some 'copy' to start work on. There was no time to work out an original 'make-up' or to choose types, so the printer was told that 'make-up' and types were to follow the style of *John o'London's Weekly*, a Newnes periodical.

*   *   *   *   *

Crocombe recruited a solitary editorial assistant. "Do you know anything about wireless?" he asked Charles Tristram at his job interview on an autumn afternoon in 1923. "Discovered by Marconi, wasn't it?" answered Tristram, "Used to transmit codes, or something?"

His vagueness didn't daunt Crocombe, who asked Tristram if he'd care to join the editorial staff.

"It sounded all right," wrote Tristram afterwards, "and I agreed, little dreaming that this was the beginning of the most interesting twenty-one years of my life."

In those seven days Crocombe, Tristram, and Herbert Parker went into top gear to sort out features, advertisements, and of course the all-important billings for the programmes of the six BBC stations - 2LO London, 5WA Cardiff, 5IT Birmingham, 5NO Newcastle, 2ZY Manchester and 5SC Glasgow.

Crocombe decided on a weekly front-page feature with the heading *What's In the Air?* (He later described it as "a bad title!") The ubiquitous Reith was invited to pen 1200 words every week for this purpose, but for its debut, Crocombe's pal, Arthur Burrows, was asked to make the initial contribution to this regular feature.

Radio Times   Issue 1   28 Sept 1923

Burrows' style was rather more informal than that of his General Manager, and he began:

HULLO EVERYONE!

We will now give you *The Radio Times.* The good *new* times. The Bradshaw of Broadcasting.

May you never be late for your favourite wave-train.

Speed 186,000 miles per second; five-hour non-stops.

Family season ticket: First Class, 10s. per year.

*   *   *   *

[All this, presumably, is "by the way"; not "In . the. Air." — EDITOR]

*   *   *   *

So I am instructed to write about programmes and not "talk like an Uncle"!

*   *   *   *

Let me tell you about our plans.

Wait, though! I–I'm just a little bit uneasy. My predecessor in the broadcasting business made a mistake of this character with painful consequences.

You probably remember the incident.

A Company, with distinguished Directors, having lofty ambitions, established a power-station at Westminster. Despite quite a stirring programme there were no oscillations, owing to the government intervention. The Director (Guido Fawkes) and his colleagues somehow lost their heads, and the long-anticipated report failed to materialise.

When WE broadcast Parliament - and it's bound to happen this century or next - the process will be a more dignified one than that planned in 1605. The fate of the culprits may be another matter.

*   *   *   *

Arthur R. Burrows

We must assume that Messrs Bradshaw were flattered that Burrows sought to make comparisons with their popular railway timetables!

Opening up issue one the reader would discover first a reprint of Major A. Ratclyffe Dugmore's broadcast talk on *Photographing Wild Animals.* But there was much else to digest. A background piece to the broadcast of a new song by composer Hayter Preston to be transmitted that week; a page of gossip and photographs "about artistes and others"; a handful of shorter pieces concerning such matters as *Wireless and Writers, Other People's Opinions,* and *The Choice of Receiving Set.*

The BBC's chairman, Lord Gainford, contributed a message to "Listeners":

This periodical will each week produce in advance the Company's programmes in a compact and attractive form for the convenience of the public. There will therefore be no chance that particularly interesting or unusual programmes will escape notice.

The BBC's musical director, Stanton Jeffries, wrote about *The Broadcasting of Music*; Chief Engineer, Peter Eckersley, wrote an amusing account of the Troubles of Simultaneous Broadcasting which he titled *"What are the Wild Waves Saying?"*

Children were not ignored, for as well as *The Children's Corner - Happy hours to come* (the work of 'Uncle Rex of 2LO' - otherwise chief announcer Rex Palmer), 'Uncle Jack' contributed a column dedicated "To the Kiddies of Newcastle". Other 'uncles' would address other 'kiddies' in issues to come.

That staple diet of all papers - the letters page - was much in evidence in issue one, with a mixture of views that had been received at Savoy Hill. Wisely, Crocombe did not only include messages of support:

In memory of TANNHAUSER Murdered by the London Wireless Orchestra 19th September 1923

The above is a photographic reproduction of a "listener's" postcard. The Director of Programmes does not resent criticism of this kind, and the Editor likes it, for it provides amusing "copy" for *The Radio Times*.

From issue 2
5 Oct 1923

> Frankly it seems to me that the B.B.C. are mainly catering for the "listeners" who own expensive sets and pretend to appreciate and understand only highbrow music and educational "sob stuff." Surely, like a theatre manager, they must put up programmes which will appeal to the majority, and must remember that it is the latter who provide the main bulk of their income.
>
> Yours faithfully,
>
> Birmingham   P.J.

And whither Reith himself in this rich literary mix?

The General Manager - by One Who Knows Him, together with a portrait of Mr. J. C. W. Reith, occupied a single column of the new paper's 36 pages. As to who the 'one who knew him' could have been we can but speculate.....

Into this mixture was sprinkled a few cartoons; a page of funny stories "told by wireless", all demonstrating signs of the new Editor's influence; and a grand competition for readers to vote on their favourite six items from the forthcoming week's broadcasts. The prize fund contained the princely sum of £21, which was to be divided into prizes of £2, £1 and ten shillings awarded to "listeners" of each of the six stations.

(The word "listeners" appeared throughout in inverted commas - clearly it was yet to receive universal approval for its entry into everyday parlance.)

There was even a song: *Across the Bridge of Dreams* (words by Douglas Furber, music by Arthur Baynon) had won £100 in a BBC competition, and the first page of its sheet music was printed in the new publication.

For a paper put together in a week it was a highly readable and witty effort - thanks doubtless to the inspired choice of Crocombe as Editor, who was modest when writing later of his achievements:

John Charles Walsham Reith

> Not a bad effort, I submit, in view of the fact that we had only a week to think it out, gather it together, and put it to press. I had to work at my present job in addition, of course.

Issue 1   Sept 28 1923

But there were still a few details to sort out before the listening public were offered their first opportunity to fork out Two Pence for "The Official Organ of the B.B.C.". Crocombe:

> When the contents of that first number had been settled, the 'copy' written and sub-edited, the illustrations chosen, the blocks made, the first proofs measured and read, there came our press day and the night when the new paper had finally to be 'put to bed'. What a hectic evening it was! For that historic occasion I went to the printing works with Tristram and worked on the proofs until, not far off midnight, the last page proof had been passed and the machines began their wondrous work of printing and stitching the finished copies of *Radio Times* number 1.

It hit the streets on Friday, September 28th 1923, and the modest initial print-run of a quarter of a million copies was quickly sold out.

The Radio Times had arrived!

The twopenny weekly was an instant success. Reith and his colleagues knew that the 250,000 run was much too small. The circulation soon reached the weekly figure of 600,000. Within weeks, more BBC stations had opened in Aberdeen, Bournemouth and Sheffield, all taking their appropriate places on the billings pages, and all adding to the paper's circulation.

From issue number two, Reith was press-ganged into churning out his weekly *What's in the Air?* feature, a task which he described in his diary as "an awful plague". And from the very first he didn't much conceal his feelings from his readers:

> I had hoped to evade active participation in this new venture. I imagined I was already fully busy. The Editor's views and mine apparently differ on what constitutes a week's work. Perhaps, however, he will discover that journalism is not my long suit. I wonder what he will do: there is some delicacy in the position. Perhaps he will come to me and report that he is dissatisfied with the "What's in the Air?" column and ask authority to dispense with the services of the contributor. He will get it.

In contrast to Messrs Crocombe, Eckersley and Burrows, Reith was also inclined to somewhat po-faced and schoolmasterly outbursts. The BBC's First Birthday was celebrated in November, evidently with some gusto:

> I was somewhat vexed by the insinuation made by one correspondent, who made humorous references to bottles consumed on the birthday evening. I hope the spontaneous good spirits of our announcers at 2LO on that occasion were not misinterpreted by any other listeners. This should have gone without saying.

The fee of six guineas per thousand words that Reith was eventually persuaded to accept (retrospectively, for he had begun the column without payment) perhaps eased the task for him a little.

1923 Christmas cover by Abbey

Plate 1a

Crocombe believed that a colourful Christmas front cover could significantly boost the paper's circulation. He risked trebling the cover price for the festive edition, and printed a full-colour cover, with a suitably seasonal design by the artist, Abbey, thereby establishing *The Radio Times'* credentials as a major customer for new British graphic art.

The ploy was successful, and led, not only to a regular colour cover for Christmas (together with its attendant price increase to sixpence), but to the introduction of occasional 'special' issues (at the regular price of 2d) with colour covers during the rest of the year.

Throughout 1924 a new relay station was opened every month, each bringing new listeners and, consequently, new readers. But as the pages became more densely packed with programme details, production of *The Radio Times* became increasingly more complicated. One station reputedly had its week's programmes missed out altogether when it failed to meet the print deadline on time.

by G.S. Sherwood Issue 18 25 Jan 1924

THE WAGNER NIGHT.

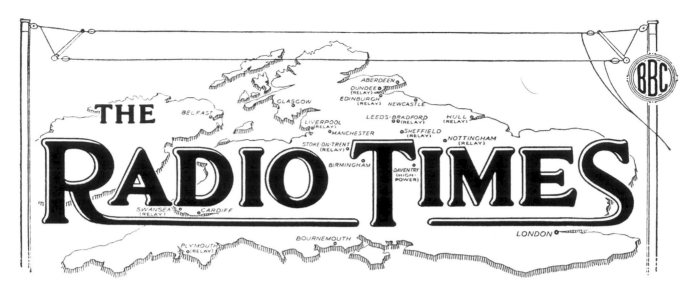

THE OFFICIAL ORGAN OF THE B.B.C.

New masthead
Autumn 1924

The growth of broadcasting had another more immediately obvious effect on *The Radio Times* Its masthead sketch-map of Britain had at first shown just the six stations on air when the paper began - but in the Autumn of 1924 the map was redrafted to include all the stations whose programmes were annotated between its covers. A magnifying glass would have been a useful gift to readers....

The BBC's views on the correct way to run their official organ did not always coincide with those of its Editor, and throughout 1924 and 1925 there were constant disagreements between the BBC and Newnes. Many at Savoy Hill felt the educational content of *The Radio Times* was inadequate, and in particular the diminishing space it allocated for the reprinting of broadcast talks.

There were calls from within for the BBC to publish additional periodicals of a more 'highbrow' nature. Education Director, J. C. Stobart, wanted an educational journal to be titled *The Radio Academy*; Eckersley wanted a serious technical paper; and the music department even went as far as producing a dummy edition of *Radio Music.*

These and other suggestions - including one that each station should be allowed to produce its own periodical - were rejected as being liable to adversely affect the circulation of *The Radio Times* itself.

Herbert Parker wrote a considered memo to BBC top brass, in which he pointed out the obvious - that *The Radio Times* was successful specifically because it understood the "general interests of the ordinary reader" - and urged executives not to rob it of content in order to launch new papers for which the public had not shown any desire.

But, much to Crocombe's relief, Reith himself continued to offer support and understanding of the difficulties of such an undertaking. On the occasion of the paper's first anniversary in 1924, he spelled out his views:

This journal of ours is, we consider, of the very greatest importance to the success of British broadcasting. It should be the connecting link between the broadcaster, individual or corporate, and the great listening public. It is so in great degree already, and by all the means in our power we shall endeavour to make it so in still greater degree. Certain limitations are imposed upon it, most of which we voluntarily accepted owing to the possibility of detriment to established journals which did not possess the fundamental and unique attraction of our comprehensive programme publication.

But we do not wish to feel that the magazine is bought in such large numbers entirely on account of the programmes. This will naturally remain the paramount appeal, but that is not good enough. If the broadcast service is to attain the maximum efficiency, and the listener to reap the greatest benefit, it can only be secured through a considerable degree of intimacy and understanding between the two parties concerned in the undertaking.

The Radio Times goes to every sort of home and is taken by every sort of individual. It cannot therefore be all to one man's taste. The embarrassments of the programme builder encompass also the Editor of this paper, but the same principles are applied by each in the combating of them.

by Abbey

" Imagine her . . . . sitting by the little open fire on which she cooks her meals, with the receiver over her ears, her eyes closed for rest."

At the end of 1924, with another 64-page bumper colour Christmas Issue looming, the BBC appointed a new Director of Publicity - Gladstone Murray - who put forward his own views on ways in which *The Radio Times* could be improved. His suggestion of an 80-page weekly "in the style of America's *Saturday Evening Post*" was turned down by Newnes as impractical. Murray's attempts to find another publisher were abortive, and he realised that Newnes operation was "so good that we should try to retain it".

With ever more transmitters opening and the consequent increasing demands for billings space within the paper's pages, an increase to 52 pages was insufficient to cope. At the end of 1925 two separate editions were introduced: one containing the programmes of the Southern stations; the other detailing those in the North. Both included the programmes of the London stations in full.

But rumblings continued over the thorny issue of editorial control, with the boss of 2LO taking umbrage at *The Radio Times* actively promoting one particular artiste for whom the station itself did not wish to provide any further publicity. Crocombe responded that the paper could not be edited by "a very scattered committee representing various interests".

The press, meanwhile, continued to object strongly to the BBC apparently accepting advertising by the back door, and voiced their opposition to advertisements for *The Radio Times* being broadcast on the BBC's stations.

At the same time the Company's shareholders argued that, by virtue of their special status, they should benefit from some kind of discount when advertising in "their" journal, and that the BBC should use some of the profits it accrued from *The Radio Times* to advertise the merits of broadcasting in other periodicals.

The Radio Times was constantly facing both internal and external pressure, and, as Lord Riddell put it, was far too often "dug up by the roots for examination, refreshment, pruning and reparation". Seasonal fluctuations in its circulation figures caused its masters on the Thames embankment further angst. Lacking the publishing experience to anticipate the winter peaks (750,000 in December '24) and summer troughs (610,000 in August '25) they assumed that their venture was "in a bad way" and in need of more root treatment.

Inevitably, the only treatment that would assure *The Radio Times* continued to grow and flourish was its complete repotting. Whilst the good men at Newnes watered, pruned and attended its needs it was but one plant of many for them. For the BBC it was the whole garden.

THE HEADQUARTERS OF BRITISH BROADCASTING.

SAVOY HILL by Henry Rushbury, A.R.A.
Specially drawn for 'The Radio Times'
Issue 198   15 July 1927

At first, in the autumn of 1925, a herbaceous border, in the form of a two-page 'educational section', was officially made the BBC's sole editorial responsibility. Publicity man Gladstone Murray assumed the role of BBC joint Editor, and immediately received a memo from a journalist colleague reiterating the view that *The Radio Times* couldn't be an "official" organ until the BBC was able to exert "entire editorial control".

The repotting proceeded......

by Fouet

CHAPTER TWO
The Vague Genius and the Entrepreneur

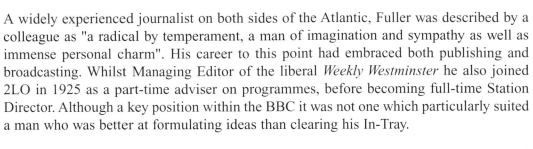

alter Fuller once lost the corrected proofs of an entire issue of *The Radio Times* in the London Underground on his way to the printers.

Aptly described as 'a vague genius', he was the second man to edit the illustrious Journal of the BBC. The first issue to be published under the complete editorial control of the BBC was on the 19th of February 1926.

A widely experienced journalist on both sides of the Atlantic, Fuller was described by a colleague as "a radical by temperament, a man of imagination and sympathy as well as immense personal charm". His career to this point had embraced both publishing and broadcasting. Whilst Managing Editor of the liberal *Weekly Westminster* he also joined 2LO in 1925 as a part-time adviser on programmes, before becoming full-time Station Director. Although a key position within the BBC it was not one which particularly suited a man who was better at formulating ideas than clearing his In-Tray.

When it came to finding a suitable *Radio Times* editor from within the BBC's ranks, 45-year old Fuller was an obvious choice. He set about transforming the production process,

Walter Fuller

delegating various stages to a handful of sub-editors. D. C. Thomson was in charge of Music, and P. Darnell looked after news. Programmes were the responsibility of a Mr. Munn, until August 1926, when H.G. Hodder, who came from the *Morning Post,* replaced him as Programme Editor.

As well as assuming editorial control, the BBC changed its financial arrangements with George Newnes. Instead of sharing the profits, Newnes now received commission on the net receipts from sales and advertisements. The BBC was the benefactor of this new deal, and was able to plough substantial *Radio Times* profits into programme making.

Fuller presided over a minimal staff from his little room on the fourth floor of Number 4 Savoy Hill, overlooking the churchyard. He shared this room with a red-haired lady assistant. Later they were to be joined by Maurice Gorham, a young man who had been on Fuller's staff at the *Weekly Westminster* before moving to the daily *Westminster Gazette.*

Within a few months of the new arrangements there was a general strike, during which the BBC became for the first time the main source of reliable news for the general population.

In common with most magazines and newspapers *The Radio Times* suspended publication, but after missing the issue of 14th May 1926, it returned to tell - in glowing terms - the story of the BBC's role in the strike.

> *"Daventry Sees It Through" - A Tribute by Fred M. White, the Famous Novelist*
> .....all the time there was the man in front of the little box standing there to "speak comfortably to Jerusalem" - an almost Jovian voice telling the King's subjects from Scilly to Shetland to take heart of grace, for all was well and none was going to suffer.

(Presumably the Famous Novelist had never actually tried picking the BBC's transmissions out of the static in these far-flung and, in those days, poorly-served parts of the British Isles.)

Fuller was allowed the editorial freedom to print a highly critical letter from MP Ellen Wilkinson accusing the BBC of giving...

> ...only one side during the dispute. Personally, I feel like asking the Postmaster General for my licence fee back as I can hear enough fairy tales in the House of Commons without paying ten shillings a year to hear more.

However Fuller added a footnote that

> ...we do not believe that [Miss Wilkinson's views] are shared by many people, even among those who are of her political colour.

MYSEL'!
As Sir Harry Lauder sees himself. Specially drawn for "The Radio Times."

by Harry Lauder, himsel'
Issue 143
25 June 1926

One result of the strike was that 24-year old Maurice Gorham found his daily paper shut down, and with the spotlight suddenly thrown on the BBC he decided to join his old boss at Savoy Hill. This move was to be substantially influential on the future of both the *The Radio Times* and the BBC itself.

In June 1926 Gorham was appointed Assistant Editor - on the 'very exceptional' starting salary of £400 a year. He was to be a major influence on the magazine's future.

Maurice Gorham

Because the paper's layout had been perforce modelled on that of another, it had not, under Crocombe, found a unique visual identity of its own. As soon as he took over, Fuller had set about forming such a style, and soon expanded the number of illustrations in the paper.

Crocombe had - for a variety of practical reasons - decided in the early days to restrict programme illustrations to a single page headed *People You Will Hear This Week*. However, the various feature articles were illustrated and, of course, the advertisements. As a result the pages didn't look so terribly bare. But Fuller saw that *The Radio Times* could provide a means of visually complementing the 'sound only' nature of broadcasting as it then was.

So in the summer of 1926, a 'new-look' *Radio Times* was launched. The narrow columns of programme listings were now broken up quite simply by the insertion of a photograph or two - either of those taking part in the broadcasts, or of something relevant to the subject of the broadcast programme itself.

Issue 91   19 June 1925

Illustrated programmes page
Issue 255   17 Aug 1928

Slowly, cartoons and drawings began to appear on the pages, sometimes to decorate the heading for an article; sometimes in place of a straight photograph of a well-known performer; and now and again to provide a whimsical reference to the programme's content.

Of course, *The Radio Times* had unique and crucial access to the programme billings for the BBC's stations. Although newspapers were permitted to print a list of programmes and times, they were forbidden to print anything other than the programmes for the newspaper's day of publication - except for the Saturday papers who were allowed to print Sunday's programmes as well.

But *The Radio Times* had everything a week in advance. Getting it, however, was not always so easy. Apart from the bare times and titles, it was generally up to the paper's staff to winkle more details of the programmes out of the production staff. And they were not always great fans of *RT*.

Within ten days of young Maurice Gorham joining the journal's small staff Walter Fuller fell ill. With no previous knowledge of the inner workings of the BBC, Gorham was left to run the paper. In his memoirs, he recalls a typical incident on his first day as Acting Editor.

> An angry woman burst into the office, stood over me with arms akimbo, abused me for ten minutes without stopping, and flounced out again, all before I had the least idea who she was.

Fuller returned from his sick-bed to oversee the paper's makeover in the summer of 1926. The erudite and enthusiastic Music Editor, Percy Scholes (who retired in 1928), and his private staff wrote the musical annotations - Scholes once described *The Radio Times* as "the musical journal with far-and-away the largest circulation in the world." And, with the aim of enticing the listener to tune in, Gorham found himself responsible for writing a few lines about all the non- musical programmes. He evolved a technique:

Percy Scholes

> From a skeleton billing, one or two names of cast, and a knowledge of the producer, I could glean enough to write about and order illustrations for any show. But that was a last resort. I still spent hours hunting producers, who one and all love publicity but hate getting down to details about what they are going to do.
>
> It was here that the secretaries came in......they were very clever; and whatever else they did, they did the work of two men. If I wanted to find out all about a forthcoming programme, I would be more likely to find the secretary in the office than the producer, and luckier, too. Not only was it more pleasant, but she would probably know more.

Others soon joined Fuller, Scholes and Gorham. Eric Maschwitz was appointed Managing Editor with the task of chivvying the programme departments and negotiating with the business side, whilst giving Fuller more time to sit back and plan ahead. And Val Gielgud, an old and close friend of Maschwitz, was also brought into the little circle, amongst other things editing *What the Other Listener Thinks*.

> I became editor of the Letters page simply by taking the letters out of his [Maschwitz's] tray when he wasn't looking, because I didn't have enough to do. I must admit I wrote most of the letters myself.

Six-foot-two-inches tall, Maschwitz and the slightly shorter Gorham were both bright and witty young men who had the eminent good sense never to take themselves - or what they did - too seriously. This was often to Fuller's consternation!

Around this time Scholes was inspired to suggest the first in a long line of 'Special Issues'. The occasion was the Centenary of Beethoven's death in 1827. The measure of its success was that it became the first number to sell a million copies, and the BBC (in the person of Reith) gave a celebratory lunch to publishers George Newnes (in the person of Newnes chairman Lord Riddell). The latter gave an amusing and what one observer described as "malicious" speech in which he made pointed reference to the *News of the World* (with which he was not unconnected) having an even bigger sale than the *The Radio Times*.

Reith was unsurprisingly unamused by this. But the paper's editor was probably even less amused by the fact that the BBC clearly did not consider his position important enough to bestow the honour of delivering a speech.

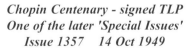

Chopin Centenary - signed TLP
One of the later 'Special Issues'
Issue 1357   14 Oct 1949

Even from its first days the special importance of wireless for listeners who were blind or partially sighted was obvious. For radio was the only medium so far invented that allowed them to enjoy it on equal terms with those with the gift of vision.

The role of *The Radio Times* received appropriate recognition when, in the spring of 1927, an experimental Braille edition was produced under the auspices of the National Institute for the Blind. Its success led to a regular weekly Braille version appearing, starting publication in the first week of May. Copies cost one penny each.

Fuller's ill health persisted. In 1927 he died suddenly from a blood clot on his brain. But his influence extended long after his death - as Percy Scholes said, "I never enter the *Radio Times* office without finding that he is still alive."

Reith appointed Eric Maschwitz as Acting Editor, and Basil Nicolls as General Editor of BBC Publications.

Eric Maschwitz

Nicolls, one time Station Director at Manchester and subsequently the Director at the London Station, was a well-built Oxford graduate with a passion for health, and who had been an administrator in India. Clearly he was expected to rise to the top in the BBC. But he had no experience in magazine or newspaper publishing, and his appointment caused some dismay within the ranks of *The Radio Times*.

by Aubrey Hammond From cover of issue 206 9 Sept 1927

Perhaps inevitably (given his temperament) Gorham was one of the first to clash with Nicolls. The job of sorting out illustrations for the paper had been left to Fuller's red-haired assistant, a task she had been content to share with Gorham. After Fuller's death she left the BBC, and Gorham judged rightly that the time had come for the appointment of a full time Art Editor. However, he rather impertinently suggested to Nicolls that he should not only occupy the position himself, but that he should continue with his other duties on the paper in return for an enhanced salary.

The Opening of the Football Broadcast Season

AUBREY HAMMOND

THE WINNING GOAL!

Nicolls' response was to agree to Gorham's expanded role, but with no alteration to his job title or his salary. Gorham's indignant retort was that he would continue with things the way they already were, thank you, and somebody else could look after the illustrations.

His reply, incidentally, was considered so irregular that the memo was burned instead of being put on file!

But Gorham was not to be defeated. He staged what he described as "a little sit-down strike". Whenever Maschwitz or Nicolls enquired about illustrations, Gorham would say "I'm sorry, that's nothing to do with me" and direct them to his beleaguered assistant, Douglas Graeme Williams.

'THE END OF THE RUN.'   By Rowland Hilder.

This picture, specially drawn for 'The Radio Times' by one of the most talented artists of the new generation, shows one of the great ultra-modern printing presses which turn out many thousand copies of 'The Radio Times' each week. The moment selected by the artist for his drawing is that at which the 'printing run' has just ended, and the tired packers are fastening the last bundles of the paper which, in a few short hours, will be bringing news of the broadcast programmes to listeners throughout the country.

Issue 208
23 Sept 1927

Plate 1b

*Christmas cover
by Edward
McKnight Kauffer
23 Dec 1927*

In fact, Gorham always secretly worked with Williams on the illustrations, and eventually Nicolls caved in. By the end of 1927 Gorham was officially the Art Editor - complete with appropriate remuneration.

Gorham's appointment marked the official beginning of what was to be a key role for *The Radio Times* for over fifty years - as one of the leading patrons of graphic art in the United Kingdom. Increasingly from 1927 the publication would commission original new artwork, not merely to illustrate the programme pages, but for covers, feature headings and illustrations, and latterly for the famous decorative borders that signalled high days and holidays within the programme pages.

The Radio Times amassed a large repertory company of illustrators, many of whom we will meet in later chapters. But undoubtedly the most enduring of these was involved right from the start.

BOTH SIDES OF
THE MICROPHONE

Eric Fraser was born in 1902, and trained as an artist at Goldsmith's College in London's East End in the early 1920s. When he left, R.P. Glossop, who had just started an agency for artists, took him on, and it was Glossop who introduced Eric Fraser to the BBC's Journal. The association was a fortunate one for both men for the next fifty odd years. Fraser's first illustration for *RT* (a humorous drawing of a family sitting together to 'listen-in') was printed in 1926 and his last in 1982, shortly before his death the following year.

Eric Fraser's last illustration for **Radio Times** *- 1982*

Fraser was just the first in a long line of distinguished draughtsmen and women whose work adorned the pages of the world's first listings magazine.

The sought-after commissions to draw for *RT* were never handed out by telephone. Another artist whose work has adorned the pages for many years, Victor Reinganum, describes the arrangement:

Gorham never commissioned by telephone, you would just get a message to come down and see him. But time was very tight then, as I believe it is now, for an illustrator. One had to work over the weekend and deliver the drawing on Monday morning, but I'm very glad that I had that sort of training because it was an extremely good discipline. This sort of short-order working didn't happen only with *Radio Times*, the advertising agencies always needed their work in a frantic hurry too.

Three guineas was the going rate and, in real money terms, I think it was rather better paid then than its illustrators are now. I lived fairly comfortably on about six guineas a week while supporting a wife and two children.

History does not relate the kind of reception Fraser's agent R. P. Glossop got when he visited Savoy Hill, but another of the agents, Jack Wall (who was, in his spare time, a successful rugby player) often found an argument about fees ended with him wrestling on the floor with Gorham and Williams before being violently hurled out into the corridor, followed by his hat. The bright young men of *The Radio Times* clearly had much raw energy to spare, until the day that Williams and Wall nearly injured themselves on the sharp-edged open drawer of a filing cabinet - after which Gorham banned fighting in his office on the principal that "it would look bad if one of them got killed". Wall, incidentally, benefitted in the end when he married Gorham and Williams' tall, slim and beautiful part-time secretary, Vere Bland, a star of staff revues.

BOTH SIDES OF THE MICROPHONE

by TP
1928

Meanwhile, Maschwitz ran a less violent but equally colourful office. He was at the time married to Hermione Gingold who was to become a major star. And his social circle evidently included many other showbiz personalities.

After he left the BBC in 1937 to write for the stage, Maschwitz's marriage ended, and a string of affairs with fashionable actresses followed. After the war broke out he was employed by MI5 to recruit potential saboteurs in the event of a German occupation, and later joined the SOE, in the rank of Lieutenant Colonel, working on black propaganda against the Germans. He also wrote some of the most enduring songs of the period: *These Foolish Things, Goodnight Vienna* and *A Nightingale Sang in Berkeley Squar*e. He was largely responsible for 'popularising' the paper during his time as editor. In 1928 he wrote:

> My ambition for the Radio Times is no purely journalistic or commercial one (my own belief in, and enthusiasm for Broadcasting would never permit this) but I should be doing less than my duty by the paper if I did not wish both its circulation and its revenue to be as great as possible.

Val Gielgud left his job as Personal Assistant to Maschwitz to become the distinguished radio drama producer, and was replaced by the impulsive C. Henry Warren - who regularly rushed home

at lunchtime to play his piano in order to relieve the stress of working for the BBC. The Business Manager was the jovial and robustly built Guy Rice, formerly secretary to the British Broadcasting Company, another of the team who didn't take his work too seriously, and devoted much of his energy to yachting and practical jokes.

If illustrations were to be one of the most distinctive features of this unique publication, there was another element that would, in time, ensure *The Radio Times* a place in history.

Yet when it came along for the first time, it was but a few lines of type, buried in the day's listings...

'Physical Jerks to Music.'

Three drawings by Arthur Watts for
BOTH SIDES OF THE MICROPHONE

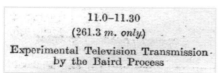

11.0–11.30
(261.3 *m. only*)
Experimental Television Transmission
by the Baird Process

Half an hour of blurred and rather wobbly 30-line pictures transmitted mid-morning without any sound certainly didn't merit more than three lines of highly sought-after space in the programme pages. But those three lines established *The Radio Times* as the world's first *Television* listings magazine.

There was much more to follow!

CHAPTER THREE
Television and Twyford Abbey Road

o begin with, the BBC hierarchy was less than impressed by the experiments being conducted by an eccentric Scots inventor, John Logie Baird. True, he made pictures move on a postcard-sized screen, but they were flickering and fuzzy, and the BBC was concerned that its reputation for the highest technical standards might be compromised if it allowed itself to be associated with the 30-line television trials.

An unofficial accomodation, whereby Baird's pictures were fed by telephone line to the BBC and rebroadcast over its transmitters, ended abruptly in 1926 when the arrangement was discovered by Reith.

Although we will perhaps never know the full extent of Reith's jealousy of Baird, a number of contemporary commentators have suggested that there was substantial animosity between the two Scotsmen. It is certainly ironic that two of Scotland's most prominent sons were unable to cooperate. Baird was forced to install his own broadcasting transmitter and aerial (callsign 2TV) and conducted his tests alone until September 1929 when 2LO began to officially transmit experimental television pictures.

**2LO
365 M.**

The Reproduction of these Copyright Programmes is strictly reserved.

The colourful electronic adventures of the 'vision warrior' from Helensburgh are recounted in a variety of volumes but they all reveal a curious amnesia on the part of the BBC when it comes to the origins of its own Television Service.

Official Corporation histories all point to the 'Television Service' beginning in November 1936. Yet the pages of the *Radio Times* from 1929 onwards are littered with references to television broadcasts. At first these were relays from the Baird Television Company's studios in London's Long Acre, but in May 1932, shortly after the BBC moved from Savoy Hill to its new purpose-built headquarters in Portland Place, the corporation built its first television studio in Broadcasting House, and appointed Douglas Birkinshaw as its first television engineer.

by Eric Fraser
Issue 313   27 Sept 1929

Eric Fraser, in mediæval mood, has here shown Walter in the pond, Walter haranguing the deaf gentleman, Walter walloping the bad boy, and Walter back again before the microphone—all in one picture.

THE DAY OF REST.
Sunday's Special Programmes.
From 2LO London and 5XX Daventry.

by Evelyn Dods   Issue 286   22 March 1929

11.0–11.30 TELEVISION TRANSMISSION
By The Baird Process
A St. Andrew's Eve Programme
THE PIPERS OF THE 1ST BATTALION SCOTS
GUARDS
(*By kind permission of Colonel E. C. T. Warner, D.S.O.
M.C., Commanding Scots Guards*)
in Piping and Highland Dancing
HELEN MCKAY (Hebridean and Lowland Songs)
WILLIAM HEUGHAN (Scots Songs)
JOCK WALKER (Scots Comedian)
(*Vision*, 261.6 m. ; *Sound*, 398.9 m.)

This 30-line service branded as the 'BBC Television Service' continued until September 1935. Because it was broadcast on the Medium-Wave transmitters viewers throughout much of the British Isles could receive it. *The Radio Times* helpfully carried full billings for these programmes in all of its editions, thus playing a neutral role in the politically charged development of this new medium.

But while Baird and Reith locked antlers, Maschwitz and Gorham continued to develop the Corporation's senior journal, joined, as it was, in January 1929 by *The Listener* under the editorship of Richard S. Lambert.

This sister paper was developed mainly as a medium of record for the reproduction of broadcast talks, but it also previewed major literary and musical broadcasts, reviewed new books, and, perhaps surprisingly, printed "A Selected List of Broadcasts for the [coming] Week". This consisted of billing information for many of the more intellectual broadcasts, and thus provided the BBC with not one, but two in-house programme listings magazines.

Astonishingly, the avowed purpose of *The Listener* (what it would nowadays undoubtedly be saddled with as a rigid 'mission statement') appeared on the front cover of the first issue - not as a piece of editorial, but incorporated into an advertisement for 'Amplion' loudspeakers.

> A medium for the intelligent reception of broadcast programmes by way of amplification and explanation of those features which cannot now be dealt with in the editorial columns of the 'Radio Times'

There is no evidence, however, that any significant numbers of readers shifted their allegiance to the new journal. Sales of *Radio Times* continued to rise steadily. But the BBC was once again plunged into a bitter fight with the Newspaper Proprietors' Association, who considered the launch of a second periodical to be - in the words of the *Financial Times* - "an illegitimate stretching of official activity".

First Listener   *16 Jan 1924*

TONIGHT AT 10.15

'The World We Listen In'

A Revue in Miniature

By

HOLT MARVELL

Lyrics by HOLT MARVELL, GEORGE POSFORD, and SIDNEY BOX

Music by GEORGE POSFORD and THEO V. NORMAN

Produced by GORDON McCONNEL

by Evelyn Dods   Issue 313   27 Sept 1929

Reith entered the fray by going on his own to meet with the thirteen or fourteen NPA representatives who had already taken their grievance directly to the Prime Minister after the Postmaster General had refused to meet with them. Reith started by giving the assembled press representatives a dressing-down for having the temerity to involve the Prime Minister before coming to him first. The tall Scot then negotiated a deal that was, in his eyes, a 'great victory' - observing pompously in his diary that the NPA chairman Lord Riddell "drove me back to Savoy Hill; he said he thought I would be Prime Minister one day".

In Reith's mind the notion of a female Prime Minister would probably have been heretic, if not downright blasphemous. Yet his Head of Talks was a member of the female sex - and she was sent in to bat next when it came to defending *The Listener*.

The Observer's editor, Garvin, penned "a wild leader" attacking the BBC's new paper - so Hilda Matheson was sent to cast her spell of charm on him at a private lunch organised by Matheson's former employer, the first woman to enter Parliament, Lady Astor.

The combination of Matheson and Astor was too much for the NPA, as Hilda recorded with some satisfaction in her diary:

> I had a useful half hour with Lord Astor before lunch, who was rather unsound and who had been a bit shaken by his Trade Union, the Newspaper Proprietors' Association. At lunch Lady A played up, as she does, put Garvin between us and whenever his speeches became too oratorical or prolonged she shut him up and made me take my innings. This was so encouraging that I was able to keep my end up and I left him with not a leg to stand on and, for him, comparatively penitent. At any rate I think we've stopped any further rant.

Of course Reith had never considered consulting with the *Listener*'s editor at any point, and Lambert was subsequently left to work out the practical implications of various compromises, which included an agreed maximum limit of ten per cent original contributed material 'not related to broadcasting'.

The fortunate addition of these last four words allowed Lambert and his team a certain elasticity of interpretation which they stretched to its limit, using for example a radio adaptation of St Joan as the excuse to run a feature on witchcraft.

Another compromise: *The Listener* should not accept any more advertisements than were necessary to supplement the cover price in order to cover its costs. The dearth of advertising matter probably contributed to the success of the publication, and it survived comparatively unchanged until 1990.

GRIZZLE,
the Children's Hour dragon

Issue 383   30 Jan 1931

*   *   *   *   *

What the other listener thinks

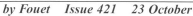

by Fouet   Issue 421   23 October

with decorations here and there by Fouet.

by Eric Fraser
Issue 379
2 January

The man in control will be able to tell at a glance what proportion of the public is listening, and where.

A selection of illustrations from
THE RADIO TIMES
1931

by R. Barnard Way
Issue 404
26 June

BEHIND THE BARS.
An impressive glimpse of the high tension generators of the London Regional transmitter, specially drawn for *The Radio Times* by R. Barnard Way.

DON QUIXOTE IN MUSIC
by Bob Sherriffs
Issue 387   27 February

by Eric Fraser
Issue 387
27 February

Producer (to Effects): 'I said a *warm*, *wet* wind from the Sout

Above: Cover of issue 476   11 Nov 1932
TEN YEARS OF
BROADCASTING
1922 - 1932

Below: by Steven Spurrier   Page 417

BOTH SIDES
OF THE
MICROPHONE

With Illustrations by
Arthur Watts

Page 414

' Create a breach of the peace '

By the Light of the Television Beam

"Steven Spurrier's impression of a scene in the Television Studio, in the flickering light of the beam, during a transmission by the Baird process. The flat boxes on stands, rather like floodlights in appearance, are the photo-electric cells that record vision, and the torpedo-shaped object is the microphone. The dancer has just stepped back through the screen, which goes up on rollers like a blind, from the 'close-up' position, and she is now placed for an 'extended' shot, giving a full-length image. In the foreground is another artist in his television make-up of white, blue, and black."

TEN YEARS OF LISTENING

IN 1922 I GOT INTERESTED IN WIRELESS

IN 1923 MY CRYSTAL SET BEGAN TO FUNCTION

& IN 1924 IT PASSED THE EXPERIMENTAL STAGE INTO THE DRAWING ROOM.

WITH 1925 CAME THE GLIMMER OF VALVES,

& IN 1926 I GOT MY FIRST LOUD-SPEAKER.

IN 1927 I GOT A LOUDER-SPEAKER

& IN 1928 A REALLY-LOUD-SPEAKER.

IN 1929 I ADDED A (NOT VERY) PORTABLE.

IN 1930 I SWITCHED OVER TO AN ALL-MAINS SET

& IN 1931 A RADIO-GRAM.

NOW IN 1932 I HAVE GOT EVERYTHING — SO I'VE TAKEN OUT A LICENCE!

by Alan Cowling

Page 419

The BBC was by now expanding beyond the severe space limitations of Savoy Hill, and in 1932 moved to the grand new Broadcasting House in London's Portland Place. A copy of the first edition of *Radio Times* was placed under its foundation stone, and the paper went to town with special editions marking the end of Savoy Hill and the move to Broadcasting House, for both the broadcasting service and its Journal.

Broadcasting House   by Mervyn Wilson   November 1938

It was time for the "brilliant if erratic" Maschwitz to move on. And for Gorham, who described him thus, to take his place. Maschwitz's heart was in showbusiness, in spite of his wartime interest in the secret services, and he moved on to concentrate on writing radio shows and movies. Gorham received the news, not from his employers, but through the *Daily Herald* whose Sydney Moseley broke the story. Indeed, that seemed to be the way changes in the BBC were generally disseminated in 1933.

From a spider's web of internal BBC intrigue, Gorham emerged as frontrunner in the competition to win a prized BBC role, much to his own surprise. He was summoned to the D-G's office, where Reith subjected him to a rather unconventional job interview. The dour Scot seemed less concerned with Gorham's journalistic abilities than his religion - "Ho. You're a Catholic, then? " And his politics:"Are you a Communist?" Eventually this brittle exchange turned to financial matters: "Supposing I offered you the editorship of the *Radio Times* with no salary, but with a commission on results: what would you say?"

Gorham's response unsettled the po-faced BBC supremo. He affirmed his willingness to agree to a commission based on circulation increase, provided he had control over a few things - like the programmes! Reith at once said that his question had not been meant seriously, at which Gorham added to Reith's unease by naming his preferred salary - a figure which appears to have surprised Reith as much as the earlier exchange had disconcerted Gorham.

In spite of this awkward interrogation - or perhaps because of it - Gorham was, in due course, named as Maschwitz's heir. He was immediately forced into a typical BBC compromise when it came to the choice of his own successor as Art Editor, a position he wished to offer to Douglas Williams. Basil Nicolls once again had other ideas, wishing the job to go to his own candidate. Another clash ensued. In the end the position was shared between the two, but fortunately for Gorham, Nicolls' man did not much like the work and soon left.

It's perhaps puzzling that Reith - with his apparent reservations over Maurice Gorham's religious and political affiliations - allowed a key position to be occupied by a man who seemed to hold the Corporation in low esteem, later describing it as "pompous, self-righteous and aloof".

But for all his weaknesses Reith was a perceptive man, and his objectivity when it came to the best interests of his beloved BBC often over-rode his personal viewpoint. Indeed when *The Radio Times* had started Reith had refused the BBC Board's offer of a percentage of its profits considering it "hardly proper" even though he later calculated that the proposal would have quadrupled his salary.

Evidently, Gorham had the imagination, fire and creative wit needed to hold the reins of the BBC's Official Journal and generally act as an antidote to a Corporation that seemed "a bit above itself". And by all accounts he was popular with his staff: former colleagues confirm that his charm and wit combined to make *The Radio Times* a happy place to work.

THE RADIO TIMES
TENTH ANNIVERSARY

Soon after Gorham took office he presided over the Tenth Anniversary Issue, which permitted itself a certain amount of indulgent backslapping, although tempered by some prescient words from Filson Young:

> Nine more such strides and it will be celebrating its centenary; and perhaps some writer of 2023 will look up the files and turn to these pages to see what we said about ourselves when we were ten years old.
>
> It will amuse such a reader to realise that we considered our 10th birthday as a very considerable event in the annals of Broadcasting and of journalism.

The anniversary outburst of self-congratulation was perhaps an isolated incident in a period when the BBC sought to court respectability at any cost. Sometimes this took odd forms, as with the lengths it went to prevent its staff from benefiting from publicity in any form. (Remnants of this policy have survived into the 21st Century).

Cover by Richard Levin
RT *10th Anniversary*
Issue 522   29 Sept 1933

Thus Gorham was under a regularly changing variety of instructions to omit names from *The Radio Times*. In spite of considerable public curiosity, the announcers were to be afforded complete anonymity. For a time this stretched to the names of staff producers, conductors and performers - whose names were not permitted to sit alongside those of their more freelance colleagues in the programme billings.

But Gorham himself was keen to allow 'names' into the hitherto largely anonymous *Radio Times*. He allowed a number of contributors their own by-lines: - by 1934 A. A. Thomson was writing his weekly humorous *Strolling Commentaries*; Filson Young provided *The World we Listen In...* which concentrated on radio matters, always encouraging listeners to be discriminating in their choice of broadcasts; 'Uncle Mac' wrote *Hullo Children!*; and the children's page also included a current affairs commentary *There and Here* by Commander Stephen King-Hall.

Later, a regular 'women's feature' appeared in the shape of Irene Veal's *I Saw Yesterday* column of fashion and cookery snippets, and a quirky column penned by R.M. Freeman in the guise of *Samuel Pepys, Listener* writing about radio in the style of the great seventeenth century diarist.

The popular *Both Sides of the Microphone* feature which consisted mostly of a number of paragraphs of news and gossip about the programmes and their personalities had been started by Maschwitz in May 1928 and was wittily illustrated by Arthur Watts who went to enormous lengths to get his illustrations to the paper on time, even when he was on holiday. A great winter sports enthusiast, when vacationing in Poland he met his deadline by skiing twenty miles to the nearest post office. He died tragically in a plane crash in the mountains of Italy in 1935 and was a hard act to follow.

By this time Gorham was penning the weekly feature, and chose as his illustrator a young Scotsman from Arbroath, Robert Stewart (Bob) Sherriffs, whose style was quite different to Watts'. When Sherriffs enlisted for the army, in 1940, Victor Reinganum took his place. Reinganum was in the A.F.S. and stationed in Welbeck Street just round the corner from the editorial offices. He drew in his spare time.

Gorham's *Radio Times* was a rounded magazine carefully designed to have appeal beyond the wireless enthusiast. The introduction in January 1933 of a weekly crossword was just one such element. ("Though *Missing Words*, *Limericks*, *Diabolo* and *Put-and-Take* have vanished into limbo, the Crossword still remains as popular as ever" was how *The Radio Times* heralded its first puzzle.)

The overall effect of Gorham's policy was the creation of a friendly, fashionable and fun publication. One of the 'bright young things' of its era. Gorham described his editorial philosophy in the summer of 1934:

> The two-fold function of the *Radio Times* is, I take it, to achieve the largest possible circulation and to give the most helpful kind of service ancillary to broadcasting. For both these purposes, it is essential to consider the really average listener; the person we have been accustomed to personify, in the office, as 'the cabman's wife'. This really average listener will probably buy the paper primarily for the programme pages; that is why they will always remain the backbone of the paper....... to make such listeners read as much as possible of the *Radio Times*, and to make what they read there help them to understand and appreciate their broadcast programmes is our obvious goal. To attain it, it is necessary to avoid being highbrow but not necessary to be cheap.

Not all the new ideas of the early 30s were to be successful. In March 1934 the BBC embarked on a disastrous attempt to persuade the public to use the 24-hour clock. *The Radio Times* started printing the programme times in both 24-hour and 12-hour clocks - and at once its circulation suffered, despite the free cardboard 'clock' it gave away to readers.

The experiment had its roots in a report issued by a government committee in 1919, chaired by Lord Stonehaven, which had suggested the adoption of the 24-hour clock for official purposes. The public was unimpressed, and in August the scheme was abandoned - "in view of the Government's decision that it will take no action to secure the extension of the use of the twenty-four hour clock..."

With the Christmas 1934 edition readers were presented with another unusual free gift. The leader of the immensely popular BBC Dance Orchestra, Henry Hall, had written and composed a song, titled "*Radio Times*", which was played regularly on the BBC's stations during the Christmas period. A facsimile of Hall's original manuscript was included as a gravure supplement to the 21st December issue, "written clearly enough for you to play it on your piano".

Inevitably Hall's toe-tapping hit incurred the easily-roused wrath of the Newspaper Proprietors' Association, who - perhaps with some justification - accused the BBC of advertising. Pressure was applied to Henry Hall and he stopped playing the song.

For some time *The Radio Times* had been uneasy about the enforced regionalisation of its content. With the increased availability of powerful and sophisticated multi-valve receivers, coupled with the introduction of the new high-powered 'Regional' BBC transmitters, many listeners were now choosing to tune in to BBC stations beyond their immediate locality.

by Victor Reinganum
Radio Times
Supplement Xmas 1934

24-hour clock billings   RT 10 Aug 1934

767 kc/s   391.1 m.

WEDNESDAY
Midland Regional

12.00 *Regional Programme*
(*See page* 381)

15.00 (3.0)   Interval

17.15 (5.15) The Children's Hour
A Story of Charlie the Field-Mouse, by ROBERT TREDINNICK
Songs by GERTRUDE FARMAN (soprano)
THE MIDLAND STUDIO ORCHESTRA Directed by FRANK CANTELL
' Bushrangers ', a talk by E. G. HILTON

18.00 (6.0) *Time Signal, Greenwich*
' The First News '
Weather Forecast, First General News Bulletin and Bulletin for Farmers, followed by Regional Announcements

18.30 (6.30) REGINALD FOORT
At The Organ of The Regal, Wimbledon
(*National Programme*)

19.00 (7.0) THE GERSHOM PARKINGTON QUINTET
ETHEL BARKER (contralto)
(*National Programme*)

20.00 (8.0) Seaside Songs
THE MIDLAND WIRELESS SINGERS Under the direction of EDGAR MORGAN

20.30 (8.30) THE COVENTRY REPERTORY COMPANY
(*By arrangement with Bennett Theatres, Ltd.*)
present
Two Short Plays
By H. C. G. STEVENS

1.   SIR HERBERT IS DEEPLY TOUCHED
Characters :
Parker
Sir Herbert
A Young Man

2.   TO MEET THE KING
Characters
A Nurse
Ronnie's Mother
Ronnie
A Doctor
Produced by A. GARDNER DAVIES
Relayed from
The Opera House, Coventry

21.00 (9.0) *Time Signal, Greenwich*
' The Second News '
Weather Forecast
Second General News Bulletin

21.15 (9.15) FRED CLEMENTS presents
The Arcadia Follies

TELEVISION
By the Baird Process
11.0-11.30 p.m.
(*Vision,* 261.1 *m.; Sound,* 391.1 *m.*)
MAISIE SENESHALL (Songs)
GUSTAVE FERRARI (French Songs)
LAURIE DEVINE (Dances)
GAVIN GORDON (Songs)

The printing arrangements were therefore changed with the first edition of 1934 (dated 5th January) and once again all the programmes from all the BBC's stations were printed in one edition. To facilitate these changes the three-column programme pages were expanded to include a fourth column, and, for the first time, television programmes were given a section, albeit tiny, of their very own in the daily layout.

The programme layout constantly placed pressures on the Editor. The requirements of the sales department made it necessary to give advertisements as prominent a position as possible, whilst allowing the programmes their due. Although, theoretically, the BBC's regional scheme replaced the old network of single town stations with a handful of high power transmitters (offering both the National and the localised Regional programme) there were anomalies which made life difficult for *The Radio Times*.

To take an example of the layout from the mid 30s, the National Programme came first with two pages of billings. Then two full-page advertisements, followed by a full page for the basic Regional Programme, as broadcast by London, Plymouth and Bournemouth. Turn over for Midland, West, North and Northern Ireland Regionals - a half-page devoted to each. And finally, a full-page headed 'Scottish Programme', which also shoe horned in the programmes for Scottish National plus Aberdeen and Newcastle, which were neither National nor Regional but transmitted locally a mixture of both.

The makeup of the paper had to allow for the fact that the billings department never knew until the last minute how long the billings for each station's programmes were going to be. And despite much editorial pressure the programme departments never learned to send their full details in time. It was therefore sometimes necessary to turn over twelve pages in order to get all the programmes for just one day - what Gorham described as "an infliction on the reader". In spite of this, circulation and revenue continued to rise. By 1936 three million copies were being sold each week, and the profits from BBC Publications were reaching around £400,000 a year.

*Cover
Issue 643
24 Jan 1936*

This took into account, not only the surplus from *The Radio Times* and *The Listener,* but the losses incurred by the international listings magazine *World-Radio,* as well as Year Books, concert programmes and pamphlets. Gorham reckoned that by the outbreak of war *Radio Times* was generating an annual surplus of some £600,000.

In early 1936 the death of King George V caused *The Radio Times* to go into mourning, with a special issue - published on 24th January - devoted to the King's funeral. Although hurriedly put together after the 'ordinary' edition had already gone to press, this issue is a fine example of the BBC's relationship with the Monarchy. It devoted 12 of its 48 pages to the Royal death, with an edited reprint of the May 1935 feature on the King's role as 'Chief Broadcaster', and a page detailing the Order of Memorial Service broadcast from the Concert Hall of Broadcasting House on the Sunday before the funeral.

35

By now *The Radio Times* was one of the most eye-catching of an ever-growing selection of magazines to be found on bookstalls up and down the country. Its artistic policy ensured that special editions had attention-grabbing front covers that resulted in ever-increasing sales.

Colour cover by Philip Zec Issue 633 15 Nov 1935 Plate 1c

The covers of this period have often been the objects of study for students of design and graphic art. So memorable were some of these covers that even now - over sixty years later - many are still familiar, thanks to their subsequent appearances in books, magazines and even postcards. For example, Philip Zec's cover for the 'Fireside Number' of 15th November 1935, showing a stylised couple sitting in 'modern' armchairs beside a roaring fire was copied in 1981 for the dust wrapper of Susan Briggs' nostalgic volume *Those Radio Times*.

Probably most memorable of all the 'thirties designs was Gilroy's laughing cat. Created to adorn the front page of the 'Humour Number' published on 9th October 1936, the disembodied cat - with its Alice in Wonderland connotations - caught the public imagination. Readers carefully cut out the cat face and pasted it to office walls, school jotters, and even bits of cardboard to produce cat masks! John Gilroy (creator of the famous 1920s "Guinness is Good For You" posters) is said to have used his own cat as the model for his drawing.

Colour cover by John Gilroy Issue 680 9 Oct 1936 Plate 1d

From its inception the high spot of the paper's year was always Christmas; each year bringing another innovative pullout or gimmick, and always a striking colour cover. In 1936, for example, a gravure supplement provided high quality pin-up photographs of 'the Announcers' (all chaps of course) tastefully tinted in sepia and green.

Even the crossword went festive: A. Cash's 1936 version using the letters from the paper's title to make a most unusual grid.

Crossword   Issue 690   18 Dec 1936   *Solution at end of chapter*

Crossword 198 'RADIO TIMES'

ACROSS

3. The fool's is just paper (3)
5. Printers may find them enshrined in enshrined (3)
10. Tan a cat to get this surprisingly harmonious result (7)
11. In an elevated position (4)
12. He, if any one, ought to be able to lead us a dance (*two words :* 5, 4)
13. No. 12 is this of many listeners (4)
14. The very embodiment of British broadcasting (*two words :* 8, 9)
15. Transmission by an extensive product of the metal industry, perhaps (12)

16. Before Raleigh this radio comedian was universal (*two words :* 5, 4)
17. ' Was it first ? ' it is asked in bed (among other places) (3)
18. A fishy solution, or what Tauber said to the Scottish girl when she asked him what he did (9)
23. This coloured broadcaster is evidently no nudist (7)
29. A teaser for you ? ' Yes, and you'll have to wait till 1937 for it (6)
20. To the writer this has its point, of course (3)
31. A good-for-nothing (*double hyphen :* 4, 2, 4)

32. Everything is unostentatiously shallow (3)
33. Get the measure of a fellow (3)
34. The piano is thus distributed among a coloured people (10)
36. Good for eating, they will be found it's a hundred to one in the steamboat (6)
37. The more occasional this broadcast the better (3)
38. Transmit, not necessarily by wireless (4)
39. Only on top of the world will woman get repose, it seems ! (7)

DOWN

1. Mythological example of insatiable feminine curiosity (7)
2. Florence is but Nancy isn't (7)
3. An up-to-date one even has a wireless set (7)
4. Is put with the Southern Railway for meticulous selectors of words (7)
5. The general demonstrates how to expand (7)
6. Adapting to a purpose (7)
7. Red nose would appear to be necessary to do this to a negotiable instrument (7)

8. Contracted, but not to do anything (6)
9. This is one of the earths, but it doesn't say what the mineral salt is in (7)
19. They should have ready ingress to the studios (7)
20. Cricket would be impossible with this, and yet it is in cricket that we meet them (*hyphen :* 2, 5)
21. Light cavalry soldiers (7)
22. Unsullied broadcaster apparently urging the bird to motion (7)

23. An untanned skin, but a week at Brighton wouldn't make any difference (*two words :* 3, 4)
24. The graduate takes a weapon and gets equality (7)
25. and 26. Sound partnership of South Africa and New England (4)
27. The loan advanced by Ireland for broadcasting purposes (7)
28. ' Say farewell as I do ', says Maria de Laguna (5)
35. and 36. A heartless beast (4)

(Compiled by A. Cash)

The solution to last week's crossword is on page 100

Television was soon to develop. The inventors, technicians, politicians - and of course the BBC - played out their various power games. The first round of the struggle ended on 2nd November 1936 with the launch of the BBC's High-Definition Television Service.

The role *The Radio Times* was to play in the promotion of television was clear right from the start - a special 'Television Number' was published on 23rd October 1936. A slightly muted editorial by the Deputy Director-General, Sir Charles Carpendale, suggested that he had deliberately avoided painting too bright a picture because "The thing is so big .... we do not need to magnify its approach".

Gerald Cock, the BBC's first Director of Television, contributed 'a personal forecast of the future of television' in which he predicted that feature films - because they were made to be shown on a large screen to a large audience - would not be suitable programme material for television.

by Eric Fraser
Television Number   23 Oct 1936

As an extreme case I believe viewers would rather see an actual scene of a rush hour at Oxford Circus directly transmitted to them than the latest in film musicals costing £100,000 - though I do not expect to escape unscathed with such an opinion.

From page 6

Two pages and a helpful floor plan guided viewers around television's new abode, Alexandra Palace. And another two pages introduced viewers for the first time to 'the principal personalities of the television staff', including the first three announcers, Leslie Mitchell, Jasmine Bligh and Elizabeth Cowell.

The week after the 'Television Number' Londoners received their own edition of *Radio Times*. This was a key moment in the

TELEVISION PROGRAMMES IN FULL in 'THE RADIO TIMES'

The regular programme service from the London Television Station at Alexandra Palace begins on November 2, and there will be television broadcasts every day (except Sundays) from 3 p.m. to 4 p.m. and from 9 p.m. to 10 p.m. These programmes will be printed in full in the London edition of THE RADIO TIMES, which circulates in the area within which reception of the television programmes is anticipated.

Other editions circulating outside the London area will still contain news of television developments likely to interest readers all over the country.

paper's history - for not only was it the first time that an edition was produced for just one city, and not only was it the first programmes, but also it appeared with a different cover from the edition that circulated throughout the rest of the UK. Indeed, it was the only prewar issue to boast two different covers; regional covers did not occur again until the late 1940s.

The new London edition was not labelled as such - instead in the top right-hand corner of the front page there appeared in bold type the words TELEVISION PROGRAMME. That unique front cover carried with it a photograph of television announcer Elizabeth Cowell in the Baird 'spotlight studio'; television was not to usurp radio from the cover again for another fifteen years.

For the remaining weeks of 1936 the London edition appeared with two pages of television programmes at the back. But, in January 1937, London readers found a new magazine slipping out from within their regular *Radio Times*. It was an elaborate sepia-tinted photogravure self-contained supplement of anything up to 16 pages, printed separately by Rembrandt Photogravure in Watford.

Issue 683
30 Oct 1936
London edition

FULL TELEVISION PROGRAMMES WILL BEGIN ON MONDAY
The picture above shows Elizabeth Cowell, television announcer, in the spotlight studio at Alexandra Palace

The *Television Supplement* can fairly be said to have been the very first proper television listings magazine. It came complete with full-page pin-up photographs of the new television 'stars' and articles about the programmes and personalities, including *News for Televiewers* by 'The Scanner' which was the TV equivalent of the main paper's popular *Both Sides of the Microphone* feature attributed to "The Broadcasters" but written by Gorham himself.

There were also plenty of advertisements for television receivers, and a classified section which was clearly aimed at the better-off, including, as it did, the rather surprising categories of 'Cars for Sale' and 'Houses for Sale' mixed in with the lists of 'Television Demonstrations' and 'Radio Set Servicing'.

The whole philosophy of the *Supplement* was based on the fact that *The Radio Times*' Russian-born Advertisement Manager, Ralph Judson, was convinced that there was sufficient London-only advertising to make it viable.

From the first double-page spread of TV billings

Gorham took on Harold Rathbone as his 'television man'. And it appears that Rathbone wrote much of the *Television Supplement* himself. Gorham described him as 'a television enthusiast and a first-rate journalist'. But Rathbone joined the RAF and became one of the BBC's many war casualties.

Monday

3.0	**Opening of the BBC TELEVISION SERVICE**

by

Major the Right Hon. G. C. TRYON, M.P., H.M. Postmaster-General

Mr. R. C. NORMAN (Chairman of the BBC)

and

the Right Hon. the Lord SELSDON, K.B.E. (Chairman of the Television Advisory Committee) will also speak

3.15	Interval Time, Weather
3.20	BRITISH MOVIETONE NEWS
3.30	Variety

ADÈLE DIXON
Musical Comedy Star

BUCK AND BUBBLES
Comedians and Dancers

THE LAI FOUNS
Chinese Jugglers

THE BBC
TELEVISION ORCHESTRA

Leader, Boris Pecker

Conductor, HYAM GREENBAUM

Produced by DALLAS BOWER

Adèle Dixon is now playing lead opposite Laddie Cliff in the West End musical comedy *Over She Goes*. Amongst recent radio shows she has played in are *Lots of Love* and *Cottage Loaf*. Buck and Bubbles are a coloured pair who are now playing in *Transatlantic Rhythm*. They are versatile comedians who dance, play the piano, sing, and cross-chat. An Oriental juggling act, the Lai Founs consist of four men and two women who specialise in plate-spinning.

4.0	CLOSE

At the close of this afternoon's programme a chart arranged in co-operation with the Air Ministry will forecast the weather

The production of the *Supplement* was somewhat more haphazard than that of the main paper. After it had gone to press, Rathbone and Gorham would go out to Watford armed with pocketfuls of full-page photographs which they would "bung in" whenever advertisements fell down or programmes on which double-page spreads were based were suddenly cancelled.

Judson's optimism proved ill-founded, and the *Supplement* gave way in 1938 to the return of a double-page spread for television, this time appearing in all editions of the magazine, thereby stimulating nationwide interest in the new medium.

In 1936 the printing arrangements for *The Radio Times* underwent a major change. From the start Newnes and Pearson had printed it at their works in Exmoor Street, off Ladbroke Grove in West London. But in 1936 the contract expired and was put up for tender. Unexpectedly, Newnes failed to win it back and it was awarded instead to Waterlows - who had just suffered a half-million pound loss, having fallen victim to an elaborate Portuguese banknote fraud.

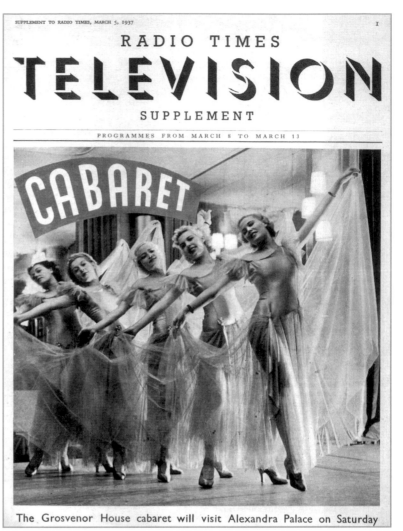

SUPPLEMENT TO RADIO TIMES, MARCH 5, 1937   I

RADIO TIMES

TELEVISION

SUPPLEMENT

PROGRAMMES FROM MARCH 8 TO MARCH 13

CABARET

The Grosvenor House cabaret will visit Alexandra Palace on Saturday

Cover of Television Supplement   5 March 1937

Waterlows constructed a new purpose-built plant at Park Royal, between Acton and Wembley in north-west London. The massive building was due to be officially opened by the Duke of Gloucester, just before Christmas 1936, but he fell ill and the BBC's chairman, R.C. Norman, did the honours instead.

To underline the coming of the new, the magazine was given a design overhaul - with new typefaces, a new masthead, and perhaps most significantly of all the word 'The' was dropped from the title - thus on 8th January 1937 it officially became simply

RADIO TIMES

An elaborate brochure to mark the official opening was produced for the benefit of the list of distinguished guests. The brochure describes the building in Twyford Abbey Road in lyrical terms:

> It is a handsome building of brick and steel construction covering an area of two acres.
>
> This building, with its two acres of space, is one of the most modern expressions of the sound artistic principle of fitness for purpose applied to a highly technical branch of industry.

No statistic is left out: from the 15,680lbs of ink used to print each issue to the 700 tons of paper; from the 750 printing plates to the 850 tons of hydraulic pressure at 6,000 lbs per square inch that was necessary to produce a clean print impression on each of the 730 reels of paper.

Concerned perhaps that such statistics were not colourful enough, and having regaled guests with the voltages, miles of electrical wiring, dimensions and weight of each press, it went on:

> When the week's issue of the *Radio Times* is completed, if the copies were placed side by side it would cover a distance of 442 miles (from London to Dundee). If spread out in pages, side by side, it would make a pathway of 18,564 miles and would stretch from London, over the Atlantic, across the continent of America, then over the Pacific Ocean - girdling three-quarters of the circumference of the earth. An average issue, if piled in bundles on top of each other, would reach a height of 7.5 miles, and each week's edition would require a train of ninety ten-ton trucks to remove it.

In concocting these similes, the writers apparently failed to take into account the adverse effects of the world's oceans on the pulp paper upon which *Radio Times* was printed....

Waterlows themselves dubbed the presses at Park Royal as "six of the most wonderful presses, and the largest magazine presses in the world".

They were almost immediately pushed to their limits by the Coronation Number of 7th May 1937, celebrating the crowning of King George VI, following the abdication of Edward.

110 pages inside a striking full colour cover by C. R. W. Nevinson (the famous war artist) plus an additional 8-page gravure supplement of which 4 pages were full colour. The issue was packed with features about the Coronation, and in particular the BBC's plans for its coverage - the first Coronation ever to be broadcast, and one which was to be seen as well as heard, thanks to the siting of three television outside broadcast cameras on the Coronation route.

Plate 2a

*Coronation colour cover
by C. R. W. Nevinson
Issue 710   7 May 1937*

**Supplement cover
by Steven Spurrier**
Plate 2b

The supplement, with a colour cover by Stephen Spurrier, included a double-page colour map of the Coronation route, and a four-page illustrated feature, 'How the King is Crowned' by S. P. B. Mais.

The Coronation issue sold 3,540,547 copies, which was at the time understood to be the largest ever recorded by a weekly magazine in any country.

Change was in the air. For the BBC itself, just over a year later Reith bowed out to become chairman of Imperial Airways. And across Europe the clouds of war were gathering.

The BBC and its Organ were to face their greatest challenges.

by Bert Thomas

CROSSWORD 198: Solution

CHAPTER FOUR
Broadcasting Carries On

s the signs of impending war became more and more difficult to ignore, the BBC began making plans. Some of these plans were of a practical nature. Where would the Corporation's staff be based to ensure their greatest safety? Others were philosophical, and included the apparently important question of the *Radio Times* masthead.

For some time the BBC had employed, as its motto, the phrase, *Nation Shall Speak Peace Unto Nation*. This phrase was prominently incorporated into both the BBC's coat-of-arms and the masthead of its official organ in the autumn of 1928.

Masthead Mid 30s

But, as the prospect of war became more tangible, the motto fell out of favour. And when the new masthead was under consideration, prior to the opening of Twyford Abbey Road, it was clearly important for Gorham and his staff to know which motto to use. Gorham described the dilemma:

> The rival [motto] appeared to be 'Quaecunque', which was popularly supposed to mean 'What you will', but really stood for the first word of a phrase that goes on 'Whatsoever things are holy, whatsoever things are good...'. But so far as I was concerned there was a great difference between the two, and not only in length, though this was an important factor in a cover design. If the BBC dropped the peace slogan on the cover of its programme journal and replaced it by something vague, a lot of people would think it regarded war as a certainty.

Gorham sought the highest authority before taking such a step, and, after being stonewalled by a dazzling assortment of BBC managers, he was eventually given a 'ruling' that the BBC in fact had two alternative mottos, but that 'Quaecunque' was preferred and although 'Nation Shall Speak Peace unto Nation' had not been abandoned, its use had been discontinued.

Masthead 1937

Colour cover by C. Walter Hodges Issue 795 23 Dec 1938

Plate 2c

Doubtless infuriated by this fudge, Gorham opted for a new masthead which failed to include either motto, instead prominently displaying the sub-title, Journal of the *British Broadcasting Corporation* and using only the graphic element of the Corporation's new emblem in its design.

As the Twyford Abbey Road presses began to roll, in January 1937, the Editor was already compiling a list of 'essential' staff who could carry on production of the paper in what was euphemistically described as 'an emergency'.

The Christmas edition of 1938 appeared with the usual splendid full-colour cover - a traditional scene by C. Walter Hodges. It was to be the very last time that the paper would boast a full colour wrapping for the next *twenty-six* years!

The BBC's programmes started to reflect the seriousness of the situation. In 1939 regular news bulletins in French, German and Italian intruded on the evening's programmes on many of the Regional Programme wavelengths.

A programme page for the last day of broadcasting under the pre-war system, with the prominent inclusion of late evening news broadcasts in French, German and Italian. This was the last day when the National and Regional programmes were broadcast in full.
Issue 830   25 Aug 1939   page 57

★ ★ ★ ★

Cover of above
Issue 830
25 Aug 1939

As issue number 830 (containing the BBC's radio and television programmes for the week August 27th to September 2nd 193), was being laid out neatly on newsagent's counters, its editor was enjoying the sunshine in the garden of his weekend retreat at Monkstown, near Dublin, and creosoting his kitchen table.

This peaceful scene was shattered by a telephone call from his deputy, Gordon Stowell, summoning Gorham back to London at once. Russia and Germany had signed their pact, and it was clear that the long postponed crisis had come at last.

After a boat and train journey, Gorham arrived back to find the office in a high state of tension as evacuation plans were being put into effect.

Most programme departments were sent to Wood Norton, near Evesham in Kent, where studios and offices had been 'secretly' constructed. Although the general public were never allowed to know that their programmes were coming from Evesham (or, in the case of Variety shows, from Bristol) it seems certain that the Germans knew the BBC's location well in advance of the outbreak of hostilities.

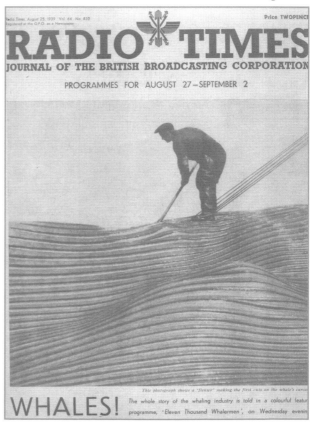

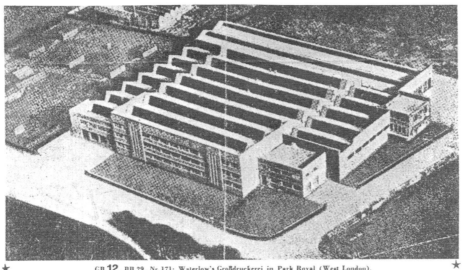

GB 12, BB 29, Nr.171: Waterlow's Großdruckerei in Park Royal (West London).
Großdruckerei der Radio Times.

It was on the Luftwaffe List

This photograph, taken from German air force files in Berlin, shows that the Waterlow plant, on which the "Radio Times" is produced, was scheduled for destruction. It was damaged, but only slightly.

Luftwaffe photo of Waterlows taken from 'World's Press News' 18 Dec 1947

The plan for *Radio Times* was that its staff should work at Waterlow's plant in Park Royal, because in theory the N.W.10 district of the capital would be well outside the main target area for bombing.

In reality, the printing works were on the Luftwaffe list of targets - as this photograph, taken from German air force files in Berlin, shows.

However, the plant was only ever slightly damaged, which was just as well for the *Radio Times* employees who worked there.

A last minute change of plan, however, kept the Editor and the Programme Planners (both of whom had been destined to billet at Evesham) in Broadcasting House, a decision that met with Gorham's hearty approval, since his wife had already enrolled for duty with her neighbourhood Air Raid Precaution force.

The BBC's plan for the outbreak of war involved a complex change from peacetime broadcasting conditions that had enormous repercussions for the way in which the programme journal appeared.

Prior to 1st September 1939, BBC radio provided a National Programme for the whole of the UK, on both a long and medium wavelength. The Regional Programme appeared in seven different versions (London, Midland, North, West, Wales, Northern Ireland and Scotland) using eight wavelengths - plus the Aberdeen and Stagshaw programmes (each a combination of National and Regional transmitted to the North-East of Scotland and England respectively).

From 6pm on 1st September, a single BBC programme was broadcast - known as the "Home Service" - using just two separate wavelengths, with all of the BBC's transmitters up and down the country using one or the other. German aircraft were thus unable to use individual BBC transmitters for electronic direction finding since the grouping of many stations on the same wavelength tended to confuse the equipment, and local transmitters were shut down when enemy raids were imminent.

The shutdown of a local transmitter might mean weaker signals from an adjacent one, but at no time did all of the BBC's transmitters go off simultaneously, and so with a little effort listeners were always able to hear their programmes.

But the inevitable side-effect of grouping all transmitters on the same frequencies meant that they perforce had to radiate exactly the same programme, and so the *Radio Times* suddenly found itself having to fill its pages with the billings for just one station, television also being closed for the duration.

This was further complicated in the early days of the war by the fact that the whole system of submitting programme billings in advance was scrapped. Instead Gorham sat for days on end beside programme planner Harman Grisewood (brother of announcer Freddy) as the latter cobbled together a schedule containing news every hour on the hour and little else.

Sandy Macpherson

A stock of pre-recorded programmes had been prepared and wherever there were gaps in the plans (and there were many) either a programme of gramophone records was inserted, or the microphone was once more handed over to BBC theatre organist Sandy Macpherson, who sat alone in the vast St George's Hall playing music at all hours of the day and night.

The BBC's decision to put its programming on a wartime footing was taken on the morning of Friday, 1st September 1939. On that same morning copies of issue 831 were on sale in newsagents around the UK. This issue contained programmes for September 3rd-9th that would not be heard or seen. And work had already started on issue 832, which was clearly to suffer a similar fate.

Cover of issue 831   1 Sept 1939

As the morning progressed, the entire staff sweated over the removal of desks, chairs and filing-cabinets, as vans that were normally used to distribute the publication took the *Radio Times* furniture to its new locations. They adjourned to a pub in New Cavendish Street for a farewell lunch before dispersing to their new offices.

The Editor then had the task of completing the emergency issue. Most of it had already been put together in proof form, but Gorham still had to compose his leader.

The Six o'Clock News told of the invasion of Poland and the bombing of Warsaw. The over-use of the word 'emergency' in the news reports irritated Gorham - his article 'Broadcasting Carries On!' (telephoned to Waterlows page by page) is peppered with the word 'war'. This gave the Editor some uneasy moments during the next thirty-six hours, since Britain had *not yet declared war*, and in the event of a last-minute change of heart on the part of Germany, nothing could have prevented the emergency issue from being published the following Monday full of references to war.

But indeed, on Sunday 3rd September, the Prime Minister broadcast to the Nation, and declared that a state of war existed between Britain and Germany.

The next day, issue number 831A hit the newsstands.

Cover of issue 831A   4 Sept 1939

After the comforting normality of advertisements for *Cadbury's Milk Tray, Double Crown* tinned peaches and *Allenbury* children's foods, Gorham's lead article described hopes for the future:

> Just as broadcasting will go on, so will the *Radio Times*. Our plans, too, were laid long ago, and here again the difficulties, though formidable, can - we hope - be overcome. The number of the *Radio Times* that was published only last Friday has become out of date. This number is published to correct it. As we have explained, the programmes printed in the subsequent pages may have to be altered, but they will not be altered radically. The general framework of the day's broadcasting will be as it is given here. You can expect to get your news at every hour '*on* the hour', as the Americans say.

The final paragraph injects a note of caution, as well as exhibiting the signs of having been written in haste:

'It's rather hard to tell you who is winning, as all the horses are camouflaged'

by Bob Sherriffs
Issue 831A

Like broadcasting itself, the *Radio Times* will be coming out under difficulties during these dark times - difficulties of editing, of collecting programme information, of production and (most of all) of distribution. It is probable that paper will be hard to get and we may have to reduce the size of the paper. In fact, it is hard to tell now what unexpected difficulties may arise. All we can say is that we shall do our best to bring you full and correct information about all the doings and plans of the BBC, and that, like other departments of the BBC, the *Radio Times* - incorporating *World-Radio* - is carrying on.

Carry on it did - with that week's second Crossword, and then an ominous full-page article on 'First Steps in First Aid'. Lots of photographs of the BBC's troupes of variety artists, actors, musicians followed; the final instalment of a Sydney Horler mystery serial; a piece by woman's editor Irene Veal on the improvements in the status of women in the period 1914–1939; and an amusing feature by Strolling Commentator A.A. Thomson preceded Bob Sheriffs' first wartime cartoon, which was given a whole page to itself.

Then came the new-look programme pages, stretching the endless lists of gramophone records to their limit by printing them as two columns to a page instead of the previous four, and somehow taking three pages for a complete day's billings. The term 'Home Service' had yet to appear in print, and in fact no name was yet given to this new wartime service.

The first wartime billings
showed a distinct lack of anything much beyond
gramophone records and Sandy Macpherson.
RT issue 831A

The first wartime edition ran to a respectable 40 pages - complete with *Nat and Reg* cartoon and a blank 'Stop Press' page ("Any late programme alterations will be inserted on this page").

Within a few days Issue 832 was published - on Friday as usual - another 40 pages. This created something of a record in the publishing business, with three numbers of a weekly publication put 'to bed' within five days.

Many features resumed as normal, including *Round and About*; the *Letters* page; *The World we Listen In*; and a detailed listing of European radio stations together with programmes from American short-wave stations, both of which features moved over from the sister publication *World-Radio* which was now incorporated into *Radio Times*.

World-Radio had been edited by Reith's brother-in-law and, in the early days of wireless, had given the BBC a useful income, mainly from wireless enthusiasts in the days when listening-in to foreign stations had been fashionable.

By the end of the 30s, sales had been dropping off, and the BBC were only too grateful for the excuse of war to wring the publication's neck and stuff its giblets into the pages of the successful paper.

Although the, by now, very bored staff of *Radio Times* hoped for some respite in the glamour of foreign programme billings few were ever to make it in time for inclusion. In contrast to the elaborate - and, it must be said, largely accurate arrangements the BBC devised for passing programme information to its programme journal - foreign stations' details were either late, inaccurate, or non-existent.

Gorham had taken the decision not to include the programmes of the German stations, an entirely reasonable one in the light of the propaganda that flowed from all of their wavelengths during the so-called 'phoney war' - the period between the declaration and the outbreak of serious fighting.

Fortunately for the BBC's listeners still coming to terms with air raid warnings and gas masks, the unleavened domestic diet of gramophone records and theatre organ was by now being supplemented by some real programmes at the production villages in Evesham and Bristol (jointly given the affectionate name 'Hogsnorton' after the mythical village created by broadcaster Gillie Potter).

The serialisation of J.B. Priestley's new novel *Let the People Sing* - which was a major coup for the BBC - resumed, as did some popular programmes like *The Children's Hour*, *Band Waggon*, and *Songs from the Shows*.

And the 'Stop Press' page proudly (and with perhaps an air of some relief) announced:

THEATRE ORGAN

Sandy Macpherson, the BBC Theatre Organist, who has been doing a grand job entertaining listeners during these first days, is now to have some help with it. Before long Dudley Beavan and Reginald Foort are both to start regular wartime broadcasts.

Issue 832   11 Sept 1939

Radio Times (incorporating World-Radio), December 22, 1939   PRICE TWOPENCE

RadioTimes
ChristmasNumber
2ᴰ

A Merry Christmas to all Listeners

by James Hart
Xmas 1939

By Christmas things had settled into a more regular pattern; a colour (red) had been introduced into the masthead making the front cover more attractive. And there was still the luxury of a seasonal design for the 52-page issue of December 22nd which, although a little smaller than previous Christmas efforts, still contained all the essential ingredients. Once the 'phoney war' ended things were to be very different.

As troops of the British Expeditionary Force found themselves stationed in France - waiting for, but not yet experiencing battle action - the BBC announced plans to reintroduce an alternative radio service, designed primarily to provide programmes suitable for the fighting forces to listen to, and as a means of raising morale amongst the now rather bemused troops.

Already a commercial station, Radio International, with an office right beside the BBC in London's Portland Place, was entertaining the troops from a transmitter at Fecamp. Quick to seize on the potential of a captive and largely bored audience, Radio International produced and distributed its own programme magazine, *Happy Listening,* which was provided free to servicemen.

Thus on 7th January 1940 the single Home Service was joined by the programme rather coyly described as "For The Forces". *Radio Times* reorganised its pages to accommodate the newcomer, and for the first time produced a French edition to compete with *Happy Listening* (which didn't survive long as Fecamp was closed down a few weeks later on the orders of French command).

With a cover price of 1.50 francs (no troop freebies from the BBC!) the BEF edition carried all the home and forces programmes, as well as its own version of *Both Sides of the Microphone*, cheekily titled, *Orders of the Week: News and gossip about your radio programmes by 'Compere'*. It also replaced the advertisements from the home edition with ones specifically aimed at a military readership, even giving prices of everything from State Express cigarettes to Brylcreem in French francs.

By the spring of 1940 paper rationing had taken care of some of the typographical largesse exhibited in the early months of the war. With an average of just 32 pages available, no longer were a day's billings for the Home Service stretched extravagantly to fill three. A page-and-a-half was allocated to the Home Service, with, at first, another half-page for the new Forces Programme and, from March, a full page for the new service. And an early casualty of the war was the crossword - no room now for such peacetime frivolities.

In fact, the typography and layout of the programme pages established at this time, was to remain the model for the next forty or so years, with few changes, even after hostilities had long ceased.

48

1a   Christmas 1923   by Abbey

1b   Christmas 1927   by Edward McKnight Kauffer

1c   Fireside Number 1935   by Philip Zec

1d   Humour Number 1936   by John Gilroy

2a   *Coronation Number 1937*

2b   *Coronation Supplement 1937*

2c   *Christmas 1938   by C. Walter Hodges*

2d   *Christmas 1940   by John Gilroy*

Within a few months of launching the BEF edition the phoney war came to an end. On 10 May 1940 German forces invaded the Netherlands, Belgium and Luxembourg, and Winston Churchill became the Prime Minister. France subsequently fell in June as the British troops were evacuated from the battered beaches of Dunkirk - and the German Luftwaffe began their systematic aerial bombing of Britain in September. The *blitzkrieg* had begun.

Production of *Radio Times* became hazardous, with frequent daytime air raid warnings and regular evacuations of staff to the (relatively) safe shelter of the Concert Hall in Broadcasting House, or for those caught at Waterlow's, to the trench shelters. The printing plant was first to suffer bomb damage, and Gorham was there when it happened. He wrote:

> We were nearly all of us there (in the trench shelters) when Waterlows was bombed. Two of the canteen staff were not, and I had the experience I had always imagined and never really expected - running out to give a hand with the casualties and then returning to the shelter and going on passing the page proofs.

Cover of British Expeditionary Force edition
Number 865   26 April 1940

Advertisements
Above edition
26 April 1940

Colour cover
by John Gilroy
Issue 899   20 Dec 1940
Plate 2d

In 1941 Maurice Gorham was given the opportunity to run the BBC's North American Service. It was the first time in his fifteen years at *Radio Times* that the BBC had offered him another job. He took it, figuring that running the overseas service aimed at the USA and Canada just might offer more bearing on winning the war than editing the listings paper.

On 11th May 1941 Gorham left his £1,600-a-year job as Editor. His deputy, Gordon Stowell, was promoted to 'acting' editor, with Douglas Williams as his 'acting' deputy in turn. Officially all wartime moves were classed as temporary, as Gorham was given the option of returning to his old position upon the cessation of hostilities. It was an option he did not take, instead setting up first the Allied Expeditionary Force Programme and then becoming architect of the peacetime Light Programme before taking up the position of Head of the Television Service when it resumed in 1946.

★ ★ ★ ★ ★

As hostilities spread, the wartime paper found itself not only listing programmes but sometimes supplanting *The Listener* as a journal of record, as in February 1941 when it devoted four precious pages to the whole of Winston Churchill's "Give us the tools, and we will finish the job!" speech, broadcast on 9th February. This it considered of sufficient importance to trail the contents in the front cover space usually reserved for the date!

Issue 908
21 Feb 1941

PRICE TWOPENCE

MR. CHURCHILL'S BROADCAST
IN FULL (pages 6 to 9)

RADIO TIMES
JOURNAL OF THE BRITISH BROADCASTING CORPORATION
(INCORPORATING WORLD-RADIO)

Canon
F. A. COCKIN,

who will be taking part in the special religious broadcasts for the first days of Lent. See the article on page 3.

ALSO ───────

Laurence Olivier
and Vivien Leigh
In all-star Services Variety (p. 10)

'The Admirable Crichton'
Cecil Trouncer and Mary Hinton in Barrie's comedy

'The Happy Hypocrite'
Revival of the Max Beerbohm story (p. 15)

Ridgeway's Roadhouse
Philip Ridgeway on parade (p. 16)

Flanagan and Allen
With the Revue Orchestra (p. 19)

Mozart's 'Requiem'
BBC Chorus and Orchestra (p. 21)

'Don Roberto in the South'
Feature about R. B. Cunninghame Graham (p. 24)

Oxford v. Cambridge
Commentary on the Varsity Rugby Match (p. 28)

St. David's Day Celebrations
Four broadcasts of special interest to Wales (p. 30)

Canon Cockin photographed outside the Wren house in Amen Court that he occupies as a Canon of St. Paul's Cathedral. In the background are the ruins of Paternoster Row, burnt during the great fire in December.

In the years leading up to the war, average weekly circulation had started to drop from its pre-war peak of 2.88 million in 1936. By 1941 it was as low as 2.28 million. But, as radio became increasingly the only form of safe entertainment available, sales rose again, and by the end if the war in 1945 had risen above 4 million.

Paper rationing continued to bite into the wartime version of the BBC's official journal. It dropped in size to 32 pages, then 28, then 24 and sometimes as few as 20. Grace Harbinson, who was by now in charge of editing the programme billings, was faced with the task of ruthlessly cutting down the information producers supplied in order to fit the day's programmes for each of the two stations into a single page, while retaining sufficient space for a few advertisements. Yet the pages continued to be enhanced by illustrations.

The front cover - once a playground for graphic imagination - was given over to text, with just enough space for one small illustration. Inside however, thanks to superhuman effort and very small typefaces, Stowell managed to retain several of the regular features. Programme gossip and news could still be found in *Both Sides of the Microphone*, which generally opened the magazine. The remaining few pages of features included Irene Veal's *I Saw Yesterday*; A A Thomson's *Strolling Commentaries*; the letters column; and *Miscellany*, a 'people' feature written from the outbreak of war until 1942 by former actor, Guy Fletcher.

Issue 982   24 Jul 1942

50

Fletcher's work for *Radio Times* included 112 interviews with prominent radio personalities for the *People You Hear* column before writing *Miscellany* until his death, on 15th February 1942, after a long illness.

Guy Fletcher was one of the more old-fashioned of the paper's writers: he held that "the only story worth telling was that of Cinderella". His sixteen novels were all modern variants of that fairytale. His sense of humour was legendary, and his charm and popularity were uncontestable. After his death *Radio Times* paid tribute to him in affectionate terms: "Everybody who met him liked him. Everybody who met him was better for having known him."

His column was taken over by C. Gordon Glover, and renamed *Introducing.....*

'THE TORCH'. A burning cathedral is the grim background to the play tonight at 10.10 by G. Rodney Rainier, which brings together the man who built the cathedral and the German airman who destroyed it.

by G. Rodney Rainer
Issue 919   9 May 1941

By 1942 the Christmas number had become as austere as the other 51 issues of the year. Rather than being specially commissioned, the cover illustration was taken from Piero della Francesca's painting of "The Nativity".

Stowell described the mood in his caption:

Now that the gay material trappings of Christmas have been stripped away and all its strident overtones are silenced, what remains? Only the story of the angels, ringing out more clearly than before.

by Cecil Bacon
From cover
of issue 1055
17 Dec 1943

The following year the Christmas cover depicted a soldier on the field of battle clutching a spring of holly - a poignant drawing by Cecil W. Bacon who for the next decade was to be one of the most frequent contributors of the *Radio Times* cover design.

Bacon was born in Battle, Sussex in 1905, and studied at Hastings School of Art. After a spell in the RAF he was transferred, in 1942, to the Ministry of Information. In 1946 he began a career as a freelance illustrator, drawing for *Radio Times*, *The Listener* and *London Transport*, as well as illustrating a variety of books. Much of his work will be apparent in the pages that follow.

by Piero della Francesca (1420-92)
From cover of issue 1003
18 Dec 1942

Laurence Gilliam introduces a new feature, which presents week by week outstanding news stories

by Eric Fraser
From front cover
Issue 969
24 April 1942

As the fortunes of war changed, so the BBC's provision of programme services altered. The General Forces Programme superseded the Forces Programme on 27th February 1944. The new channel was a mixture of the BBC's short-wave General Overseas Service and material designed for listeners at home.

The main reason for this change - to provide the same programmes simultaneously to troops and their families at home - was spelled out (with the aid of rather a lot of commas) on the front page of *Radio Times*:

Now, for old and young, rich and poor, at home and scattered of necessity over the earth's surface, the wireless set will, we hope, become a symbol of the hearth, a gathering place for affectionate reunion. Those drawn round it, though divided in space, will be united in mood. To be sharing the same news, the same tunes, the same jokes, the same prayers and hymns, will, we believe, quicken the feeling of nearness and of kinship. It will create a spiritual link.

BLACK-OUT			
London	. . .	. 11.2	to 4.57
Plymouth	. . .	. 11.13	to 5.20
Cardiff	. . .	. 11.15	to 5.10
Leeds	. . .	. 11.23	to 4.49
Glasgow	. . .	. 12.3	to 4.31
Aberdeen	. . .	. 12.4	to 4.12
Belfast	. . .	. 11.46	to 5.1

June 1943

'MR. HANDLEY ! ! !'

An impression by David Langdon on the all-conquering Miss Hotchkiss in action. Office life on the ITMA plane will again be revealed this evening at 8.30

by David Langdon   October 1944

SUNDAY General Forces Programme

FEBRUARY 27   296.1 m. 1013 kc/s   342.1 m. 877 kc/s

6.30 a.m. SOLO AND ORCHESTRA
Gramophone records

7.0 NEWS

7.15 BOSTON PROMENADE ORCHESTRA
on records

8.0 News Headlines
followed by
News read at dictation speed
for Forces newspapers overseas
and
Announcements

8.15 CAIRO CALLING
for the Middle East Forces. Messages recorded by members of the Services for their relatives and friends in Great Britain, introduced by Peter Haddon

8.45 ORCHESTRAL MUSIC
on records

9.10 GREETINGS FROM SOUTH AFRICA
Messages recently recorded by R.A.F. personnel for their relatives and friends in this country

9.30 SUNDAY SERENADE
Scottish Variety Orchestra (conductor, Ronnie Munro), with Janette Sclanders, Ann Rich, and Ian Gourlay

10.15 FOR ISOLATED UNITS
Sunday Service from Ruchill Church, Glasgow: conducted by the Rev. George Knight, B.D., Minister of Ruchill Church, formerly Chaplain of the Scottish Church in Budapest

10.30 CALLING ALL CANADIANS
A feature programme of special interest to all Canadian Forces, containing news from Canada and news of Canadians on the fighting fronts

11.0 Announcements
followed by
News Headlines

11.2 Weekly Newsletter

11.12 London Calling
General Forces Programme summary

11.15 'THE GOOD-HUMOURED LADIES'
Ballet Suite by Scarlatti played by the London Philharmonic Orchestra, conducted by Eugene Goossens. (Gramophone records)

11.30 MORNING SERVICE
from St. Martin-in-the-Fields, conducted by the Vicar, the Rev. E. S. Loveday
This is the first of a new series of popular services which will consist of five well-

known hymns from the Army Prayer Book, and short prayers, reading, and an address by the Rev. E. S. Loveday, who has often broadcast from St. Martin's to Forces overseas.

12 noon NEWS

12.15 p.m. 'KAY ON THE KEYS'
Kay Cavendish with her piano

12.30 TOMMY HANDLEY in 'ITMA'
with Horace Percival, Fred Yule, Dorothy Summers, Sydney Keith, Dino Galvani, Bill Stephens, Bryan Herbert, Jean Capra, and Paula Green. Orchestra conducted by Charles Shadwell. Script and lyrics by Ted Kavanagh. (Recording of last Thursday's broadcast)

1.0 News Headlines

1.1 BBC ORCHESTRA
Conductor, Sir Adrian Boult. Frederick Grinke (violin)
Violin Concerto in A (K.219) *Mozart*
(BBC recording)
Mozart's Violin Concerto No. 5, in A (K.219), is the fifth of six concertos written by him during 1775 and 1776. He was about twenty at the time of the first, and since he was then practising the violin hard—he was actually quite an accomplished player—it is presumed that he composed them as much for his own use as for use by others. This concerto is scored for small orchestra, two oboes, two horns, and strings, and the solo part is written with superb understanding of the genius of the instrument.

1.30 THE BRAINS TRUST
with spontaneous answers to 'Any Questions?': A. Beverley Baxter, M.P., Lieut.-Commander R. T. Gould, Mrs. E. R. Arnot Robertson (author), Dr. Malcolm Sargent, Emanuel Shinwell, M.P. Question-Master, Dr. Dudley Stamp. (Shortened edition for Overseas of last Tuesday's recorded session)

2.0 NEWS

2.10 FORCES FAVOURITES
Records chosen by British Forces serving overseas

2.30 RADIO NEWSREEL
Close-ups from the world's battlefronts

2.45 FOOTBALL RESULTS
read at dictation speed
followed by
2.59 News Headlines

3.0 MUSIC WHILE YOU WORK
Primo Scala and his Accordion Band

3.30 PALESTINE HALF-HOUR
for Forces in Palestine, Persia, and Iraq, with Stanley Black and his Orchestra. Guest artist, 'Hutch'. Introduced by Georgie Henschel

3.55 LIGHT MUSIC

4.0 NEWS

4.15 BOOKS, PLAYS, AND FILMS
Ivor Brown talks about the theatre

4.30 HARRY FRYER
and his Orchestra

4.55 London Calling
General Forces Programme summary

5.0 CALLING MALTA
with Anne Shelton, Nat Allen and his Orchestra, and 'Home Town'. W. Macqueen-Pope interviews Anna Neagle. Introduced by Avis Scutt

5.30 VARIETY BAND-BOX
John Blore and his Dance Orchestra, Harry Welchman, Olive Groves, Pat Frost, Violet Carson, Kathleen Moody. Introduced by Margaret Lockwood. From the stage of the Queensberry All-Services Club. This week's edition dedicated to the 'Iraq Times'

6.15 BBC SCOTTISH ORCHESTRA
Conductor, Guy Warrack
Overture : Euryanthe................*Weber*
Ballet Suite..................*Rameau—Mottl*
Hungarian Dances..........*Brahms—Dvořák*
Poème lyrique ; Valse de concert, Op. 47, in D................*Glazunov*

7.0 NEWS

7.15 FORCES FAVOURITES
Records chosen for their women-folk at home by British Forces serving overseas

7.45 'ALL TOGETHER NOW'
A special broadcast to mark the first day of the General Forces Programme, now linking listeners at home with the Forces overseas
Throughout the war, radio has been the British serving man's constant link with home. Now that listeners in this country can share the Serviceman's programme, the link is strengthened by the knowledge that they are all listening together. From homes throughout the British Isles, relations and friends here tell the men overseas what the sharing of the General Forces Programme will mean to them and to all listeners at home.

8.15 THE HAPPIDROME
with Bennett and Williams, Helen Hill, Rawicz and Landauer, Tommy Handley, and Harry Korris as 'Mr. Lovejoy' assisted by Cecil Frederick ('Ramsbottom') and Robbie Vincent ('Enoch'). Happidrome Orchestra and Chorus, conducted by Ernest Longstaffe. (BBC recording)

9.0 News Headlines

9.1 SUNDAY HALF-HOUR
Community hymn-singing, led by Cardiff Civil Defence Choir : conductor, Hubert Williams. Organist, Harold Spear. From the Memorial Hall, Cowbridge Road, Cardiff

9.30 PARLIAMENTARY SUMMARY
by E. W. A. Atkinson

9.40 LIGHT MUSIC

9.45 WORLD NEWS and NEWS FROM HOME

9.55 Announcements
followed by
News from Canada
cabled from the CBC News Rooms

10.0 'CONDUCTORS AT THEIR BEST'
Sir Thomas Beecham : a programme of records

10.25 EPILOGUE
Lead us, heavenly Father (A. and M. 281) ; St. Luke 4, vv. 1-13 ; Be thou my guardian (A. and M. 282) ; Hebrews 2, v. 18

10.30 MUSIC WHILE YOU WORK
Phil Green and his Band

10.59-11.0 News Headlines

All programmes, except those between 8.15 a.m. and 11 a.m., are broadcast also on short wave for listeners overseas

Big Ben *at* 11 *a.m., with the quarters broadcast at frequent intervals as programme requirements allow.* Greenwich Time Signal *at* 7 *and* 8 *a.m. and* 12 *noon, and at each hour thereafter except* 8 *and* 10 *p.m.*

The first **General Forces Programme** *billing page   27 February 1944
from issue 1065   25 Feb 1944*

★ ★ ★ ★ ★

The story of the BBC's 'Overseas Services' deserves a volume of its own, but the programmes that were beamed furth of Britain were rarely referred to in *Radio Times*.

When the Corporation began experimental broadcasts directed at listeners abroad, the 'Empire Service' transmissions were listed in the sister publications *Radio Supplement* and its successor *World-Radio*.

Radio Supplement had made its first appearance on 17th July 1925 as the BBC publication carrying "Dominion and Foreign Programmes", and was clearly aimed at the listener who wished to 'pull in' stations from as far afield as the USA.

Like its companion, *Radio Supplement* was published for the BBC by George Newnes. In 1927 it changed its name (but little else) to *World-Radio,* and was taken over entirely by the BBC in the late 'thirties, probably when the printing of the journal was switched to Twyford Abbey Road. Its final edition appeared on 1st September 1939, by which time it also included skeleton listings for the BBC's television programmes.

Radio Supplement
Issue no.1
17 July 1925

As *World-Radio* was amalgamated into *Radio Times* on the outbreak of war, a new paper was created to carry programme listings for listeners abroad. A programme sheet titled *BBC Empire Broadcasting* had been aimed mainly at listeners in the scattered British colonies but, as the political situation demanded that London's voice should be most audible across the continent of Europe, a more general publication was called for.

BBC Empire Broadcasting *August 1939*

by Victor Reinganum August 1945

The story of radiolocation, one of the great scientific achievements of the war, will be told tonight at 9.30

London Calling made its debut in the first weeks of the war, appearing in September 1939. The Airmail edition was printed in a higher quality paper by W. Speaight & Sons Ltd in Fetter Lane (just off London's Fleet Street) it had the unmistakeable look of *Radio Times*.

For readers in Europe, there was even a four-page supplement printed in French, German and English. Eventually there would be separate editions of *London Calling* for Europe, and programme sheets in many of the languages used in the BBC's external broadcasts, including such delights as the French *Ici Londres* which, surface-mail editions of *London Calling* was printed by Waterlows in Twyford Abbey Road.

The first editor of *London Calling* was Tom Henn, and in 1944 he moved to *Radio Times* to replace Gordon Stowell. He inherited the most truncated of publications, by now reduced to 20 pages per issue. Even the bright red masthead was now appearing in black as a result of ink shortages.

First London Calling 24 Sept 1939

On the morning of June 7th 1944 - the day after D-Day when Allied troops landed in France en masse - the BBC began broadcasting to the Western Front forces its 'Allied Expeditionary Forces Programme' - the brainchild of General Eisenhower - a joint programme aimed at British, American and Canadian troops.

Towards the end of May Maurice Gorham was brought back from the BBC North American Service to be in charge of the new AEF Programme, giving him but a couple of weeks to plan a new service that would go on the air at 5.55 every morning and stay on the air until 11pm.

Gorham arranged for a special edition of *Radio Times* to be printed and distributed free to the occupation army. The first inkling of this came ten days after D-Day when some copies of the Home edition carried a prominent banner on the front page promising an AEF edition the following week.

Front page banner Issue 1081   16 June 1944

This is the Home edition of Radio Times: from next week you will receive an A.E.F. edition containing details of your own A.E.F. programmes as well as those of the BBC's Home Service and General Forces Programme.

Radio Times (incorporating World-Radio) September 29, 1944
Vol. 85 No. 1096 Registered at the G.P.O. as a Newspaper
AEF EDITION

PROGRAMMES FOR October 1—7

RADIO TIMES

Masthead Issue 1096 29 Sept 1944

From 23rd June 1944 the AEF edition carried details of all the programmes from Gorham's new station. A bespoke version: it had its own edition of *Both Sides of the Microphone*; its own letters column; it often had its own cover and it prominently displayed the bold words **AEF EDITION** in the top left-hand corner above the masthead where the Home edition bore the words **PRICE TWOPENCE**.

In September 1944 *Radio Times* celebrated its 21st Birthday. Muted celebrations they were as the Editor duly recorded:

The Royal Air Force Dance Orchestra and the R.A.F. 'Skyrockets' Dance Orchestra will be heard from the London Coliseum at 4.30 p.m.

> ...in normal circumstances the event would no doubt have been celebrated with an enlarged issue. It would have revealed in pictures as well as words the story of this, the first radio programme paper in the world, from its inception - when the project narrowly escaped being turned down on the grounds of expense - to its present unique position as a trusted household friend in some three to four million British homes.
>
> But these are days of strict paper rationing. Moreover, wartime values are not those of peacetime, and events of infinitely greater significance to the world demand everyone's first and closest attention. So we must content ourselves this week with an expression of thanks to listeners for the continued support of *Radio Times* for twenty-one years, and an assurance, in the face of that support, of our own sense of high responsibility in the continued endeavour to make the journal worthy of it.

With just twenty pages at his disposal, Henn's two celebratory paragraphs appeared on the front cover of the Home edition, and on page three of the AEF version. He devoted just one further page (in the Home edition only) to an article by long-term staff man, Charles Tristram, who had been Leonard Crocombe's Chief Editorial Assistant at the birth of the paper. He was one of only two staff members to see *Radio Times* into adulthood - the other being T. R .Warner from the Advertisement Department.

Amongst Tristram's recollections was a confession:

> Once, owing to an extra rush of work, all the programmes of one broadcasting station were omitted! Another time, a messenger who had been sent to the printers with a batch of 'copy' at the last moment left it in the train. Most of the matter was irreplaceable and consternation reigned. Happily, after much frantic telephoning and what seemed like an eternity, the parcel was recovered, but only in the nick of time.

By Christmas 1944 the Allies continued to occupy more territory on the Continent, and as they travelled mobile radio stations went with them. These Army Broadcasting Stations would be set up as near to the front line as possible and armed with improvised transmitters, mixers and equipment often constructed from bits and pieces captured from or abandoned by the enemy in the desert.

As well as relaying the General Forces Programme, these stations improvised programmes of their own. Some went as far as improvising their own editions of *Radio Times* as well.

Cover of Forces' **Radio Times**
Northern Italy No.1 1 March 1945

Paiforce edition No. 38
Forces' Radio Times   *20 Jan 1946*

However crude these issues - produced voluntarily by the troops themselves - they incorporated the essential ingredients that made *Radio Times* in those days. One version, boasting *Both Sides of the Microphone* (whose writer went by the pseudonym of 'Watome') appeared complete with his grave warning, "The printer's knowledge of English is about as good as ours of Italian."   Illustrations were cheerfully 'borrowed' from old copies of the home publication. And copies included a form upon which to "Request for Audition for Broadcasting". An article on 'Television' was contributed by Walton Anderson, himself a pre-war producer and star interviewer at Alexandra Palace - now one of the Services' team running the British Forces' station in northern Italy.

Other versions followed, and soon it became *de rigeur* for Forces Radio stations to provide their own distinctive printed programme, always with the title *Radio Times*. Such ventures continued to flourish as late as the 1960s.

★ ★ ★ ★ ★

By 1945, *Radio Times* could afford to retain few regular features. Two-and-a-half pages of advertising and fourteen of programme billings (which also incorporated advertisements) left but three-and-a-half pages for editorial matter. The cover (which from 9th February 1945 had a new, larger masthead with the simple addition 'Journal of the BBC') included a small illustration and a third of its space devoted to a summary of the week's programme highlights.

A leading article connected with a programme highlight usually occupied page three, which just left space for *Both Sides of the Microphone*, the *Letters* - and a couple of features if you were lucky and could squeeze one of them into the corner of Sunday's General Forces Programme page.

'YOU'VE SAID IT,' a play about 'Careless talk,' will be broadcast this evening at 7.0

by Victor Reinganum
Issue 1112   19 Jan 1945

On 4th May 1945, *Radio Times* appeared as usual: twenty pages, with a small cover illustration of Anthony Trollope's "Doctor Thorne" drawn by Steven Spurrier. The features inside included one on that serial play; a short article about bacteriologist Louis Pasteur written by Sir Alexander Fleming; a preview of a new serialisation of Shakespeare's *King Henry the Fourth*. The programme pages covered the period May 6-12.

But at three minutes past two on the afternoon of 7th May 1945, German radio carried a broadcast by the German foreign minister declaring his country's unconditional surrender. The war - in Europe at least - was over, and the following day was declared VE Day.

The BBC had of course been planning for such a contingency, and as programme schedules were revamped *Radio Times* once again found itself having to hastily update printed information and produce a special issue in less than the usual time.

Thus, on Thursday, 10th May, the *Radio Times* Victory Number was published, containing programmes for that and the next eight days. For the first time in many years a special illustrated cover was designed by Terry Freeman, incorporating the V-sign as twin bursts of spotlights above the London skyline.

Within its 24 pages this well-decorated special issue celebrated the cessation of conflict with a leading article by the Archbishop of Canterbury, and a two-page *Both Sides* illustrated with Cecil W. Bacon's drawings of prominent British landmarks.

The programme pages included prominent illustrations that paid tribute to each of the forces in turn: the Royal Navy, the Army and the RAF - as well as the Merchant Navy and the 'people of Britain'.

Victory cover by Terry Freeman   Issue 1128   10 May 1945

The following week, eight days' worth of programmes were again crammed into 24 pages, and *Radio Times* carried a large photograph of Broadcasting House illuminated by floodlighting for the first time since the blackout had been imposed at the beginning of the war.

Now it was time for *Radio Times* to consider its role in peacetime.

CHAPTER FIVE
Sound and Television

Changes to British Broadcasting now came thick and fast as it shed battledress and donned its civvies.

On 20th July 1945, the final AEF edition appeared, with a front-page article by Gorham alerting listeners to the imminent launch of his next project - the BBC Light Programme, of which he was the first controller. As the AEF Programme ended, the wartime transmitter arrangements ceased and Regional broadcasting was resumed.

On 27th July 1945 a new-look *Radio Times* appeared with a cover article by the BBC's Director-General, W. J. Haley describing the new programme arrangements. It was to be just the first of a whole series of re-arrangements of the paper's contents which were to continue through a rather unstable decade.

*Cover
Issue 1139
27 July 1945
N/NI edition*

*The Light Programme's first day
From above issue*

An extra four pages allowed for a summary of the new regional programmes as well as short features about some of the more prominent regional broadcasts. And for the first time listings for Gorham's latest infant - the Light Programme.

From front cover of issue 1153   2 Nov 1945

by Victor Reinganum

Since the print restrictions continued well into the 1950s, it would have been quite impossible for *Radio Times* to return to the glorious pre-war days of printing all the programme details for all of the BBC's domestic services in one thick publication. It was therefore decided that, alongside the re-establishment of regional broadcasting, the journal itself would also mirror the new pattern of the Home Services by appearing in six distinct geographical editions. These were: London, Midland, West of England, Welsh, Scottish and a combined edition serving the North of England and Northern Ireland where, owing to a shortage of available frequencies, it was necessary for both regions to share a common programme.

This unsatisfactory arrangement put noses out of joint on both sides of the Irish Sea. Although the main part of the 'North' Home Service was carried in full on an exclusive wavelength by a transmitter at Moorside Edge (which covered Lancashire and Yorkshire) the North-East and Border country - served by the transmitter at Stagshaw - was "twinned" with Northern Ireland.

This was largely a result of the BBC mandarins' desire to introduce a highbrow Third Programme in order to boast an 'improved' post-war service - two wavelengths from the UK's international allocation were needed for this, leaving insufficient wavelengths to service the needs of both the Light Programme and the seven Home Services.

London edition — *Issue 1265* **9 Jan 1948** - *Spot the difference...* — *Northern Ireland edition*

This broadcasting shotgun marriage continued for a further eighteen inharmonious years. But at least *Radio Times* was able to provide a separate Northern Ireland edition from 2nd January 1948, although most curiously this new edition was not initially badged as such, having at first - like the London edition - no 'edition' name on the cover, and its billing pages merely referring to the station as 'The Home Service' (as with the London edition - the London Home Service was never referred

Tonight at 9.30

THE MAN IN BLACK
introduces
'Appointment with Fear'

by Mendoza   September 1945

to as such except on rare occasions.) A printer's device (little horizontal bars on the spine) was used to allow those 'in the know' a means of visually differentiating between the London and Northern Ireland versions.

This arrangement lasted for about a year, after which the Home Service pages were branded 'N. Ireland Home Service' and the front page fell in line with its regional brethren by carrying the words 'NORTHERN IRELAND EDITION' in the top left-hand corner above the masthead.

Although inevitably the subject of a Parliamentary Committee of Enquiry, television was given the go ahead in October 1945 to come out of hiding and resume its activities more or less unchanged. None other than the ubiquitous Maurice Gorham supervised its return!

Television had always held a special fascination for Gorham, and on 2nd November he was appointed Controller of the Television Service.

He and his small team determined that the service should return the day before the Victory Parade. Thus BBC-tv resumed on 7th June 1946, and *Radio Times* was faced with the dilemma of how to deal with it.

In pre-war days *Radio Times* had never quite been sure what to do with TV. After initially including it as an afterthought in the edition distributed in London, and the financial burden of the photogravure *Television Supplement*, television had been somewhat grudgingly afforded a double-page spread in all editions of the 90-odd page paper.

Whilst this had provided much-needed publicity for the infant service, and had stimulated an unfulfilled desire amongst the bulk of the readership who lived far outside the range of 'Ally Pally', in the immediate post-war period of severe newsprint shortages it was hard to see where TV could be found space in a thin 24-page magazine.

The solution was twofold. An extra 4 pages could accommodate the Television Service billings and editorial; and if this was confined to a separate 'Television Edition' which was produced in only limited quantities (approximately a third of the normal 'run' of London editions), then the newsprint ration could be eked out sufficiently.

TELEVISION PROGRAMMES IN 'RADIO TIMES'

These programmes for the first two days of post-war television appear in every copy of the London edition of 'Radio Times.'

In future the week's television programmes will be published as a separate section in one of every three copies of the London area distribution. The present shortage of newsprint prevents our publishing full programmes in every copy as was done before the war.

Listeners with television sets should ask their newsagent for the television edition of 'Radio Times.' (Listeners with television sets who live more than forty miles from Alexandra Palace should ask their newsagent to order a copy for them.)

Any reader with a television receiver who finds it difficult to obtain a copy of the television edition of 'Radio Times' should write at once to BBC Publications, Scarle Road, Wembley, Middlesex, giving the name and address of the local agent.

MAKE SURE OF YOUR TELEVISION EDITION NOW

TV edition panel
Issue 1183
31 May 1946,
London edition

Victory Number cover
by H. S. Williamson
Issue 1183   31 May 1946
London edition

The great Victory Parade and the resumption of television clearly merited a special cover, and H. S. Williamson provided a fitting visualisation of the victorious troops marching through the streets of the capital.

Within the Victory number, news of television's reincarnation was only to be permitted the meagre three-quarters of a page that was reserved each week for a regional contribution. Into this had to be squeezed the billings for the first two days of programmes and a tiny photograph of the two lady announcers Jasmine Bligh and Winifred Shotter along with an equally tiny picture of ballet dancer Margot Fonteyn who was to star in the Re-Opening programme.

From page 4
of Victory Number

The first Television edition the following week was emblazoned by a 16-point bold standfirst that proclaimed it to be the...

...but no other indication on the page that the visual medium had returned! The list of important programmes on the cover were all on radio, and the entire television coverage was shoved into the ghetto of pages 24-27 where a new feature *Teleflashes* by The Scanner made its first appearance. A letters column titled *Viewers' Views* was to appear in subsequent issues.

PROGRAMMES

Vision 45 Mc/s   **JUNE 9-15**   *Sound 41.5 Mc/s*

IN THE TELEVISION GARDEN
The late Mr. C. H. Middleton in the small garden he made on the grass slopes of Alexandra Palace. It became an allotment during the war, and F. Streeter is determined to turn it again into a 'thing of beauty'. Mr. Streeter starts work in the garden on Sunday at 3.10 p.m.

LEONARD SACHS takes the chair, and the tankard, at a presentation of the Players' Theatre entertainment 'Late Joys. Join them in the choruses of the nineties on Monday night at 8.55

SUNDAY
JUNE 9

3.0   FILM

3.10   'IN OUR GARDEN'
F. Streeter revisits the television garden in the grounds of Alexandra Palace and gives viewers some practical hints

3.30   CARTOON FILM

3.35-4.0   FOR THE CHILDREN
The Hogarth Puppet Circus presented by Jan Bussell and Ann Hogarth
Fred Woodward as Hank the Mule
Eric Cardi, conjuror
Presentation by A. Miller Jones

★   ★   ★

8.30   FILM

8.40   'THE IMPORTANCE OF BEING EARNEST'
A Trivial Comedy for Serious People, by Oscar Wilde
John Worthing, J.P. .... Robert Eddison
Algernon Moncrieff .... Mackenzie Ward
Rev. Canon Chasuble, D.D. .... David Horne
Merriman, a butler .... J. B. Stringer Davis
Lane, a manservant .... Alban Blakelock
Lady Bracknell .... Margaret Rutherford
Hon. Gwendolen Fairfax .... Margaret Vines
Cecily Cardew .... Dorothy Hyson
Miss Prism .... Betty Potter
Scenes: Algernon Moncrieff's flat in Half Moon Street, W., the garden at the Manor House, Woolton, and the drawing-room at the Manor House, Woolton

artists from the Players' Theatre, who include
Don Gemmell
Joan Sterndale Bennett
Bill Shine
Bill Rowbotham
Hattie Jacques
Betty Lawrence (at the piano)
Under the genial chairmanship of Leonard Sachs
Presented for television by Philip Bate

9.25   'TRANSATLANTIC QUIZ'
In this first televised edition viewers will see the London end of the famous contest between Professor D. W. Brogan and Jan Struther, with Quiz-Master Lionel Hale, and the New York team—Christopher Morley and John Mason Brown, with Quiz-Master Alistair Cooke
Produced by Mary Adams

10.0-10.10 News (sound only)

3.5   'THE SILENCE OF THE SEA'
A television play of the story by 'Vercors,' 'Le Silence de la Mer.' Translated by Cyril Connolly
The uncle .... J. H. Roberts
The niece .... Antoinette Cellier
The German officer..Kenneth More

(Continued overleaf)

Settings by Barry Learoyd
Produced by G. More O'Ferrall
Robert Eddison is appearing at the St. James's Theatre, and Dorothy Hyson at the Haymarket Theatre

10.10-10.20 News (sound only)

MONDAY
JUNE 10

3.0   FILM

3.10   HARRY ROY AND HIS BAND
with
Eric Whitley
Eve Lombard
Harry Kaye

3.40   WRESTLING
A demonstration of heavyweight wrestling
Harry Anaconda v. Bert Asserati
Arranged by S. E. Reynolds
Commentator, E. R. Voigt

4.0-4.15   BANK HOLIDAY AT ALEXANDRA PALACE
The television camera takes you into the grounds

★   ★   ★

8.30   SYLVIE SAINT-CLAIR
the French singing star
JACK and EDDY EDEN
in songs at the piano

8.45   FILM

8.55   'LATE JOYS'
Viewers are invited to a Music-Hall entertainment of the late 1890's. Sing the choruses with

TUESDAY
JUNE 11

3.0   IRENE PRADOR
(At the piano, Evel Burns)

'THE HOGARTH PUPPETS' Jan Bussell and Ann Hogarth manipulate their amazing puppets. They are presenting a circus show for children on Sunday afternoon at 3.35

Page 25 of issue 1184   7 June 1946   Television edition

The programme pages adopted the same typefaces and design as had been used for the *Television Supplement* back in 1937, and were well illustrated with photographs of some of the lucky participants in the resumed service

by Robert Adam
Issue 1188
5 July 1946
TV edition

TELEVISION EDITION   BBC PROGRAMMES FOR July 7 — July 13

RADIO TIMES

JOURNAL OF THE BBC   PRICE TWOPENCE

Radio Times incorporating World-Radio
July 5, 1946. Vol. 91 · No. 1188.
Registered at the G.P.O. as a Newspaper

ALPINE BRITAIN. 'The Alpine world of Britain begins at 2,000 feet—lower still as we travel north.' Here is a view of the cloud-hung Cairngorms, seen across the valley of the Spey. This richly-varied region, lying in the heart of the Scottish Highlands, was one of those visited by Stephen Potter for his Sunday-evening programme, 'In Search of Alpine Britain.' (Study by Robert M. Adam)

'The Stormy Petrel'
The Early Life of Maxim Gorky

'Doctor Faustus'
Christopher Marlowe's tragedy in 'World Theatre'

'Vic Oliver Introduces'
for the last time

Admiral Lord Louis Mountbatten
receives Freedom of the City of London

Sport
Inter-Varsity Cricket at Lord's
King's Prize at Bisley
Speedway Racing at West Ham

Gregor Fitelberg
conducts the BBC Symphony Orchestra

In Belgium Today
Another 'Window on Europe' feature

'Exercise Bowler'
Scenes from the London play

A further return to normality was signalled by the first 'ordinary' peacetime cover to be adorned entirely by an illustration. The issue for 5th July 1946 featured a striking 'photographic study' by Robert M. Adam of the Cairngorms, seen across the Spey valley.

PROMENADE CONCERTS

52nd Season opens Saturday July 27

Sir Henry Wood 1869-1944

A fortnight later an attention-grabbing sketch of Sir Henry Wood occupied most of the cover, celebrating the 52nd season of Promenade Concerts and re-establishing *Radio Times* as a major commissioner of new artworks.

From cover of issue 1190
19 July 1946
TV edition

BBC

From cover of issue 1198
13 Sept 1946   **ITMA**

'The Third Programme' was conceived as being unashamedly intellectual, a programme designed to satisfy the aims of a public service in providing a minority audience with programmes that might be to their taste.

It was launched on 29th September 1946, and created for the hard-pressed editor of *Radio Times* even more problems than the resumption of television had - for the new service was to be available throughout the UK, and this meant carrying its programmes and editorial in all six editions.

Further calls on Waterlow's scant newsprint resources were necessary, but somehow Henn managed to cram everything in to 28 pages for all but the Television edition, which was granted 32.

Cover of issue 1200
27 Sept 1946

First Night
for the Third

By starting the programmes on page two, a layout was adopted where the first pair of facing pages gave programmes for the Home Service (on the left) and the Light Programme (on the right).

The next pair of pages incorporated the Third Programme and a summary of regional variations titled 'Today in the Home Services' on the left page, and editorial matter on the right. Thus four-and-a-half pages (including the front cover) were available for editorial, two-and-a-half pages for advertisements and 21 pages for programmes. A neat juggling act!

By the end of 1946 another four pages were being doled out from the rations (prematurely as it happened), allowing the Television edition a luxurious 36 pages and the others 32 pages. This meant that the journal no longer "opened up" to reveal programme pages. Instead a page of advertisements with a facing page of editorial now appeared, as had been the norm even through the 20-page wartime issues.

3a   *Christmas 1957   by James Hart*

3b   *Eamonn Andrews 1958   by Laurence Bradbury*

3c   *Christmas 1958   by Eric Fraser*

3d   *Easter 1959   by Laurence Bradbury*

4a   *Part of double centre-page advert 1962*   RT

4b   *Christmas 1963*   TV Times

4c   *Christmas 1963*   *by Victor Reinganum*   RT

4d   *Christmas 1963*   The Viewer

Third Programme

Sir Edward Elgar,

from the drawing by Batt. The Elgar Memorial Fund Concert in honour of Queen Mary's eightieth birthday will be broadcast from the Albert Hall tonight

by Oswald Batt
Issue 1232   23 May 1947

But in the first months of 1947 a national fuel crisis caused emergency measures to be taken by the government, and these included the suspension of weekly periodicals, along with television, and sound broadcasting for part of the day including a complete suspension of the Third Programme.

Consequently *Radio Times* failed to appear on 21st and 28th February. Publication resumed on 7th March 1947 with this apology....

Radio Times, in common with all weekly periodicals, has had to suspend publication for two consecutive issues. We could not give readers a warning in our own columns that for the second time since No.1 was published on September 28 1923, *Radio Times* would not be pushed through the letter-box or collected from the bookstall on Friday morning. (The first break in publication occurred at the time of the General Strike in 1926.) *Radio Times* with its weekly circulation of more than 6,250,000 copies takes six days to print, and the suddenness with which the restrictions were imposed did not allow us time to insert a stop-press notice in our issue of three weeks ago.

But we are back again, and home will seem more like home with *Radio Times* on the table by the wireless set.

This six-day printing process followed a geographical pattern, with the issues that had the furthest distance to travel being printed first. This arrangement was further complicated by the fact that the pages for the London edition had to be set first, since it was from these basic pages that the regional variations were then made. Grace Harbinson would oversee the national programme billings but sub-editors were assigned to the Light, Third and each of the regional Home Services. Generally, the order of printing was:

North of England Edition
Northern Ireland Edition
Scottish Edition
Welsh Edition
West of England Edition
Midland Edition
Television Edition
and finally the *London Edition,*
        which had been set first.

How 'The News' is Put Together
Issue 1261
12 Dec 1947

FROM THE BOOKSHELVES . . .

5.15 p.m.
'Books and Writers'
Reviews of recent fiction and other new books

10.15 p.m.
'Armchair Detective'
Thrills from new crime and mystery fiction

Issue 1221   7 March 1947

Scottish Home Service

The billings editor generally went to Waterlows on the first press day to check proofs. (Until 1964 this job was carried out by Grace Harbinson who also sometimes wrote programme notes for the paper under the by-line Maureen Chamberlain.)

As *Radio Times* began to settle back into something approaching its pre-war style there were plenty of opportunities in 1947 for 'special' covers: the return of the 'Radiolympia' exhibition in September warranted a stylish drawing by James Hart; the 25th Anniversary of British Broadcasting issue published on 7th November had a striking interpretation of the BBC's coat of arms complete with the reinstated 'Nation Shall Speak Peace Unto Nation'; the following week, the Royal Wedding of Princess Elizabeth and Prince Philip, carried a simple photograph of the happy couple.

'P.C. 49'

Above left:
Radiolympia
by James Hart
Issue 1250
26 Sept 1947
Scottish edition

BBC 25th
Anniversary
Issue 1256
7 Nov 1947
Scottish edition

Royal Wedding
Issue 1257
14 Nov 1947
North of England
and Northern
Ireland edition

MONDAY

The Light Programme

Above: by James Hart   April 1947

Issue 1263   ***North/NI edition by Braby***
26 Dec 1947

As 1947 turned into 1948, *Radio Times* took advantage of its regional system to provide an entirely different cover for the Scottish edition, recognising the added significance of Hogmanay to listeners in that nation. All the other editions had a cover illustration by Braby with the caption 'Ring out the old, Ring in the new' - but Scotland boasted an illustration by Imrie incorporating the traditional greeting, A GUID NEW YEAR TO ANE AN' A'.

...and the Scottish edition by Imrie

The idea of separate covers (which had begun with the AEF edition) continued. From time to time various regional editions would boast their own, associated with special local programmes or events such as the Welsh Eisteddfod or the Edinburgh Festival. Regional covers were sometimes produced in order to eliminate reference to a special event, which local listeners (or later viewers) were <u>not</u> to be party to.

Paper supplies continued to fluctuate and Henn and his team continued to scratch their heads for the best way to cram everything in between the covers.

The arrangement whereby programmes started on page two had not been successful, so the Light and Third were made to share a single page of billings, thereby allowing feature material to once again occupy the first few pages. During 1948 the basic editions had reverted to 24 pages, and even an event as momentous as the 14th Olympic Games being held in London in July had to be content with that number.

by Cecil Bacon   Issue 1293   23 July 1948   Television edition

Having perforce celebrated its 21st birthday in muted fashion *Radio Times* was allowed just a little more space to celebrate its Silver Jubilee in September, with an 'enlarged number' (enlarged, that was, by a mere four pages). Tom Henn's birthday editorial traced the by now well-worn path of the paper's history, and ended with some words about its inadequate size....

Issue 1302
24 Sept 1948

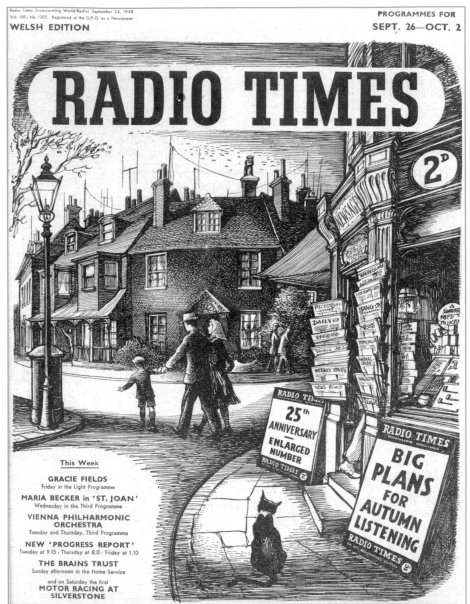

Radio Times (Incorporating World-Radio) September 24, 1948
Vol. 100 : No. 1302. Registered at the G.P.O. as a Newspaper
WELSH EDITION

PROGRAMMES FOR
SEPT. 26—OCT. 2

RADIO TIMES

2ᴰ

This Week

GRACIE FIELDS
Friday in the Light Programme

MARIA BECKER in 'ST. JOAN'
Wednesday in the Third Programme

VIENNA PHILHARMONIC ORCHESTRA
Tuesday and Thursday, Third Programme

NEW 'PROGRESS REPORT'
Tuesday at 9.15 : Thursday at 8.0 : Friday at 1.10

THE BRAINS TRUST
Sunday afternoon in the Home Service

and on Saturday the first
MOTOR RACING AT SILVERSTONE

25th ANNIVERSARY ENLARGED NUMBER

BIG PLANS FOR AUTUMN LISTENING

Tom Henn

The Radio Times enters the new period of service to listeners at a disadvantage. There is not enough paper to provide the sort of *Radio Times* which the present scope of broadcasting demands. We have to work within the strained economic fabric of a country still emerging from the greatest war of all time. We are not grumbling; merely stating a plain fact. By regionalising the contents of *Radio Times* on the same pattern as broadcasting has been regionalised we have solved many of our immediate problems. But it leaves us still very short of space for articles and illustrated features which, as we know from readers' letters, add considerably to the enjoyment and understanding of all forms of broadcasting. But we are in the happy position of being able to say today that every listener who wants a copy of *Radio Times* can have one every week of the year - and that is a pleasant beginning to the next twenty five years.

The paper situation began to ease in the spring of the following year and on 4th March periodicals were permitted an additional four pages a week bringing RT up to 28 (or 32 for the TV edition).

Once again, Henn experimented with new ways of presenting the programme information and this time hit upon an idea that would be developed further in the coming years. The weekend programme pages were doubled, with daytime programmes (up to 5pm) on one pair of pages and evening programmes on the next pair. This not only allowed for more detailed billings for the programmes that tended to attract the highest audiences but also - and crucially for the magazine's continuing financial stability - permitted more advertising matter to be placed alongside programme billings.

Double page spread - pages 24 and 25 of issue 1325   4 March 1949

Just four months later came the good news that paper rationing was to be eased further and *Radio Times* was now able to expand to 40 pages.

Alas,
something
went
horribly
wrong.

PROGRAMMES FOR
JULY 3—9

RADIO TIMES

JOURNAL OF THE BBC   PRICE TWOPENCE

A NEW
CHILDREN'S PROGRAMME
Monday to Friday in the
Light Programme at noon

BERLIN STORY
The airlift was a year old on June 28:
Sunday's Home Service programme tells
the story of that year

CHARLIE CHESTER
and 'Stand Easy !' are back on
Wednesday in the Light Programme

'THE SCARLET PIMPERNEL'
Baroness Orczy's famous adventure story
as the Tuesday Light Programme serial play

'MURDER ON THE EXPRESS'
A play by Maurice Maxwell, written for
broadcasting. Tuesday, Home Service

Australia's
CHAMPION BAND
Sunday evening, Light Programme

THE ULSTER DERBY
Commentary from The Maze on Saturday
in the Home Service

OPEN GOLF CHAMPIONSHIP
Reports from Monday to Friday in the
Home Service : details on page 16

SPEEDWAY RACING
Belle Vue v. West Ham
Saturday in the Light Programme

'THE CANTERBURY TALES'
Chaucer's famous stories in thirteen parts
Prologue on Monday and Friday in the
Third Programme

BROADCASTING HOUSE IN LONDON, THE HUB OF BRITISH RADIO

NOW 40 PAGES, WITH MORE PROGRAMME DETAILS, MORE ARTICLES AND MORE PICTURES

Issue 1342   1 July 1949   Northern Ireland edition

The regional editions rolled happily off the Twyford Abbey Road presses each with forty pages of a new make-up which allowed four pages - two double spreads - for each day's radio programme details. Henn's weekend design was now extended throughout 7 days, the type size was increased wherever possible and there was a general tidying up of the magazine's look.

Your *Radio Times* is larger this week and different. There is now more paper available, enough to add another twelve pages and for some time past we have been exploring ways and means of using it so that you will have the best possible service. All the suggestions you have sent to us have been studied and the result of our deliberations is presented inside.

But when it came to printing the London edition it would appear that Waterlows had run out of paper. History does not relate - and memories do not recall - the exact nature of the problem. But in extreme haste, late on the Tuesday afternoon the decision was taken to send the London edition to be reset by the printers at the Kemsley House headquarters of the *Daily Graphic* and strange-looking tabloid sized copies of a 24-page London edition rolled off the newspaper's presses - a million in London and two million in Manchester.

The following week, it was back to 24 pages and a shamefaced front-page apology.

Owing to circumstances outside the control of the BBC it was necessary last week to produce an emergency edition of RADIO TIMES for London and the Home Counties. This week, as a temporary measure, we have had to reduce the size of RADIO TIMES to twenty-four pages, but with our next issue we will introduce our new standard forty-page journal with its twenty-eight programme pages

Finally on 15th July, London readers - who unusually had their own front cover for once - were able to experience the 40-page design for the first time. In fact by the end of 1949 the size was nudging up again - 44 pages for most editions and 48 pages for the Television edition were not uncommon. And the crossword - for many readers one of the highlights of the paper - had been reinstated and enlarged, with such pre-war compilers as Leslie A. Roberts making a welcome return.

This evening at 7.0 for the five-hundredth time In Town Tonight stops the roar of London's traffic to present interesting personalities

by Victor Reinganum   Issue 1362   18 Nov 1949

GOETHE'S 'FAUST'

by Eric Fraser
From cover
of issue 1359
28 Oct 1949

In fact, the crossword was one of the few signs of a more relaxed mood within the pages. The austere face of the late '40s and '50s was reflected in the unsmiling nature of so many *Radio Times* features of the period. If Gorham's paper had been a bright, young thing, Henn's was utilitarian and sombre. There were few regular features, and - largely due to the severe space constraints - what space there was tended to be occupied by worthy words concentrating on important and prestigious broadcasts. Items like *Strolling Commentaries* and *I Saw Yesterday* no longer had a place in the magazine.

'THE SOUNDS OF TIME'

The broadcast at 9.15 presents the story of the years from 1934 to 1949 through the medium of notable recordings selected from the archives of the BBC's Recorded Programmes Library. John Snagge introduces the programme on page 8

by Victor Reinganum   Issue 1366   16 Dec 1949

Until December 1949, television continued to take a back seat in the BBC's broadcasting arrangements, mainly because its sole medium power transmitter covered only London and some of the Home Counties.

But just before Christmas, the high power station at Sutton Coldfield, near Birmingham, brought TV to the densely populated English Midlands.

THE TOYTOWN CHRISTMAS PARTY takes place in Children's Hour at 5.0 this afternoon with the Mayor as the host—a gay gathering at which even Mr. Grouser is prevailed upon to tell a story. This illustration was drawn by the late S. G. Hulme Beaman, creator of Toytown

By Sydney Hulme Beaman Issue 1365

From page 47

Radio Times had been eagerly anticipating this event for some time, even going as far as putting an impressive photograph of the partly-completed 750-foot Sutton Coldfield mast (the first of its kind) on its cover in July.

Issue 1365   9 Dec 1949   Television edition

SATURDAY — December 17

TELEVISION comes to THE MIDLANDS

Opening of the Sutton Coldfield transmitter

Speeches by
The Postmaster-General, the Rt. Hon. Wilfred Paling
and the Vice-Chairman of the BBC Board of Governors
the Dowager Marchioness of Reading

TONIGHT AT 8.0

11.0-12.0 NEWSREEL
(Composite edition)

★   ★   ★

3.0-4.5   Patrick Barr,
Linden Travers, and Susan Bligh
in the film
' WEDNESDAY'S LUCK '
Scotland Yard is faced with an unusually intelligent gang of criminals, and deals with them in its own special way

8.0 First transmission from the new BBC Television Station at Sutton Coldfield
(See displayed panel above)

8.15   STARS IN YOUR EYES
A Variety revue featuring :
Leslie Henson, Binnie Hale
Stanley Holloway, ' Hutch '
Mary Meade, Jolly
' Dynamite ' Jefferson
The New China Troupe
and The Starlets
Eric Robinson and his Orchestra
Décor by Richard Greenough
Devised and produced
by Henry Caldwell
(*Specially staged at the King's Theatre, Hammersmith*)

9.15   ICE HOCKEY
Earls Court Rangers v. Nottingham Panthers
A visit to the Empress Hall, London, to see the third period in this Autumn Cup match
Patrick Burns helps viewers to follow the play

9.45   NEWSREEL
(Repeat of Friday's edition)

10.0-10.15 NEWS (sound only)

For the 9th December issue a photograph of the completed mast adorned the cover, and inside was a variety of articles about television, including *This Thing Called Television* by Norman Collins, who by then had replaced Gorham as Controller of BBC Television.

And for the first time, television programmes were printed in all copies of the Midlands edition, with half-page summaries of the TV programmes also included in the North and Welsh editions which bordered the Midlands and in which areas a few lucky viewers with powerful aerials and favourable conditions were able to view BBC TV. Also, for the first time, the top right-hand corner of the Midland edition no longer carried the words 'BBC Programmes' but instead the bold **SOUND AND TELEVISION** which was to appear on all editions as they expanded to include detailed television listings.

Although the BBC was in many ways responsible for the increased emphasis on Christmas as a national holiday festival, it had recognised that in Scotland the majority still viewed Hogmanay as the secular holiday. Indeed, in that nation the public holiday that was generally given on Boxing Day south of Hadrian's Wall was awarded on 1st January.

Accordingly in December 1949, and doubtless under considerable pressure from Melville Dinwiddie, the BBC's Scottish Controller, *Radio Times* altered its normal arrangements to give Scottish readers a special 44-page "Hogmanay Number" of their own. It had a distinctive cover illustration by Cecil Bacon, and eight days of programme details starting on Saturday 31st December with a decorative page-header by Bruce Roberts.

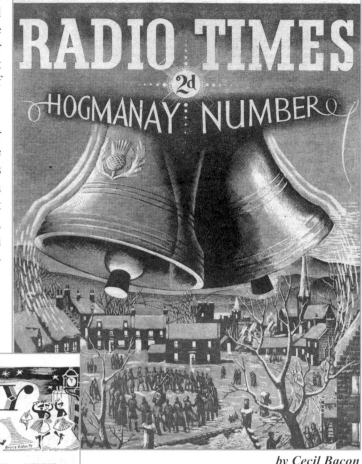

by Cecil Bacon
Issue 1368
30 Dec 1949
Scottish edition

From pages 14/15 of issue 1368
Hogmanay page-header by Bruce Roberts

Broadcasts for Schools
BEGIN AGAIN TODAY

by Margaret Levetus
Issue 1431   13 April 1951

by Cecil Bacon

North of England edition & Television edition   *Issue 1378   10 March 1950*

Early in 1950, broadcasting stations around the world adopted a new frequency plan, agreed upon before the war but only implemented afterwards. *Radio Times* made full use of its regional editions to inform listeners of the new places on the radio dials where Home, Light and Third were to be found through a Cecil Bacon design that was appropriately adapted for each edition...

In March the staff of *Radio Times* were able to leave their assorted wartime billets - in particular the Grammar School in Scarle Road, Wembley where many of the staff had been posted - and return together to their headquarters at 35 Marylebone High Street in west London.

The austerity of post-war Britain began to take its toll, and resentment of poor pay and conditions in a number of areas of industry began to bubble over into industrial disputes. This included the print industry, and in the autumn of 1950 a dispute between the London Master Printers and the London Society of Compositors, which had begun in May began to adversely affect production of *Radio Times*.

9.30 SPEEDWAY RACING
The World Speedway Riders'
Championship for the
Sunday Dispatch Trophy
Commentary by Robin Richmond on
the concluding heats of the final
From the Empire Stadium, Wembley

Issue 1404

Illustration by Eric Fraser   Issue 1404

+ S T. J O A N +
BY BERNARD SHAW

74

The paper failed to appear on 8th September. And the following week - on 15th September - a truncated 20-page issue covering nine days of programmes was published in a single edition. There was no editorial - save an explanation of the circumstances on the cover. Each day's radio programmes were afforded just two pages, with a single page at the back for the week's television billings.

Worse was to come. And although the paper temporarily returned to normal with the 22nd September issue the dispute was not over, and the 6th October issue was produced in just two editions - 'Sound' and 'Sound and Television' with only the programmes of the London Home Service displayed fully.

Radio Times then disappeared from bookstalls for three weeks before returning on 3rd November with another 20-page, nine-day emergency special edition.

On its front page, Tom Henn apologised for the paper's enforced absence:

> During the last three weeks many listeners have written chiding us for not having produced *Radio Times* elsewhere in the United Kingdom or in Europe; some have asked why we had not produced in a typewritten-printed form in which some other publications appeared and even why we had not the energy and foresight to produce it on duplicating machines. As we said earlier, the BBC is not a firm of printers and the dispute was outside our control but we assure listeners that every effort was made to continue the regular publication of the journal. The problem was simply one of printing 8,000,000 copies each week. Despite all efforts this did not prove possible by alternative methods.

Although the dispute was at an end and *Radio Times* quickly returned to normality, readers had been quick to show their irritation that the paper could not have made alternative arrangements. Henn and his colleagues had in fact tried very hard to find a way of producing the paper and had gone as far as having plates made up abroad - but the printers back in England refused to handle them.

The exercise had not been totally futile, however, as it gave the production team adequate experience that was put into use when it came to the next printing dispute a few years later - of which more in Chapter Six.

Cover of issue 1404   15 Sept 1950

Cover by Hunter   Issue 1408   3 Nov 1950

by Cecil Bacon   Issue 1433   27 April 1951

'Festival of Britain' banner by Eric Fraser

The 1951 Festival of Britain was one of the events of that year to merit another special Cecil Bacon cover.

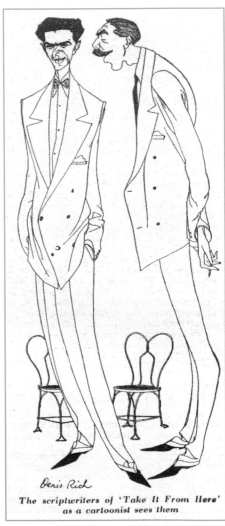

The scriptwriters of 'Take It From Here' as a cartoonist sees them

Denis Norden and Frank Muir
by Denis Rich
Issue 1464   30 Nov 1951

By this time *Radio Times* was appearing with special covers as often as it had before the war, even if they were still in black and white and readers now had to pay an extra penny for them, the price of *Radio Times* having been increased - for the first time - to threepence.

March 1951

> When you have finished with 'Radio Times'
> **SAVE IT FOR SALVAGE**
> *Paper is scarce and it can be used again*

Television continued to expand, and in October the opening of the Holme Moss transmitter on the Pennines near Huddersfield brought TV within sight of millions of new viewers in the North of England - along with the now obligatory cover photograph of the new mast. The summary of television programmes was now extended to all editions that didn't carry full TV listings.

Eight million copies of *Radio Times* for 8th February 1952 had already rolled off the presses when the announcement was made of King George VI's death on 6th February. It was too late to withdraw the issue as copies were already *en route* to newsagents, so in the space of a few hours, a four-page supplement was prepared and distributed throughout the Kingdom by air, express train and road.

This contained the revised BBC programmes for February 9-16, along with the order of a Service of Memorial to be broadcast from the Concert Hall of London's Broadcasting House on 10th February and a sketchy outline of programmes for the day of the King's funeral on 15th February.

Supplement cover
Issue 1474
8 Feb 1952

The new television transmitter for Scotland at Kirk o'Shotts midway between Glasgow and Edinburgh was temporarily brought into service in order to transmit pictures of the King's funeral. However the official launch of TV in Scotland was made on 14th March and this time the paper's newly-appointed art editor, R. D. Usherwood found for the cover illustration a more imaginative alternative to a photograph of yet another tall, thin hilltop mast.

As was becoming increasingly the case, Cecil W. Bacon was the favoured illustrator for this special front page.

by Cecil Bacon
Issue 1478
7 March 1952
Scottish edition

The following week, the Scottish edition increased to 52 pages, which had become the norm for those editions that contained full television billings. Soon afterwards full television billings were included in *all* editions of the London edition, and the Television edition was abolished.

Issue 1485   25 April 1952
Television, Scottish
& Northern Ireland editions
An example of regional covers. With no Scottish or Irish interest in the F.A. Cup Final, local alternative covers were produced.

≈≈≈≈≈≈≈≈≈≈≈≈≈

The lot of the Billings Editor was never a happy one. Constantly coaxing, cajoling and wheedling billing details from recalcitrant producers, and balancing their desire for maximum space with the constraints of page layouts was surely not a simple task.

DON'T BLAME THE B.B.C...

Don't blame the B.B.C. for *all* the noises that come out of your set. Some are caused by worn out valves. When valves wear out, you get distortion, loss of power, fewer stations. That's why the B.B.C. advises listeners to have their receivers and valves checked regularly. See your own dealer today, and you'll hear the difference when you

Re-valve with
Mullard

Mullard Ltd., Century House, Shaftesbury Avenue, W.C.2

Illustration by Ronald Searle
Issue 1520   26 Dec 1952

Frequently programmes would be changed at the very last minute, and the unlucky billings sub-editor out at Park Royal would have to improvise a paragraph or illustration to fill the gap.

Rarely did the subs make mistakes of their own, but Hilary Cope Morgan, who looked after the Third Programme pages at this time before taking over from Grace Harbinson as overall Billings Editor, relates how on one occasion, producer Anna Karin had adapted a Mary McCarthy novel which was a skit on campus life. All concerned were satisfied with the programme's title, but all concerned were wrong and thus the book's correct title *The Groves of Academe* was printed as:

THE GROOVES OF
ACADEME.

Misprints of this nature were, however, very few and far between in a journal which prided itself not only on its huge circulation, but also on its accuracy.

In the summer, television extended to the Welsh and West of England editions with the opening of the transmitter at Wenvoe and another Cecil Bacon design, which this time incorporated his drawing of the transmitting mast!

RADIO TIMES
JOURNAL OF THE BBC   PRICE THREEPENCE

WELSH EDITION   BBC Programmes
                                      AUGUST 10—16

TELEVISION COMES TO
SOUTH WALES

Official opening of the new BBC Television transmitter at Wenvoe. The ceremony will be performed by the Postmaster-General and televised on Friday at 7.45

This special issue contains articles by the BBC Controller, Wales, and the BBC Director of Television; a two-page pictorial survey, 'This is Television'; and full television programmes for Friday and Saturday

by Cecil Bacon   Issue 1500
8 Aug 1952   Welsh edition

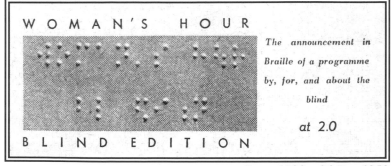

WOMAN'S HOUR

The announcement in Braille of a programme by, for, and about the blind

at 2.0

BLIND EDITION

Issue 1520   26 Dec 1952

✳ A ✳ HAPPY ✳ NEW ✳ YEAR ✳

**by George
Mackie
Issue 1501
15 Aug 1952
Scottish edition**

**by Cecil Bacon
Issue 1529
27 Feb 1953
Scottish edition**

Another instance when Scotland went its own way was with the 1952 Edinburgh Festival which featured on the cover of all editions for the issue of 15th August. Whereas most of Britain had a cover featuring a photographic study of Princes Street in Scotland's capital, the Scottish edition had a special cover drawn by George Mackie.

Television - from the start of 1953 - assumed a new importance in *Radio Times* with the TV programme details no longer confined to the back-pages ghetto but instead allowed to follow naturally on from the six radio pages, in much the same way as the Third Programme had followed the Home and Light when it was introduced.

At the same time, TV billings were - from the issue of 16th January 1953 - extended to all editions which in practice meant merely adding them to the Northern Ireland edition since this was the only part of the United Kingdom left without its own television transmitter. By 1st May this had been rectified with the opening of a temporary transmitter at Glencairn, near Belfast, housed in an old pre-war outside broadcast vehicle!

52 pages were now the norm in the run-up to the Coronation. The BBC celebrated thirty years of broadcasting in Scotland with yet another CWB cover illustration. This particularly striking design incorporated the three BBC centres in Scotland under the shadow of a radio and a television transmitter mast. By now Bacon was clearly a expert at drawing such structures.

The Coronation Number demanded a very special cover, but the Waterlow presses were not designed for full colour operation. Nevertheless Eric Fraser made use of the limited technology to create the first colour cover of peacetime.

The process involved tinting the front (and of necessity back) pages yellow and running a red crown motif at the top and bottom the page, growing fainter as it approached the centre. This yellow and red paper was then run through the normal presses where the black-ink detailed illustration was added.

Uniquely, Fraser carried the design of lion and unicorn over to the back page where in a jocular form they sat down together for a feast of Batchelors tinned foods!

The Coronation Number included five pages containing the complete text of the service. Cecil Bacon was not overlooked for this issue as he designed the map of the Coronation Route which occupied the centrefold. And veteran artist Walter Hodges drew the page decorations for the Coronation evening programme pages.

This special issue sold 9,012,358 copies - a new record for *Radio Times* but one that would soon be broken.

Colour cover by Eric Fraser
Coronation Number   Issue 1542   29 May 1953

From far and near the festive throng
    Arrived on the festive morn
And along with the throng (some millions strong)
    Were the Lion and the Unicorn.

They had fought, these two, in a story book
    To make a Nursery Rhyme,
But now, for a long time friends, they took
    Their seats together, on time.

    And as the procession came toward
        The stand where their places lay,
    The shouting soared and the Lion roared
        And the Unicorn neighed Hooray!

The hours have sped and it's time they fed.
    They walk back licking their lips.
They had breakfasted while the dawn was red
    And lunched on a bag of chips.

And so, for the end of a perfect day,
    Their supper, like ours, includes
A specially gay and delicious array
    Of Batchelors Wonderful Foods.

Batchelors
WONDERFUL Foods

Printed in England by WATERLOW & SONS LTD., Twyford Abbey Road, Park Royal, N.W.10, and published by the BRITISH BROADCASTING CORPORATION at 35 Marylebone High Street London, W.1 —May 29, 1953

Back cover of Coronation Number   May 1953

CHAPTER SIX
Television and Sound

om Henn died from lung cancer in 1954 and Douglas Graeme Williams - who had joined as Gorham's Art Editor in 1933 - took over as Editor. He did not approach the job in the same ways as had Henn, Stowell and Gorham, preferring himself to be thought 'a gifted amateur' rather than a professional.

With the size of the publication now stabilised at 52 pages - adequate space to cover sound and television programmes - it seemed *Radio Times* was in for a period of smoother sailing, like the Royal Yacht 'Britannia' shown on Cecil Bacon's unusual cover of 7th May. Unusual because apart from the normal standfirst of price and edition and the title *Radio Times* there were no other words - the picture representing the return home of the Queen from her tour of the world simply spoke for itself.

by Cecil Bacon   Issue 1591   7 May 1954

Rarely had an Art Editor ever risked using pictures only to convey the message! But throughout the decade *Radio Times* was blessed with the risk-taking talents of Ralph Usherwood.

'Ush' - born Ralph Dean Usherwood - was born in London on 27th October 1911, and had shone at Worcester College, Oxford where his talents allowed him to produce cartoons of his contemporaries for student magazine *Isis* (these were later published as a book) whilst captaining the University's cup-winning lacrosse team.

Upon graduation in 1934 he was headhunted by the then renowned Cloister Press in Manchester, where he developed a passion for printing and the theory and history of typography, spending some time in Germany studying contemporary practice.

Ralph Usherwood

At the outbreak of war he had been a conscientious objector but, on seeing so many of his best friends in peril, had joined the RAF - training as a flying boat pilot at the ripe old age of 30. After the war he had worked for Odhams Press for two years before joining the staff of *Radio Times*. In his decade as Art Editor, he presided over what was probably the most fruitful artistic period of the magazine.

by Bob Sherriffs

Tom Jenkins
and the Palm Court Orchestra
by Hunter

Another fine example of Usherwood's eye for a striking front page was Geoffrey Fraser's Welsh edition cover for the 1954 Eisteddfod, incorporating the flags of all of Wales' counties and text which was only in the Welsh language.

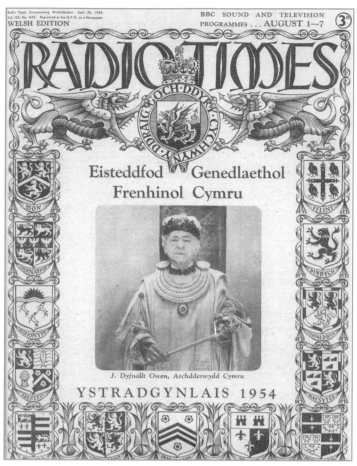

by Geoffrey Fraser
Issue 1603
30 July 1954
Welsh edition

With seven editions and more pages, it now took eight days to print. On the day one issue was put to press, the galley proofs of the next issue's programme billings were available for the first time, thus allowing just a week to get everything ready for the printer.

Art Editor R. D. Usherwood explained how this printing schedule affected the freelance illustrators:

> There was thus just a week in which to get everything ready for the printer. By the first day the layout of the programme pages had been drawn up and space allocated for illustration. This was when the artist was commissioned. He had three days - and four nights - in which to complete his work. The process engraver was left a day and a night in which to make the blocks.
>
> All the artists were employed on a freelance basis to do the work for which they were thought best fitted. Scripts of plays, features and information about programmes were made available for the art editor to read, and the content of the text suggested a particular artist to him. The size of illustration was determined by page layout. When the artist was commissioned he was told the exact proportions to which he must draw and given the deadline for delivery. There was no time for roughs or alterations; a drawing was either good enough or - very rarely - unusable. It was essential that the original drawing, whatever its size, should scale to the correct dimensions, for the typographical layout to contain it had gone ahead of it to the printer. Block and type came together on press day - and by that time galleys were available for another week.

The informal story of radio entertainment as related by artists and others who have had a hand in making it

Television reached out along the southern coast of England on 12th November 1954 with the opening of the Rowridge station on the Isle of Wight, but by now the novelty of mast-laden covers had worn off, and in any case that happened to be Remembrance Week and so the issue was wrapped in a cover design by Cecil Bacon (of course) depicting London's Cenotaph.

The Christmas issue broke new records with sales of 9,253,025 copies. But *Radio Times* was beginning to face competition. The copyright in the BBC's programme listings was jealously guarded by the Corporation, and newspapers who had once threatened not to print its programmes were now strictly forbidden to print more than a day at a time, except at weekends when papers published on Saturday were permitted to print Saturday and Sunday programmes.

by Cecil Bacon   Issue 1617   5 Nov 1954

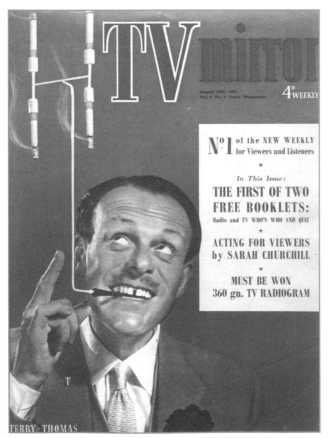

First issue of TV Mirror   *29 Aug 1953*

As the infant television had begun its march across the country, weekly papers began to pay attention to the medium and its characters. Prominent amongst those was *TV Mirror*, gravure-printed with attractive colour covers (and back-page advertisements). It was published by the Amalgamated Press who crammed its 28 weekly pages with large well-printed photographs of the major stars of this new medium, alongside detailed stories and interviews with them. Making its appearance on bookstalls on 29th August 1953 it continued until around 1957.

And the new commercial television was just around the corner, with a launch planned for the autumn of 1955. Round about this time somebody suggested to Geoffrey Strode, who was the General Manager of BBC Publications, that the BBC should register the name *TV Times*. Strode scathingly replied that he didn't think TV would catch on.....

But *Radio Times* did make some efforts to tap in to the market for colour pictures of the TV stars, and for three years published lavish *Radio Times Annuals* - which, with full colour covers and 96 gravure pages, did something to counter the attractions of the new rivals.

Radio Times Annual *1954*

1955 got off to a bad start. A threatened rail strike would have caused major disruption to the distribution of *RT* - and so production of the issue for 14th January was brought forward and an abridged 24-page issue with a layout based on that of the late 'forties was produced. As it turned out, the threatened strike did not happen in January and the latter editions of the 14th January issue were printed at full 52-page size. The rail strike *did* take place in June when the government declared a State of Emergency and it was back to abridgement for the issues of 10th and 17th June.

The subject of the covers had up to this point generally been radio-based, but with over four million TV licences now sold, *Radio Times* began to shift its front page emphasis - an early example being Peter Scott's programme *Wildlife in the Antarctic* which earned itself pole position on 4th March 1955.

Issue 1634   4 March 1955

First issue of TV Times *20 Sept 1955*

In September, Independent Television made its debut in in the London area. The BBC stoically avoided any mention of this newcomer, but *Radio Times* gave more cover space to TV than hitherto. Meanwhile 'on the other side', weekday ITV contractor Associated-Rediffusion made arrangements to produce a listings paper for ITV generally, and on 20th September *TV Times* appeared for the first time. With cover stars Patricia Dainton (from ITV's new daily serial *Sixpenny Corner*) and American comedienne Lucille Ball, and a cover price a penny more than its BBC rival, the first 40-page issue sold in far more homes than had the means to view the new TV.

There was also more humour in *TV Times* - with cartoons, plenty of star portraits and a brighter layout it was clear that *Radio Times* could no longer sit on its laurels. Fortunately, the copyright situation prevented either paper from taking each other on head-to-head and in households with 'the new TV' both papers found themselves cheek-by-jowl on fireside coffee tables.

Radio Times
Issue 1684
17 Feb 1956

Problems in the print industry once again affected the production of *Radio Times* (and most other British magazines including the rival *TV Times*) in the early months of 1956. The issue for 20th January was to be the last 'normal' one for more than two months. The following week's 40-page issue carried this ominous notice:

At the time of going to press a dispute in the printing trade has made it necessary to publish this week's *Radio Times* in one edition.

This edition contains all the BBC Television and Sound programmes including Regional changes in the Home Service.

Two weeks later the single-edition *Radio Times* was further reduced to 24 pages and the now familiar 'abridged' layout, although nine million copies were still rolling off Waterlow's presses.

THE RADIO SHOW

Above: Issue 1658   21 Aug 1955

But not so the following week.

The dispute had really begun to bite and it was no longer possible to print in London as the strike had closed down Twyford Abbey Road.

But this time Douglas Williams and his staff were prepared for a battle. Williams and four key members of the *Radio Times* production staff, including Art Editor R. D. Usherwood, Billings Editor Grace Harbinson (who conveniently spoke French) and two sub-editors were put on a plane for Paris. There, *Radio Times* was to be produced for the next six weeks on the presses of Société Cofosco, a small but efficient firm whose business was founded on the printing of pornographic magazines and race cards.

Programme information was compiled in London and much of the material simply mailed to Paris. Typesetting of the paper was done in all manner of places (including a monastery) and the end result was a bizarre four-page broadsheet publication whose typefaces had the distracting habit of changing font and size in the middle of a column.

But unlike the previous dispute, this time *Radio Times* did not need to suspend publication and even somehow managed to retain some original illustrations.

Cover
Issue 1686
2 March 1956

EDUCATING ARCHIE

The French compositors struggled manfully to keep up with the stream of text in English - indeed some of it in Welsh! But now and again their concentration must have lapsed....

> **3.0 Greenwich Time Signal**
> Conducted by
> Lt. Col. S. Rhodes, M.B.E.
> Edith Lewin (mezzo-soprano)

Page 4
Column 4
Issue 1686

The dispute came to an end at Easter, and Billings sub-editor Hilary Cope Morgan (Tom Henn's former secretary who knew her way around *Radio Times* better than most) had the wit to have printing resumed on the Wednesday instead of the usual Thursday in order to avoid having to pay a fortune in overtime for the printers to have to work on Good Friday.

The fruit of their labours, and the first normal issue for ten weeks, published on 6th April. Its 48 pages and seven regional editions showed that things were - as the editor announced with some relief on page three - "Back to Normal".

On 28th March Geoffrey Strode, issued the following memo:

From: General Manager, Publications. To: All Publications staff.

LONDON PRINTING TRADE DISPUTE

Work was resumed yesterday after a stoppage lasting 6 weeks. During that time nearly 60,000,000 "Radio Times" were printed in France and flown or brought by sea to this country for distribution by road. Ten issues of "London Calling" were produced in Malta and the European Service periodicals were printed in France and Germany. "The Listener" after a break when four issues were not published started up again under most difficult conditions.

Thirty-four members of the staff made 136 journeys by air and 16 by sea, sometimes at only a few hours notice.

This historic achievement was possible because those of you who were called upon, whether here or overseas (and like the civilian in the last war many who stayed at home suffered greater hardship than those overseas) put into their work a keenness, energy and self-sacrifice that is beyond praise.

The editorial staff who worked for many hours in a small French printing works, standing because there was nowhere to sit; the man who spent long hours on a snow-covered airfield; the PBX operator who worked for hours beyond her duty time, and the staff of the Operations Room who would not leave until the last aircraft had been cleared are examples of devotion to duty rarely encountered in business today.

The effort which was necessary to give the public the service they have come to expect from the BBC has been costly in human endeavour and money. We must all strive to get back to normal conditions as quickly as possible.

The praise from the public, the wholesale and retail newsagents and our colleagues has been overwhelming. All I can add is - thank you very much.

(G.S. Strode)

28th March, 1956.

Geoffrey Strode

Waterlow's presses in Park Royal were now working at their absolute limit and were becoming inadequate for the huge circulation that *Radio Times* enjoyed. The seven Crabtree rotary magazine printing presses had been installed to cope with a print run of three million. Now over nine million weekly copies were demanded. The seven machines had already been converted into fourteen, but this still limited the maximum size of the paper to 52 pages.

BBC Television Programmes

The BBC's sales target was 10 million copies and they wanted a paper that could grow to 76 pages. The problem was solved by building a second plant especially for the production of *Radio Times*, at the other end of the country from Park Royal, thereby allowing production to be divided more or less on a north-south line. A site in the new town of East Kilbride, ten miles to the south-east of Glasgow was chosen and three more Crabtree presses installed on a site that boasted its own dedicated railway siding.

In August 1956, the new works at Peel Park Place, College Milton, East Kilbride, Lanarkshire were commissioned. The last 48-page Scottish edition to be printed south of the border (for the foreseeable future) was published on 24th August, and the following week a special 60-page issue was printed in Scotland.

To celebrate this achievement, the Scottish edition was allowed to have extra pages each week, complete with purely Scottish advertisements and feature articles. There was even a Scottish *Letters* column.

Scotland continued to enjoy extra pages for the rest of the year, although it did sometimes look rather odd when the first numbered page - page 2 - appeared on the sixth printed page, and the page numbers mysteriously vanished after number 51!

The first **Radio Times** *to be printed in Scotland*
Issue 1712   31 Aug 1956
Scottish edition

ONE OF THREE ROTARY MAGAZINE PRESSES
INSTALLED AT THE NEW FACTORY OF
MESSRS. WATERLOW & SONS LIMITED, EAST KILBRIDE, GLASGOW
FOR PRINTING "RADIO TIMES"

Crabtree Press
Issue 1735, page 52
8 Feb 1957
Scottish edition

East Kilbride advertisement
Page 2 of above issue, 1735

by Val Biro   Issue 1729   28 Dec 1955

Radio Times now began to rely on photographs of familiar faces rather than commissioned artwork for its covers. But on some high days and holidays the illustrators were still sometimes to be seen, Val Biro's New Year's Eve cover being a good example.

With the issue of 15th February 1957, much about *Radio Times* changed. For a start, television (both BBC and ITV) was no longer required to close down for an hour between six and seven in order to allow mothers to get their children to bed. This hour, known affectionately as the 'toddlers' truce' had been the subject of considerable lobbying on the part of the ITV companies who naturally wanted to maximise their audience at this time. When the government caved in and allowed them to abolish the 'truce' the BBC obviously also benefitted. The change in programme hours led to a major relaunch of BBC Television and, in turn, a similar revamp of *Radio Times* itself.

With the establishment of the Waterlow's plant at East Kilbride, it was now possible to spread the print load and extend the size of the paper nationally beyond 52 pages. East Kilbride was to print the Scottish, North of England and Northern Ireland editions; Twyford Abbey Road would be left to handle Midlands, Welsh, West of England and London editions.

The biggest change for readers was in the makeup of the paper. At the front were the feature articles as usual - but now the rather po-faced items were supplemented by a lighthearted regular feature *Round and About*, with snippets of news about both radio and television programmes, and the byline 'The Broadcasters'. This was of course a natural continuation of *Both Sides of the Microphone* and was penned at various times by Rowan Ayers Nick Hosalti, future editor C. J. Campbell Nairne, and Elwyn Jones.

A right-hand title page (facing a page of advertising) then introduced the BBC Television Programmes, with an 'At a Glance' highlights column and a feature article about some major TV programme of the week. There then followed all the television listings, most of them allowing a double page spread for each day in order to maximise the advertising content that was spread around the TV billings.

Another right-hand title page followed for *BBC Sound Programmes* with a similar layout to the TV title page. The radio billings then followed, still with the four-page-a-day layout. More advertising, a page for women and finally the letters page now dubbed *Points from the Post* and finally the all-important crossword made up the remainder of the new 60-page magazine.

The masthead was also subtly altered. Since 1954 the grey band that incorporated the words RADIO TIMES had also contained below it in small type the words JOURNAL OF THE BBC and PRICE THREEPENCE. Now prominent in the design were the letters BBC centred at the top with TELEVISION AND SOUND on either side of it - and the PRICE THREEPENCE was centred below. Now the title could be read as 'BBC RADIO TIMES'.

But some things never changed. Victor Reinganum contributed a typical cover illustration for the National Radio Show issue (no longer was it 'Radiolympia') in August.

A few weeks later BBC Radio underwent some changes. The wavelengths used by the Third Programme were also to be time-shared with a new radio service, which would provide varying kinds of adult education and hobby programmes. Network Three (as the new service was called) was launched with a flourish in the issue of 27th September, and another cover designed by Cecil Bacon.

by Victor Reinganum   Issue 1763   23 Aug 1957

by Cecil Bacon   Issue 1768   27 Sept 1957

Readers might be forgiven for being a little confused about the new arrangements when confronted on Network Three's second day of existence by a little box on the page where Tuesday's Network Three programmes belonged.

For this special week *Radio Times* ran to 68 pages and included a large map helpfully pinpointing the locations of the BBC's shiny new VHF Radio transmitters, together with detailed information about VHF frequencies in the region appropriate to the edition.

September 27, 1957

Network Three

No programmes are being broadcast today in Network Three as the time has been allocated to the Third Programme for an opera broadcast

Issue 1768   Page 42

by Cecil Bacon   Issue 1772   25 Oct 1957

In October BBC Television celebrated its 21st Anniversary (although of course it hadn't actually been on the air for 21 years thanks to the wartime gap) with another Bacon cover, plus an appropriately celebratory message from the Director General Sir Ian Jacob, and another by Gerald Beadle, the Director of Television.

For the first time since the early wartime Christmas covers *Radio Times* again made use of red and black for one of its most memorable Christmas designs - James Hart's red-breasted robin perched under a snow-topped masthead led into 52 pages of festive fare and elaborate page decorations. And of course the Christmas Crossword with the blocked squares formed by a Christmas tree shape.

Christmas cover
by James Hart
Issue 1780   20 Dec 1957
Plate 3a

Another innovation of the late 'fifties was the introduction of *Radio Times* Pull-Out Supplements, four colour-tinted pages in the centre of the magazine that urged readers to "Pull sharply away from staples" in order to retain the supplement when its parent issue had long since been used to light the fire. The injunction to pull 'sharply' was important since to pull 'gently' usually meant either tearing the supplement asunder or disembowelling the entire magazine!

These intriguing little fold-outs in pastel shades of yellow, pink and blue dealt with everything from Third Programme music plans to Eileen Fowler's keep fit exercises. Sometimes they were just big advertisements - a pink pullout in February 1958 heralded the arrival of a new weekly periodical for women, *Woman's Realm*.

The first post-war use of colour on a 'normal' cover was in May when Laurence Bradbury designed a striking royal blue illustration that acted as a backdrop for a photograph of Eamonn Andrews in a tuxedo - all dressed up for the Home Service programme *Toast of the Town*. Perhaps the bright colour was intended to divert customers' eyes from the cover price which from this issue went up by a penny to fourpence!

Radio Times was having to increase its visibility on the news stands. The commercial channels' *TV Times* was now on sale in London, the Midlands and the North of England; and was joined by Thomson newspapers' *TV Guide* in Scotland and Berrows' *Television Weekly* in Wales and the West of England. All of these titles had brightly coloured mastheads, and by now *TV Times* was printed using photogravure giving it an altogether superior look to its grey letterpress BBC rival. So a fortnight later, there was another colour experiment - this time the often-used frame of a television screen was set behind a T. L. Poulton sketch of explorer Sir Vivian Fuchs - but instead of the usual black surround for the TV screen it was turquoise blue.

Cover by Laurence Bradbury Issue 1799 2 May 1958 Plate 3b

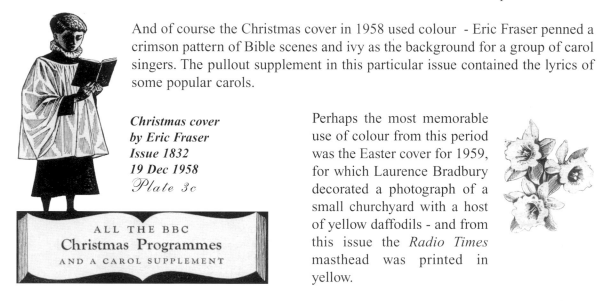

And of course the Christmas cover in 1958 used colour - Eric Fraser penned a crimson pattern of Bible scenes and ivy as the background for a group of carol singers. The pullout supplement in this particular issue contained the lyrics of some popular carols.

Christmas cover by Eric Fraser Issue 1832 19 Dec 1958 Plate 3c

ALL THE BBC
Christmas Programmes
AND A CAROL SUPPLEMENT

Perhaps the most memorable use of colour from this period was the Easter cover for 1959, for which Laurence Bradbury decorated a photograph of a small churchyard with a host of yellow daffodils - and from this issue the *Radio Times* masthead was printed in yellow.

Easter cover by Laurence Bradbury Issue 1846 27 Mar 1959 Plate 3d

Ironically, the introduction of yellow to the masthead meant that there would be no more coloured covers, since the second plate required to add the yellow ink was clearly as much as the presses could handle on an everyday basis. And apart from daffodils, there wasn't much of a yellow nature that would appear to have any relevance to the programmes.

But the yellow was necessary to distinguish *Radio Times* from its ITV competitors, since all of these had red tops - except for Scotland's *TV Guide,* which was naturally blue.

Another skirmish in the printing trade in June 1959 resulted in yet another of those 'all edition' issues, and also for one week only a reversion to a plain black and white masthead. (*TV Times* suffered worse during this particular dispute - for four weeks it appeared as an 'all-editions' broadsheet publication, printed in Glamorgan.)

Yet another disruption to the normal process came in February 1960 when the threat of another nationwide rail strike made it necessary to publish a single edition for the whole country - although this time complete with the now familiar yellow masthead.

★ ★ ★ ★ ★

The dawn of the sixties brought about a series of changes (of varying significance) to the appearance of the familiar journal of the BBC. The first was in its regional editions, and was partly a result of changes in technology.

When regional broadcasting was resumed after the war, the Home Services were defined by the transmission 'footprints' of the medium-wave transmitters, which dotted the map. These had been placed for not editorial but engineering convenience. Thus the so-called West Home Service was radiated by transmitters at Brighton, Bexhill and Folkestone, in the extreme south-east of England.

by Peter Kneebone Issue 1864 31 July 1959 North of England edition

East Anglia suffered even more anomalies - the North Home Service had a transmitter at Cromer in north-east Norfolk, the Midland Home Service was radiated by Postwick (just a few miles

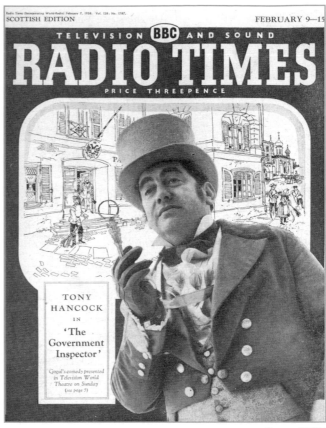

Issue 1787
7 Feb 1958
Scottish edition

south of Cromer) and most of East Anglia was covered by the London Home Service from Brookman's Park.

The introduction of VHF Radio, broadcast on very high frequencies from transmitters covering clearly defined local areas, made it possible at last to clear up many of these anomalies. Beginning in 1955, transmitters were built with the priority of serving places where medium wave coverage was either poor or editorially inappropriate.

Equally, the areas served by television transmitters did not often correspond exactly to those of medium wave radio, and with the increase in regional television opt-outs some adjustment was necessary. A result of this was that, towards the end of 1959, the BBC's regional boundaries were redefined. The former West Region was now made to acknowledge its cousins along the south coast - and renamed the South and West Region. Accordingly the edition became the SOUTH AND WEST EDITION although it was several more years before its radio service came to be described as the South and West Home.

Local programming was provided for East Anglia on VHF radio and latterly on television and so that edition became the MIDLANDS AND EAST ANGLIA EDITION.

But perhaps *Radio Times*' most significant innovation in 1959 was the launch of *Junior Radio Times* - a four-page 'pull-out' designed for children which made its premiere appearance on 28th August. (Pull sharply away from staples. Carefully, now. Don't hurt yourself...)

An impressive amount of material was crammed into the four pages. A brief listing of the week's children's programmes on television and radio (which was regionalised), some features on the programmes themselves plus Barry Bucknell's 'do-it-yourself' feature, a junior letters column, Curiosity Corner which pointed up assorted bits of TV trivia, a weekly serial story (starting with Elisabeth Beresford's "Penny for a Traitor" and the first regular strip cartoon since the demise of Nat and Reg during the war - Peter Kneebone's eccentric *Tom and Vera*.

Junior Radio Times was to reinstate some of the pre-war verve in the paper - if the articles for grown-ups were serious and lacking in recognisable by-lines, here were four weekly pages that had a comforting familiarity about them.

Tom & Vera Strip no.1 Issue 1858 28 Aug 1958

Stories abounded with Geoffrey Webb and Edward J. Mason's serialised yarn woven around the adventures of the youngest members of radio's popular *The Archers* serial, titled *Manhunt in Ambridge*; C Gordon Glover's *May the Silver Barley Blow* and Aubrey Feist's period story *The Dagger and the Rose*. And in April 1960 *Tom and Vera* gave way to a weekly *Captain Pugwash* cartoon by John Ryan, based on his popular TV series.

Issue 1819   19 Sept 1958

But in general the paper's huge circulation was quite simply a result of its sole ability to publish the BBC's television listings a week in advance. With the noble exceptions of *Round and About*, the crossword and *Junior Radio Times*, the handful of feature articles were rarely designed to make its contents more popular. Following in the tradition of Percy Scholes and Ralph Hill, Felix Aprahamian contributed a *Music Diary* and a small space (now usually a single column) was made available for regional programme notes.

The covers, too - now more than ever crucial to sales - were not exactly blockbusters. As late as the autumn season of 1959, covers were devoted variously to a production of Greek tragedy; and radio's *Take it from Here* and *The Navy Lark.*

But Williams knew that the status quo was no longer an option if *RT* was to survive and keep its massive circulation. It was again time for a rethink.

Issue 1925
30 Sept 1960
From page 4

The last of the old-style yellowtops to appear was published on 30th September 1960. Inside was exciting news for readers - "A restyled and enlarged Radio Times".

Top designer Abram Games had been brought in to give the publication a complete makeover from front to back. Nothing had been sacrosanct. Even the day of publication was to be altered.

Games' restyled *Radio Times* had a bold masthead that gave much greater prominence to TV. It was to carry a different band of bright colour each week, allowing for at-a-glance identification of the current week's issue (assuming that you remembered which colour this week's was, that is...).

Programmes would now run from Saturday to Friday allowing for the first time the full weekend of programmes to be contained in one issue. The *TV Guide* in Edinburgh had in fact pioneered this idea the year before when it had experimented with a Monday to Sunday week. But the experiment had failed, probably because it meant printing the weekend programmes too far ahead for accuracy.

TV and radio listings were re-integrated, but now television programmes would come first with radio's four pages following (under the aegis of former Art Editor Ralph Usherwood who had been sidelined to make way for change). And instead of a lead-in of feature articles, there would be a page of programme previews before each day's listings, thereby creating a self-contained mini-magazine for each day of the week - a logical style which was not only to survive into the next century, but which was eventually to be adopted by all listings magazines.

Issue 1926
6 Oct 1960

Junior Radio Times was brought to an end - with the rather hollow promise that in the new *Radio Times,* "There you will find old friends and familiar names".

In fact the only element which survived the transition unscathed was the weekly *Captain Pugwash* cartoon strip.

The first of the new-style issues was published on 6th October 1960. From now on, Thursday was to be publication day with the printing schedule advanced by a day all round. Below a loud orange masthead, Janie Marden and a puppy were the cover stars, immediate stamps of the paper's new character - along with the new cover price of fivepence.

The 64-page issue included a new *Pick of the Week* with a page 3 listing of the forthcoming television and sound highlights. Inside, Douglas Williams enumerated the changes and went on to explain the reasoning behind them:

These changes are the result of a great deal of thought and planning in which the views of readers have been taken fully into account through a wide-scale investigation made on our behalf by the BBC Audience Research Department.

Here was a new notion - market research - that was to drive all future decisions about changes to the magazine's makeup.

The visual appearance of the paper was undoubtedly more up-to-date. Larger type for programme times was one immediately obvious change. Compare the style of the October 8th billing from the last old-style issue with the new:

From page 23   Issue 1925   30 Sept 1960

From page 9   Issue 1926   6 Oct 1960

Barry Bucknell's *Do It Yourself* emerged from the pages of *JRT* to be an 'adult' feature tied in with his new television series. 'The Broadcasters' by-line still appeared now tagged to *Round and About Next Week* at the back. And there were *Pugwash* and the crossword.

Radio Times was beginning to swing with the sixties.

CHAPTER SEVEN
Changes and Colour

nevitably, the overhaul needed some tweaking. There were complaints: readers still wanted the following Saturday's programmes. And so a summary of Saturday programmes was included on the inside back page, giving the paper an eight-day life span.

The *Round and About Next Week* feature was altered to include more pictures and fewer words, and experiments were made to find the optimum locations for *Points from the Post* and *Pugwash*.

Spot colour cover by Eric Fraser   Christmas 1960

For Christmas Eric Fraser used the new masthead as the starting point for his cover and much greater use was now made of spot colour, incorporating it into the front page picture as well as the masthead (wherever possible).

Burns' Night cover
Issue 1941   19 Jan 1961   Scottish edition

Regional covers still appeared - the 1961 Burns' Night cover for the Scottish edition being one memorable example.

The Christmas issue of 1961 reintroduced a children's serial story with David Scott Daniell's tale of *Captain Barney's Cottage* and the unusual cover made use of paper sculptures of the Three Wise Men designed by Bruce Angrave, better known to readers for his irreverent cartoons.

Serial stories were to be resumed as a regular feature in the summer of 1962 when a weekly serial based on television's popular *Maigret* series was to appear, followed by a story based on the TV soap *Compact*.

Issue 1940   12 Jan 1961

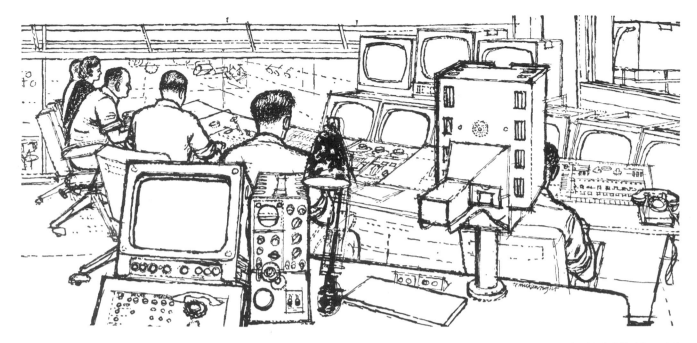

by Bob Micklewright
Issue 1981
26 Oct 1961
page 4/5

BBC Television celebrated its silver jubilee in the winter of 1961, and in its celebratory issue *Radio Times* commissioned Patrick O'Donovan of *The Observer* newspaper to write a major descriptive piece of everyday life in Television Centre, illustrated in the realistic style of West Bromwich-born artist Bob Micklewright who had been illustrating pages for *Radio Times* since 1954.

Micklewright was one of many illustrators who provided 'stock' pictures that would be used again and again on programme pages to illustrate programmes of the same genre. One such was a little drawing of the instruments of a string quartet, abandoned on four chairs. First published in 1957 the drawing was used many times but had to be re-drawn because of a technical error. Micklewright explained why:

"I put a cello leaning flat on to a chair; it should have been with the waist of the instrument against the seat of the chair.

"I've still got the letter which pointed out the error of my ways which came from a clergyman on the Isle of Wight. R. D. Usherwood – the art editor – asked me to get it right, which I did and it was used many times again after that – must have been one of the most useful drawings I've ever done. The chairs, actually, in the drawing were my own drawing-room chairs which I'd just bought."

Corrected version
by Bob Micklewright

Possibly the most unusual *Radio Times* to be printed was issued in June 1962 - it was produced for the Royal Dolls' House, and was a miniature issue 7.5cm x 6cm in size. A small print run was set up and a handful of copies distributed as souvenirs to *Radio Times* staff and associates. Since this special issue was intended to represent the United Kingdom as a whole, its pages were made up from a mixture of editions with TV pages taken from the Scottish and South and West editions and the radio pages from London.

The new style of *Radio Times* was not yet entirely satisfactory. With four pages a day given over to radio and a mere two to television, more of the total cost of producing the paper was being spent on the radio billings than television - yet increasingly more readers bought the magazine solely for its TV content.

RT miniature 28 June 1962

It was clear that radio's days of supremacy were numbered. They ended in the summer of 1962 when *Radio Times* was again revamped. With the issue of 2nd August, Abram Games' masthead was replaced with one incorporating the words '*Radio Times*' in a more gentle typeface, and the words 'BBC / tv / Sound' reversed out to the right. Inside, Williams once again went into print explaining his changes:

> We have been grateful for suggestions made by readers in their letters and now we introduce further changes in layout which will we hope, make for compactness and convenience.

The main change was the reduction of radio's billings to a double-page spread ("The whole of any day's sound broadcasting can be seen without having to turn the page") which brought down the size of the journal again. It had been running at between 60 and 68 pages but the relaunched issue contained only 52.

Issue 2021 2 Aug 1962

To cram all of the radio programmes into two pages also meant cutting down on the detailed information about programmes "In Other Home Services" and this was now reduced to details for just those Home Services adjacent to the region in question. This move proved unpopular and the full service was reinstated as soon as space became available.

Although the rest of the layout remained untouched, further alterations were made to the visual style - a greater distinction was made between radio and television pages, and a new typeface was introduced - Intertype Royal for the body matter with bold Doric for the programme headings. Clearly this decision had been made in some haste, because sufficient matrices containing these fonts had not yet been cut, and so initially only appeared on the sound programme pages of the London edition. Its use was extended to the other regions as matrices became available.

Although the BBC coat-of-arms still appeared alongside the title on page three, the words 'Journal of the BBC' were now dropped.

Colour was now becoming important again. Before the war, *Radio Times* had made regular use of spot colour on its covers and full-colour at Christmas when the occasion warranted it. The austere immediate post-war had pushed many periodicals into drab monochrome, but as the 'sixties progressed, colour was 'in' again as more modern presses were used to print magazines of all sorts. Black and white did not look good on the newsstands and bookstalls. Moreover advertisers were now being offered the facility of full colour to sell their wares, and *Radio Times* may have been able to compete with the advantage of high circulation, but for some advertisers women's magazines were a more attractive proposition because they could offer full colour.

Men Over Board!

THE game of skulls and crossbones played by Captain Pugwash and one of his crew (RADIO TIMES, July 12) is impossible. The Captain had the last 'go,' but his sailor is still one ahead. He must have slipped in an extra turn somewhere.

The state of the board indicates that neither made intelligent moves throughout the game.—*J. N. Caird, Oxford.*

Captain Pugwash by John Ryan

Something had to be done, and so in September 1962, *Radio Times* made its first crude experiments with full colour printing. In the issue of 13th September 1962, the centrefold was given over to a colour advertisement for Slumberland beds. Crude it was, since the colour portion had been printed as a section somewhat wider than the normal page, and then repeated much as the pattern on a roll of wallpaper. This was then overprinted with "Hunting for a new bed?" in black on the top portion and "Insist on a real genuine SLUMBERLAND bed" at the bottom. The colour pictures of beds were unceremoniously sliced up to conform to the page edges.

*Issue 2027
13 Sept 1962
Plate 4a*

A few weeks later, the masthead underwent a further subtle change - instead of the title on black on a block of colour, the title was now printed in colour on a white background. This was to remain the style until nearly the end of the decade.

Radio Times' experiments with colour had come a little too late to outsmart some of its rivals. While the Christmas 1962 issue of *RT* appeared as usual in a red and black Eric Fraser design, *The Viewer* (ITV's programme journal in the North-East of England, and Central Scotland) and its Dickens Press stablemate *Look Westward* (for ITV in the South-West of England) both appeared with full-colour covers (and a particularly effective colour advertisement for Gold Leaf cigarettes on the back). There were both spot colour and full-colour editorial pages inside, including a full-colour portrait of Her Majesty the Queen and Prince Philip, which must have been particularly galling for the always-loyal BBC. Even more innovative was the idea (particularly popular in Scotland) of combining Christmas and New Year programmes into one double issue.

**3.50
RACING**

The Leopardstown Chase

A handicap race over a distance of three miles

Commentary by Michael O'Hehir from Leopardstown, Eire

Broadcast by courtesy of the Leopardstown Club and Radio Eireann

Back to School

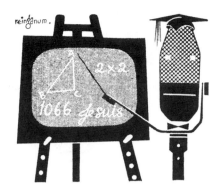

John Scupham, Head of Educational broadcasting, looks forward to the new school year in sound and television

by Victor
Reinganum
Issue 2027
13 Sept 1962

Radio Times' 56 pages (price - five pence) did not bear close comparison. It had a (rather old) blotchy 3" x 2" picture of The Queen, two pages of *Greetings from the Stars* illustrated only by a decorative title; the crossword, four pages of Christmas carol lyrics, a tiny *Pugwash* calendar for 1963 and episode one of a *Z Cars* serial story by Allan Prior. And the programmes.

This compared with *The Viewer*'s 64 glossy pages (price - ten pence): Royal colour portrait, double-page full colour feature on Dickie Henderson, Christmas short story, full-page colour picture of the cast of popular western series *Bonanza* (with a competition to win their new LP record) a centre spread of a full-colour board game based on *Coronation Street*, the crossword, a page of full-colour cartoons and a full-page full-colour pin-up of American actress and model Mikki Jamieson introducing the second week of programmes...... *And* a horoscope. *And* regional pages with large photographs of local personalities. *And* the programmes.

Radio Times did not respond immediately to these innovative ideas, coming as they did from one of its smaller rivals.

Radio Times

Every Thursday .Price Fivepence

Registered at the G.P.O. as a Newspaper

EDITORIAL
ADVERTISING AND PUBLISHING
35 Marylebone High Street
London, W.1

SUBSCRIPTION RATES, inc. postage
	12 *months*,	6 *months*,	3 *months*
Inland	£1.15.0	17/6	8/9
Overseas	£1.13.6	16/9	8/5

Subscriptions should be sent to the BBC Publishing Offices or to any newsagent

All programmes are subject to last-minute alterations

Copyright of all programmes in this issue is strictly reserved by the BBC. Unauthorised reproduction in whole or in part of any programme details included in Radio Times is prohibited.

Issue 2035

Radio Times Incorporating World Radio/ November 8, 1962. Vol. 157. No. 2035.

NOVEMBER 10—16

Radio Times
FIVEPENCE   WELSH EDITION

BBC
tv
Sound

1922 → 1962 →

THE BBC CELEBRATES
40 YEARS OF BROADCASTING

by Victor
Reinganum
Issue 2035
8 Nov 1962

Dipping its toe into the sea of colour advertising had achieved nothing. It would have to plunge in - but not yet. Black and white (with colour mastheads) were to remain the norm for another two years. Other attractions would help the magazine to sell - putting The Beatles on the cover, for example, and Dr Who.

But before either of these the BBC was forty, and of course *Radio Times* celebrated with a Victor Reinganum cover and a rather virulent shade of pink. The celebratory features were incorporated into a four-page supplement printed on buff-coloured paper, with Eric Fraser illustrations. There was incidentally no exhortation to pull away from staples, sharply or not.

The supplement avoided the introspective and self-congratulatory style of anniversaries past and invited leading violinist Yehudi Menuhin, peer Lord James of Rusholme, academic Dr Jacob Bronowski, racing driver Stirling Moss and pop singer Helen Shapiro to contribute their own personal views of the BBC's merits. Sadly the new format of *Radio Times* did not allow space for any other celebrations, although the following week the North of England edition had its own cover depicting a handful of celebrities who had contributed to 40 years of broadcasting in the north and there was a half-page article by Head of North Regional Programmes Bryan Cave-Brown-Cave.

1963 kicked off with the long-anticipated separation of the North of England and Northern Ireland Home Services. This loveless marriage had caused enormous problems for *Radio Times* who had resorted to all manner of devices to 'play down' the unwanted connection.

From Page 18
Issue 2043
3 Jan 1963
NI edition

The programme pages of the North of England edition had originally been cluttered with lines and boxes indicating which programmes were on 434m and which were on 261m - with the additional ruse of billing obviously Northern Irish material in smaller type. Equally, in the Northern Ireland edition, specifically North of England material would be given billing in smaller type.

Even so there were frequent uses of the term 'north' which had different meanings depending on where you were standing, not to mention political connotations on the island of Ireland.

Latterly, these arrangements were further complicated by the introduction of a full Northern Irish Home Service programme on VHF and the provision of the complete North of England programme on VHF in the north-east where the medium wave transmitter at Stagshaw carried the enforced mixture.

Whilst this improved the situation for those listeners prepared to invest in new receivers and aerials, it only made matters worse for the billings subs at *Radio Times* who now had to cope with two different versions of each of the Home Services.

The solution was to provide a box in the corner of the page and in the case of the English service, this was given the convoluted label "HOME SERVICE North-East & The Border" while the VHF programmes from Belfast were labelled "The Northern Ireland Service on VHF (94.5Mc/s)"

It was therefore not just radio listeners in Belfast and Newcastle who celebrated, on 7th January 1963, the announcement in *Radio Times* of "224 metres - a new wavelength for the Northern Ireland Home Service".

224 METRES | A NEW WAVELENGTH FOR THE NORTHERN IRELAND HOME SERVICE

THE BBC is glad to announce that the Home Service programmes transmitted in the medium waveband for Northern Ireland and North-east England are at last to be separated. Because of the shortage of frequency channels these two programmes have for many years been linked and transmitted on the shared frequency of 1,151 kc/s (261 metres).

From today it will be possible to provide separate medium-wave programmes appropriate for listeners in the two areas; up to now the sharing of a Home Service wavelength between the transmitters in North-east England and Northern Ireland has made it essential for the transmitters always to radiate the same programme in order to avoid intolerable mutual interference. The V.H.F. transmissions have not been restricted in this way, because there is not the same frequency problem on V.H.F., and separate programmes appropriate to the two areas have been provided to a limited extent for V.H.F. listeners only. In future medium-wave listeners will also hear these programmes.

The separation has become possible following the Government's decision that the BBC's European Service will no longer be relayed by the medium-wave station in north-west Germany using a wavelength allocated to the United Kingdom in the Copenhagen Plan of 1948. A wavelength released as a result of this change will be used at the Lisnagarvey and Londonderry transmitting stations for the Northern Ireland Home Service. Northern Ireland listeners receiving their Home Service on medium wavelengths from either of these stations should now tune to 224 metres (1,340 kc/s) instead of 261 metres (1,151 kc/s).

The BBC's Light, Third, and Network Three programme transmissions are not affected by this change.

The three sound services are also available on V.H.F. in Northern Ireland from the transmitting stations at Divis, near Belfast, and Londonderry. Although the changes in the medium waveband will give improved reception a further improvement is available by using the V.H.F. services which give better sound quality and greater freedom from interference.

The appropriate V.H.F. frequencies are as follows:

	Divis	Londonderry
Home	94.5 Mc/s	92.7 Mc/s
Light	90.1 Mc/s	88.3 Mc/s
Third/Network Three	92.3 Mc/s	90.55 Mc/s

Henry McMullan, Head of Northern Ireland Programmes, writes: 'Among the immediate benefits of the wavelength change to Northern Ireland listeners tuning to the medium waveband will be the daily five-minute News and Weather bulletin at 12.55 p.m. and the extension of the 6.15 p.m. Regional News from five to ten minutes, providing the same period of Regional News as elsewhere in the United Kingdom.

'More air time will be available for selected programmes from other Regional sources, and it should be possible to include more Scottish material (which has always had a special appeal for Ulster listeners).'

Radio Times

FIVEPENCE

WIMBLEDON FORTNIGHT

Extensive coverage in Television and Sound of the Lawn Tennis Championships starting on Monday
Dan Maskell writes on page 21

The Second Test Match

Ball-by-ball commentary in the Third Network and frequent visits in television to Lord's (Saturday, Monday, and Tuesday)

President Kennedy

His visits to West Germany and Eire will be the subject of special programmes in television starting on Sunday

Blackpool Night

A new series of summer Variety shows with stars from the theatres of the North West (Light Programme, Sunday)
See page 14

The Choice is Yours

Eric Robinson introduces a new television series of popular music featuring popular guest stars on Monday
See page 20

The Tunnel

The true story of a daring escape under the Berlin Wall in television on Tuesday
See page 27

Joan Sutherland

She sings the part of Cleopatra in the Handel Opera Society's production of *Julius Caesar* at Sadler's Wells (Wednesday, Third)
See page 32

More Faces of Jim

Jimmy Edwards presents a new comedy series beginning in television on Friday
See page 45

Issue 2067   *by Barry Wilkinson*   **Scottish edition**
20 June 1963   **Welsh edition**

Radio Times

FIVEPENCE

WIMBLEDON FORTNIGHT

Extensive coverage in Television and Sound of the Lawn Tennis Championships starting on Monday
Dan Maskell writes on page 21

The Second Test Match

Ball-by-ball commentary in the Third Network and frequent visits in television to Lord's (Saturday, Monday, and Tuesday)

President Kennedy

His visits to West Germany and Eire will be the subject of special programmes in television starting on Sunday

Blackpool Night

A new series of summer Variety shows with stars from the theatres of the North West (Light Programme, Sunday)
See page 14

The Choice is Yours

Eric Robinson introduces a new television series of popular music featuring popular guest stars on Monday
See page 20

The Tunnel

The true story of a daring escape under the Berlin Wall in television on Tuesday
See page 27

Joan Sutherland

She sings the part of Cleopatra in the Handel Opera Society's production of *Julius Caesar* at Sadler's Wells (Wednesday, Third)
See page 32

More Faces of Jim

Jimmy Edwards presents a new comedy series beginning in television on Friday
See page 45

Roy Emerson in action

Sometimes there were odd variations in regional covers (though doubtless there was a good reason). In June 1963, the Wimbledon Fortnight was hailed with a cover illustration by Barry Wilkinson (Scottish edition) or a photograph of tennis star Roy Emerson in action (Welsh edition)

When the last of the stories ended in 1963, pin-ups were introduced in the guise of *Radio Times Portrait Gallery*. A full-page photograph of some current star (e.g. Millicent Martin, James Ellis, Fenella Fielding, Eamonn Andrews) was faced by a few more snaps and a large-type (i.e. short) biography. Readers were then invited to purchase a glossy 10 x 8 inch photographic print of the picture in exchange for a mere two shillings crossed postal order (post free). This innovation was provided "As a service to our readers".

5.0
BLUE PETER

Issue 2056

In the summer the Portrait Gallery appears to have closed since an adaptation of Frances Durbridge's new novel *My Friend Charles* appeared instead, and on 25th July *Radio Times* launched its first popular post-war competition with a total of £2,000 in prize money. "Your chance to win £1000 in the FREE *Radio Times Fit-a-Feature* competition" in which various sets of eyes, noses and mouths had to be matched to photographs of stars.

The entry form for *Fit-a-Feature* included the tie-breaker: "***My suggestion for the selling slogan for Radio Times is - ....***" Here was *Radio Times* playing *TV Times* at its own game. (In fact, a remarkably similar competition appeared in *TV Times* a few years later......)

The magazine was now displaying more of the qualities expected from a child of the sixties. It certainly incurred the displeasure of its parent. Sir John Reith recorded in his diary for 7th September:

The BBC, particularly in television, has utterly discarded everything I did, and the vulgarity of the *Radio Times* week by week makes me sorry I ever started it.

*   *   *   *   *

Although his very mention in *Radio Times* would in future make that issue a valuable collectors' item, time traveller 'Dr Who' nearly didn't make it to the screen. Internal politicking over the costs of the programme's production created major hassles for its producers long before it was due to start.

Plans to feature the good doctor (at first played by veteran actor William Hartnell) on the front cover were scuppered, and Donald Wilson, the BBC's Head of Serials wrote to Douglas Williams on 5th November 1963 in some distress that the cover appearance had been cancelled partially as a result of "lack of confidence in the programme at Controller level".

However the programme did get a cover mention in the 21st November issue (three weeks after its debut) along with a half-page article inside. In contrast, once the Time Lord became a mega-star, *Radio Times* took every opportunity to increase sales by carefully placing his image upon its cover.

* * * * *

By the end of 1963, *Radio Times* had upped its cover price by another penny, and the Christmas issue did its best to compete with its rivals by attempting a multicolour cover which sadly proved to be something of a disaster.

TV Times went for a brash tug at the heart-strings with a full-colour photograph of a little girl in her night-dress apparently praying (not of course requesting, for her Mum and Dad, boxes of Gold Leaf ciggies like those in living Technicolor adorning the back of the paper). Inside it offered in full colour pop stars Gerry & The Pacemakers, all dressed as Santa Claus and sitting on Vespa scooters; plus colour pin-ups of the stars from *Coronation Street* and *Emergency Ward 10*.

TV Times
Issue 425
20 Dec 1963
Plate 4b

Radio Times *cover*
by Victor Reinganum
Issue 2093
19 Dec 1963
Plate 4c

Radio Times countered with a cover illustration (by Victor Reinganum) printed in red, green, yellow and black. The technique used the same block process normally reserved for the single colour masthead, and was evidently never intended for high-tolerance work. The result was severe colour misregistration that made the *Radio Times* look cheap 'n' nasty when sitting alongside the glitzy *TV Times, The Viewer* and their contemporaries. This time *Radio Times* would learn its lesson!

There was at least an attempt to add a bit more to the content of the Christmas issue. *Carry On Please* invited sixteen scriptwriters to combine to tell a tale each carrying on from where the previous writer had left off. Allan Prior started the story, Edward J Mason stirred up the plot a bit, and Frank Muir and Denis Norden spiced up the story - leaving readers to buy the New Year issue to find out how Roy Plomley and Ted Willis carried on the tale.

The Viewer
21 Dec 1963
Plate 4d

Pictures of The Beatles popped up wherever possible, and there was always the crossword.

5.15
DR. WHO
An adventure in space and time starring

WILLIAM HARTNELL
WILLIAM RUSSELL
JACQUELINE HILL
and
CAROLE ANN FORD
☆
The Cave of Skulls
by ANTHONY COBURN
with
Jeremy Young, Derek Newark
Cast:
Dr. Who.................WILLIAM HARTNELL
Ian Chesterton.........WILLIAM RUSSELL
Barbara Wright..........JACQUELINE HILL
Susan Foreman.........CAROLE ANN FORD
Za...........................DEREK NEWARK
Hur......................ALETHEA CHARLTON
Old mother.....................EILEEN WAY
Kal.............................JEREMY YOUNG
Horg............................HOWARD LANG
Title music by RON GRAINER
with the BBC Radiophonic Workshop
Incidental music by NORMAN KAY
Story editor, David Whitaker
Designer, Barry Newbery
Associate producer, Mervyn Pinfield
Producer, VERITY LAMBERT
† Directed by WARIS HUSSEIN

Issue 2090
28 Nov 1963

On 2nd April there were further *Radio Times* experiments with colour advertisements for Richmond cigarettes (another 'bleed' page running across pages 15 and 42 without stopping for breath) just a fortnight ahead of a *TV Times* issue with full colour cover and two editorial pages and two full-colour advertisement pages. At the same time *Radio Times* began to label the Home Counties edition as 'LONDON AND SOUTH EAST' for the first time having previously always avoided attaching any kind of geographical label to sully the edition that served the Capital City.

* * * * *

Raised voices in Wales had made repeated demands for the Principality to have its own version of BBC Television, scheduled to offer some Welsh-language programmes at peaktime.

For many years this was impossible due to the engineering constraints that have already been alluded to - in this case much of Wales received its TV pictures from transmitters across the border in England. But in 1964 the BBC was able to open new stations transmitting Welsh programmes to Welsh viewers without detracting from the service they provided to English viewers on the other side of the Severn estuary.

by Victor Reinganum
Issue 2100   6 Feb 1964   Welsh edition

The launch of BBC Wales deserved - and got - maximum coverage in the Welsh edition of *Radio Times* with a special cover designed by Victor Reinganum, and its own style of programme pages with the prominent heading BBC Wales/Cymru.

Further demands were about to be made on *Radio Times* with the imminent launch of BBC-2

Because the cost of building programme links and transmitters was high, BBC-2 followed a similar pattern of expansion to BBC-1, which meant for *Radio Times* that once again it would have to carry listings in some editions only with all the added complications of pagination size and so forth.

Issue 2109   9 April 1964
Page 11   London edition

BBC-2 began test transmissions in earnest in March, details of which were included in the London edition. The material for the test transmissions was perhaps little more riveting than that of the early television tests that *Radio Times* had publicised back in the early '30s.

BBC-2 was scheduled to launch on 20th April 1964. A fire at Battersea Power Station which deprived Television Centre (and much of West London) of electricity put paid to that, and BBC-2 actually got on the air in time for *Play School* at 11am on 21st April. But the *Radio Times* of 16th April was not to know that.

With a cover which may have induced a sense of *deja-vu* in Welsh readers, BBC-2 made its debut proper in *Radio Times* and the television pages of that edition were redesigned to allow BBC-1 and BBC-2 programmes to appear side-by-side on the page. In addition, an average of two extra pages each day was allowed ahead of the billings for articles about BBC2 programmes as well as some extra advertising matter.

Issue 2110   **London and South-East edition by Reinganum**
16 April 1964

                     South and West edition by Fraser

The night that never was - BBC2's opening schedule

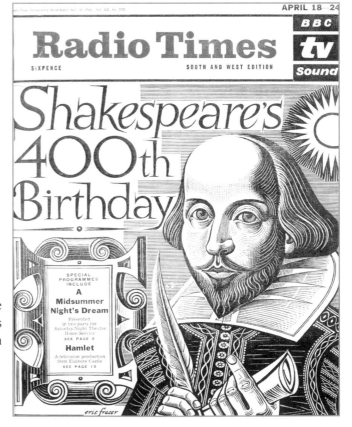

As a result the London edition ran to 68 pages, and the others just 60. On this rare occasion, London readers missed a special Eric Fraser cover celebrating William Shakespeare's 400th Birthday.

*   *   *   *   *

8.30 THE HOSPITALISATION OF SAMUEL PELLET

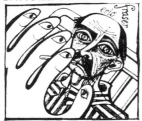

A new play for radio
by Andrew Davies

by Eric Fraser
Issue 2137
22 Oct 1964

Portrait Gallery resumed in the summer, offering more glossy ten-by-eights of such attractions as Jessie Matthews, Matt Munro, Mary Tyler Moore and Robert Reed. Still for just a two-shilling crossed postal order.

A further increase in pagination became necessary at the end of August 1964 with the introduction of radio's new Music Programme. This was a daytime service of mostly classical music and news bulletins which occupied the wavelengths used in the evening by Network Three and then the Third Programme. To begin with, the Music Programme was introduced only on a Sunday, but by Christmas it was available seven days a week. This, together with the introduction of a Saturday afternoon sports service on what was to be known as the 'Third Network', meant that radio billings could again no longer be contained on two pages. A third page was added - thus creating more space on the Light Programme page for editorial material about radio programmes to be reinstated.

* * * * *

Issue 2112   30 April 1964

THE LUCY SHOW

The zany comedienne goes on a trip with the Scouts

at 8.0

PANORAMA
The Window on the World

News came that, from its issue of 1st October 1964, *TV Times* would publish a full-colour cover and editorial pages every week. *Radio Times* fought back by publishing a full colour cover and supplement a week ahead of its rival.

The issue for 24th September 1964 featured colour photographs of veteran bandleader Billy Cotton on its cover and inside, together with colour pictures of the TV series *The Good Old Days, The Black and White Minstrel Show* and Beatle Ringo Starr with *Juke Box Jury* panelists, The *portrait gallery* offered a two-bob glossy of The Rolling Stones. *Radio Times* was learning fast.

But curiously it chose not to compete for colour advertising (although perhaps the decision to print that issue in colour was too late?) with the usual selection of garages and garden sheds on the back page.

It was one of the more endearing characteristics of the *Radio Times* that where others chose to place high profile cigarette advertisements on their back covers the BBC's journal chose instead to regularly fill the back page with small display advertisements for garden sheds, wheelchairs and corsets.

Back cover of issue 2118   11 June 1964

110

The September colour issue was a curtain raiser for the Olympic Games number in October with a stunning full-colour Victor Reinganum cover (and a full colour ad for a tartan travel rug offer from Cadbury's on the back).

With both the Olympics and a General Election to cope with in the same week, the 68 pages of the London edition were crammed to the full. As well as a two page *Plain Man's Guide* by David Butler, the usual three-page chart gave space for viewers and listeners to record the results as they came in with a full listing of all the UK 630 constituencies and the majority its incumbent achieved in the 1959 General Election.

Horse of the Year Show
This great spectacle at Wembley, which will be covered extensively throughout the week, is introduced by Dorian Williams

'Agus chunnaic mi air uairean is craigean mòr oillteil aice 'na laimh is i mar gu 'm biodh i a' seanachas is ag gaireachdaich ris a' chreutair leibideach sin. Bu bhochd an latha dhuit-sa an latha a fhuair thu Morag NicRaild'

'Tha 'Ghaoth 'San Ear'
Dealbh-chluich le Seòras Scott Moncrieff
air eadar-theangachadh le Anna NicIain
is air a dhealbhachadh le Eoghan Mac a phì
10.0

Of course, the Tokyo Olympics warranted much space, including three pages in colour. And this time *Radio Times* had sold a colour page to the National Coal Board to sell the benefits of solid fuel.

And of course this time the 72-page Christmas Number boasted a gravure-printed colour cover with a stunning photograph of a dove of peace in mosaic form - as well as a clever eight-page colour supplement (reminiscent of pre-war days) tracing the adventures of The Beat Room dancer Barbara Lord in 'Wonderland', aka the BBC Television Centre.

by Jack
Dunkley
Issue 2134
10 Oct 1964

Left:
by George
Mackie

Wittily composed by Rowan Ayers it was an outstanding piece of inventive work, combining as it did in a live-action version of Peter Kneebone's *Adventures of Tom & Vera* a great deal of humour with a lot of specially shot stills, many in colour, as Barbara stumbled her way from *The Beat Room* through the continuity studio, wardrobe, makeup, the *Z Cars* set, the weather studio, and of course the *Tardis* (where she was pictured having a meal with Doctor Who and a pair of Daleks), then on to the props store, until eventually finding her way back to *The Beat Room*.

Eat your heart out, *TV Times*!

*   *   *   *   *

by Barry Wilkinson
Issue 2140
12 Nov 1964

TOP
OF THE
pops

Tonight at 7.30

●

Alan Freeman introduces the guests, looks at today's chart, and speculates on trends in the world of Pop. The studio audience, as usual, take an active part in proceedings

Gary Cooper
He plays the hero in *Unconquered*, an action-packed film about eighteenth-century America (Sunday, BBC-1)
PAGE 11

Geraint Evans
The internationally famous Welsh baritone is one of the stars appearing in *Gala Performance* (Thursday, BBC-1)
PAGE 37

SATURDAY HERO

Stanley Matthews
In a programme on his fiftieth birthday the great footballer tells the story of his life (Monday, BBC-1)
PAGE 12

Issue 2151   28 Jan 1965   *Welsh edition*

London and South East edition

Early in 1965 came another challenge for the production staff of *Radio Times*.

The issue dated 28th January 1965 was already about a third of the way through its print run when word came of the death of wartime Prime Minister Sir Winston Churchill.

Churchill was to be accorded the honour of a full state funeral, and that meant major television and radio coverage. Those editions that went to press first were already complete. The rest were speedily reset, printed and distributed. An eight-page supplement was printed and distributed in those areas where the outdated edition was already on sale.

The replacement issue (and the supplement) had striking black and white covers with a central photograph of Churchill. Inside a double-page spread of a sketch map (which must have been drawn in record time) showed the route of the funeral procession and was followed by the Order of Service for the funeral, together with an article by Richard Dimbleby explaining why Churchill was to be buried in his family's plot at Bladon.

That was where the supplement ended, its final page empty but for a small panel explaining why there had been need for its production and the usual printer's address. In fact the versions of the supplement printed in Twyford Abbey Road and East Kilbride were slightly different since the rules surrounding the back page announcement had clearly been left to the local printers' discretion.

Editions of the main magazine which had been amended in time then carried the normal programmes and features, although several pages had to be reset in order to accommodate advertising which had been removed from the first seven pages.

And oddly *Captain Pugwash* was removed from the later editions - perhaps as a mark of respect but more probably in order to create sufficient space for a column of small display ads that had been relocated from Wednesday's television pages.

Although not yet geared up to print in colour on a weekly basis, it was now possible to produce occasional colour covers. One such appeared in April 1965. It featured Eric Fraser's first post-war full-colour illustration to accompany the Royal Shakespeare Company's televised production of *The Wars of the Roses*. There was another colour cover in July 1965 when *Blue Peter*'s Christopher Trace and Valerie Singleton appeared together in colour on the cover and inside in a Blue Peter 8-page supplement. It contained echoes of *Junior Radio Times* complete with information about pets, picnic recipes, the inevitable instructions for 'making things', puzzles, a crossword, and even a *Bengo* cartoon strip.

**Television
TOP OF
THE FORM**
●

It's boys versus girls tonight, in the final of this series, when the teams will endeavour to answer all that is asked of them in an excited, but not too serious atmosphere

AT 6.30

*by Burrell
Issue 2143
3 Dec 1964*

*by Cecil Bacon
Issue 2194   25 Nov 1965*

BBC-2 was spreading but unfortunately not in ways which coincided with *Radio Times* regional editions. In the Midlands, the Sutton Coldfield BBC-2 transmissions were initially on low power and could only be received in a relatively small area around Birmingham. So as not to raise false expectations of viewers in places like Norwich and Hereford, *two* Midlands editions were produced - one labelled MIDLAND BBC-2 EDITION and the other carrying only BBC-1 programmes.

To make it clear what was in the paper, there were now two variations on the masthead. Non-BBC-2 areas still had a masthead with *BBC/tv/Sound* on the right, but those issues which contained BBC-2 programmes had *BBC-1/tv/BBC-2* to the right of the title strip except in Wales where BBC-1 was known as BBC Wales and therefore the original strip continued to appear.

Similarly when BBC-2 was introduced in the North of England, the first transmissions were from Winter Hill, which only covered an area west of the Pennines. So a NORTH OF ENGLAND BBC-2 EDITION appeared - complete with Ken Dodd and BBC-2's publicity kangaroos Hullabaloo and Custard on its first night cover.

*Issue 2190
28 Oct 1964
North of
England
edition*

Once a transmitter had opened bringing BBC-2 to parts of the West of England, there were ten editions of *Radio Times* each week:

London & South-East
South and West
South and West BBC-2 edition
Midlands and East Anglia
Midland BBC-2 edition
Wales edition
North of England edition
North of England BBC-2 edition
Northern Ireland edition
Scottish edition

'THE LONG RUN'

THE TRAGIC LIFE OF GUTO NYTH BRAN
When Guto died in 1737 his fame as a runner had become a legend in Wales
at 10.15

by George Mackie

Another abstract colour cover for Christmas, looking much more like one from the 'thirties heydays' with a *Christmas Anthology* compiled by John Arlott; and scripts for imaginary Christmas editions of *Steptoe & Son, The Likely Lads, Dud & Pete, Meet the Wife* and *Hugh and I.*

Issue 2206   17 Feb 1966   Wales edition

A rare Welsh language cover appeared in February 1966 to mark the start of the television serial *Chwalfa* based on the novel by T. Rowland Hughes. Unusually, the masthead for this Wales edition only was printed in black. (The edition now being correctly described in relation to its geographic area rather than the language of the Principality.)

With the spread of BBC-2 around the country, and the increased competition - not only from Independent Television, but also the 'pirate' radio stations on ships and abandoned sea forts scattered around the British coastline - the BBC fought back with a series of exhibitions across the UK.

'*BBC Week*' would come to a local exhibition hall, build a temporary TV and radio studio, record some popular local programmes in front of audiences, play a few records on closed-circuit during the daytime hours, sell some BBC publications from a display stand, allow a few celebrities to be seen and provide technical advice on the reception of BBC-2. And a pair of Daleks travelled everywhere with the exhibition.

To back up 'BBC Week', a four-page supplement was produced in the style of *Radio Times* and printed by Waterlows at Twyford Abbey Road.

These pamphlets were a development of a series of four-page publicity leaflets - also produced at Waterlow's - titled *BBC-2 News*. They had been handed out free by television dealers in the run-up to the launch of BBC-2 and were still published at irregular intervals as the network spread throughout the country.

BBC-2 News generally had a large photograph on the cover of a pretty BBC girl along with a large tabloid-style headline (e.g. "BBC-2 IS TWO"; "COLOUR COMES TO BBC-2"). The centrefold detailed programme highlights in *Radio Times* style, and the back page feature was *Pamela Donald's Column*. Ms Donald was the (pretty) Dundee born "television and radio personality" who had been chosen to front the publicity for the new channel.

'BBC Week' visited a variety of towns, amongst them Bradford, Glasgow, Leicester, Middlesborough and Belfast. In each case a local BBC Week was produced, and where the regional distribution allowed there would also be major coverage in the local edition of *Radio Times* as well. In the case of the Glasgow 'BBC Week', it was sufficient of an excuse to put (pretty) newsreader Mary Marquis on the cover of that week's Scottish edition of *Radio Times*. Pretty girls on cover - very sixties.

Cover of
BBC-2 News
Number 8

Mary Marquis will be taking 'A Quick Look Round' with the BBC's Scottish news and current affairs people during BBC Week

BBC Week

RT issue 2204   3 Feb 1966

115

Colour advertisements now appeared from time to time within the black-and-white editorial pages of the journal and the print process and quality were now satisfactory - although after a little while the colour pages did have a nasty habit of sticking to the newsprint page they were facing!

In June 1966 BBC-2 opened in Central Scotland and this time the programmes were simply extended to all the copies sold in Scotland rather than create a separate Scottish BBC-2 edition.

At the beginning of October the occasion of the BBC Week in Northern Ireland was marked by *Radio Times* in a somewhat unusual manner. Although BBC-2 was not yet being transmitted in the Province, the BBC had arranged a special feed of BBC-2 into the exhibition in Belfast's Ulster Hall. So that week, *RT* printed full BBC-2 programmes in the Northern Ireland edition, even though they were not actually being transmitted!

Colour covers were still reserved mainly for special occasions - like the World Cup, held in England, in July 1966, and of course the Christmas number - now with its own title *Christmas Radio Times*. The 1966 edition contained a colour supplement with photographs of the Royal Palaces to accompany the Christmas Day television programme. Illustrations for this special supplement were by Bob Micklewright, and *Captain Pugwash* was allowed a full colour page for his own hideously complicated board game *Play Piracy with Pugwash*.

The first week of 1967 had an unusual graphic cover, which made effective use of the two-colour process for bands of snowflakes against strips of black and pink. Scottish readers, of course, had Andy Stewart and Moira Anderson instead.

Issue 2251
29 Dec 1966
Wales edition

The audience-pulling John Galsworthy *Forsyte Saga* made its debut on BBC-2 in January together with a colour cover and inside a beautiful piece of calligraphy from Cecil Bacon tracing the Forsyte Family Tree.

by Cecil
Bacon
Issue 2252
5 Jan 1967

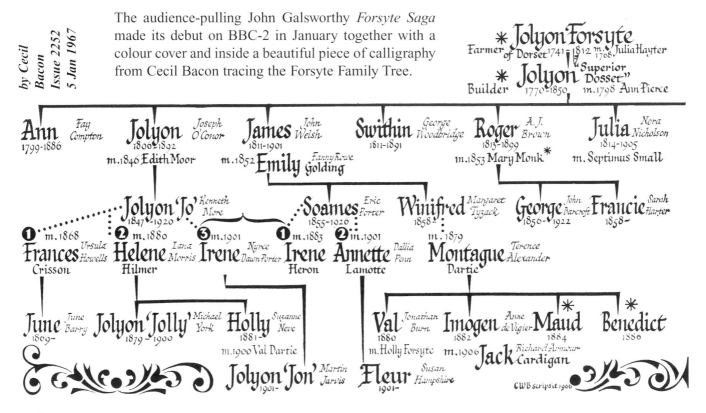

It may seem that our narrative at this point concentrates on covers rather than content. This is probably a result of the tediously unchanging innards during this period of *Radio Times'* life. With a stability of editors (only two between 1944 and 1968) and a lack of named writers or special features, there is little to be said about this period other than a commentary on its changing visage.

Indeed it was during this time that a well-known comedian suggested that *Radio Times* was perpetrating a grand rip-off on its readers by *only* changing the cover each week!

But the period of comparative stability was near an end.

From the spring, colour covers appeared frequently. But each incorporated a different design of masthead - this lack of uniformity was an indication of changes to come.

In July BBC-2 began its first public transmissions of colour programmes. After many years of unpublicised colour tests - going back as far as 1955 - colour sets were at last being manufactured and all sections of the industry and government were agreed on a technical standard.

To launch its colour transmissions the BBC chose the Wimbledon Lawn Tennis Championships from the All England Lawn Tennis Club - and so, naturally, that was the subject of the colour cover for 29th June 1967.

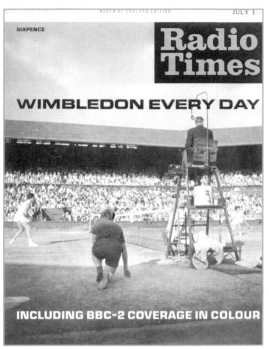

Issue 2277   29 June 1967

Inside David Attenborough, Controller of BBC-2 contributed a full page article about colour TV. During this 'launch period' colour was not being radiated by all of the BBC-2 transmitters, and so initially no mention of colour was made in the programme billings. But at the start of the paper each week there was a box listing the programmes that would be transmitted in colour that week.

To begin with this was quite a short list, with just a couple of colour programmes each day.

From cover of issue 2252

117

ON
247

5.30 a.m. NEWS SUMMARY
and Weather forecast

5.33 *Breakfast Special*
as Radio 2

7.0 TONY BLACKBURN
with a
Daily Disc Delivery
including, at 8.0,
5 of the latest 45s
hot from the press

8.32 LESLIE CROWTHER
introduces
Junior Choice
your record requests
Leslie Crowther is in ' Let Sleeping
Wives Lie ' at the Garrick Theatre,
London

9.55 CRACK THE CLUE
Duncan Johnson
invites you to take part in a
trial round of Radio 1's exciting new competition which
begins on Monday
Devised by Peter Chiswell
Repeated: 1.55 p.m.
**On page 8 you will find a speci-
men puzzle and an article explaining how you should use the entry
form**

10.0 KEITH SKUES
your resident D.J.
presents
Saturday Club
Hit discs
Top pop groups and singers
including
This week's star guests:
Dave Dee, Dozy, Beaky,
Mick, and Tich
The Bee Gees
Producer, Bill Bebb

12.0 EMPEROR ROSKO
with his
Midday Spin

**1.0 THE
JACK JACKSON SHOW**
A record roundabout
Produced by Teddy Warrick

1.55 CRACK THE CLUE
† Broadcast at 9.55 a.m.

2.0 CHRIS DENNING
says this is
Where It's At
It's here every Saturday at 2.0
It's non-stop for sixty minutes
It's all that's best in pop
It's also got KENNY EVERETT
It's produced by
Johnny Beerling

3.0 PETE MURRAY
with his pick of last week's
' Newly Pressed ' programmes
featuring the latest
pops, L.P.s, and E.P.s
Produced by Keith Boots

4.0 PETE BRADY
introduces a swinging
selection of studio sounds
and the best of the rest
on records

**5.30 COUNTRY
MEETS FOLK**
Wally Whyton
introduces folk, country and
western music on record
and, in person,
THE CREE
JAMIE, JON, AND JERRY
MURRAY KASH reviews some
current recordings
Contra bass fiddle,
BRIAN BROCKLEHURST
Produced by Ian Grant

6.32 SCENE AND HEARD
Johnny Moran
takes a trip around
the world of pop
and highlights an exclusive
interview with
George Harrison
One hour of latest news
records, reviews
and pop people talking shop
Reporter, MIRANDA WARD
Producers, Paul Williams
Ted Beston, John Walters
† Editor, BRYANT MARRIOTT

7.30 NEWS

7.34 Weather forecast

7.35—10.0
as Radio 2

10.0 PETE MURRAY
meets
Pete's People
with
GENO WASHINGTON AND HIS
RAM JAM BAND
MANFRED MANN
DANNY STREET
BOB MILLER AND HIS
MILLERMEN
Records, reviews, and news

*

CLEO LAINE and MR. ACKER BILK
In live relays from the Royal
Philharmonic Orchestra's first
JAZZ BALL in aid of the
National Society for Mentally
Handicapped Children and the
R.P.O. Trust
Introduced by LESLIE CROWTHER
The Orchestra conducted by
STANLEY BLACK
from Grosvenor House Hotel,
London
Produced by JOHN HOOPER

**12.0 MIDNIGHT
NEWSROOM**

12.5 NIGHT RIDE
Sean Kelly
with
swinging sounds
on and off the record
featuring tonight:
THE SETTLERS
† Produced by Helen Fry

2.0 NEWS SUMMARY
Weather forecast

Close Down at 2.2 a.m.

**RADIO 1
is on
247 m. only
RADIO 2
is on
long wave (1,500 m.)
and VHF
for full details
of wavelengths
see page 79**

YOUR MIDDAY SPINNER
Emperor Rosko

*Colourful is the word—cosmopolitan too. He was
born in Hollywood twenty-five years ago, son of
the film producer Joe Pasternak. He was educated
in Paris, Switzerland, Japan, and California and
served in the U.S. Navy—that was before he became
a 'pirate'. Now he's a leading disc-jockey in France.*

Day one, Radio One
Issue 2290   28 Sept 1967

The biggest change was in the autumn of 1967 and came as a result of four separate developments.

The first was the steady increase in the number of colour programmes on BBC-2 and the intention to provide a full-scale national colour service in the winter of 1967.

The second was the pressing need for *Radio Times* itself to appear in colour every week.

The third was the introduction of Radio 1 - and the fourth the creation of a handful of BBC Local Radio Stations.

Since the first 'pirate' radio ship - Radio Caroline - had appeared at Easter 1964, the BBC had been under fire for not providing sufficient popular music programming to attract the younger generation to listen to its broadcasts. The government had introduced a bill to outlaw the 'pirate' transmissions in August 1967, and it was part of the government's proposals that in return for this the BBC would respond by introducing its own pop music station.

At the same time, certain of the 'pirates' - such as Radio Essex and Radio Scotland - had provided a form of 'local' radio and proved that there was a public appetite for the kind of stations which had existed when *Radio Times* began in the twenties, bringing the voices of local people to local areas.

After a number of trials and political arguments, the government of the day had also been persuaded to let the BBC experiment with a handful of small-scale stations, which initially it would operate in a financial partnership with local government. This aspect of BBC Local Radio did not survive and, when the stations were later decreed to be permanent, the BBC took over the full responsibility for their funding.

All of the above indicated another change of makeup for *Radio Times* - the fourth under the editorial supervision of Douglas Williams who was now nearing the end of his distinguished career with the magazine.

As if to emphasise the wholesale nature of the changes, the cover of the first *Radio Times* of the new era owed more to the style of *TV Times* than the Journal of the BBC. A two-thirds page colour photograph of what at the time was best described as a 'dolly bird' wearing a paper dress emblazoned with the words "**Radio 1 on 247**" in a psychedelic font sat beside a third page panel which over a series of coloured dots highlighted the new contents in true *TV Times* style with snappy phrases like "The Swinging New Radio Service", and single-word descriptors "Cookery", "Gardening", "Motoring".

Things had come full circle and *Radio Times* was to become a magazine once again.

Gone was the dignified coat-of-arms from inside. Page three had more psychedelic lettering ("Be a Radio 1-upman") and the text was surrounded by photographs of a dozen of the new deejays.

Radio 1   Issue 2290   28 Sept 1967

TV and radio page headings had been restyled, there was a Radio 1 competition *Crack the Clue* with transistor radios to be won. The word **COLOUR** now appeared under the billings of colour programmes. The three radio pages had been rearranged with billings for Radios 1 and 2 on the first page, Radio 3 on the second and Radio 4 on the third page, which stoically refused to acknowledge the changes by including "In Other Home Services" in column 1!

And columnists were back! A centre section, with colour pages, included a *Star Story*. The first subject was American entertainer Sammy Davis Jr (who was interviewed by Russell Twisk and photographed by Charles Walls), and new weekly features on Gardening (by Percy Thrower), Cookery (with Zena Skinner), Motoring (from Bill Hartley) and Birdwatching (with Jeffery Boswall).

Each week a star with a hobby was the subject of a column titled *Meet* and the *Round and About* feature was revived - now under the by-line of "Orbiter". And a colour page each week highlighted the week's colour programmes on BBC-2.

Pugwash no longer appeared, but *Points from the Post* and the crossword were to be found inside the back page. The price had now risen by two pence - it was eightpence. And in future weeks it would boast another revised masthead - although the typeface remained the same, this new shallow design simply added a bold symbol 'BBC-tv' to the right of the title - the price, date and regional edition now being overprinted in letterpress at the top of the front page.

*   *   *   *   *

Supplement to Radio Times Issue dated November 2, 1967 (i)

LOCAL BROADCASTING ON VHF
BBC Radio Leicester
OPENS WEDNESDAY NOVEMBER 8

Welcome to your own station

'THIS IS BBC RADIO LEICESTER ...'

This opening announcement—broadcast from a small studio in Epic House, Charles Street—will be heard for the first time on Wednesday, November 8.

A few seconds later, at about 12.46, the Postmaster-General, The Rt. Hon. Edward Short, M.P., will officially open the station. He will be followed by the Lord Mayor of Leicester, Sir Mark Henig.

After months of planning and training, Radio Leicester will be on the air. And, once again, the City of Leicester will have scored 'a first'. During the following weeks and months other local stations — at Sheffield, Merseyside, Stoke, Nottingham, Brighton, Leeds and Durham—will begin broadcasting as part of the Government's local radio experiment.

'What kind of programmes will the stations broadcast?' ... 'Will there be any pop?' ... 'What times will Radio Leicester be on the air?' ... 'How many will there be on the staff?' ... 'Why will it be on VHF?' ...

These are a few of the very many enquiries I've had since

MAURICE ENNALS BBC Radio Leicester Station Manager, talks about Britain's first local radio station

hours meeting officials and members of over seventy local organisations.

First, the staff: this will total sixteen—nearly half of them with local connections—and will include a Programme Organiser (my deputy), and five Programme Assistants. Four of these will be the men who do the announcing, produce programmes, read news bulletins, present record programmes, report on local events . . . and try

BBC Radio Leicester comes from the 8th floor of Epic House in Charles Street. It is from the modern, towering office block in the heart Leicester that 'your own station' will be broadcasting daily, seven days a week, on VHF 95.05

prepare the first local programme of the day, timed for

formation-type programmes.

Also on the staff will be th[e]

A few weeks later, the first of the BBC Local Radio Stations was opened in Leicester on 8th November 1967. *Radio Times* had agreed to carry full listings for the local stations, so this meant the creation of localised editions of the paper serving specific towns.

In the first 'Midlands and East Anglia - BBC Radio Leicester edition', Frank Gillard - the BBC's Director of Radio - explained the reasons for the experiment in a half-page article, and a pull-out four page supplement ("Pull sharply away from staples") had all the programme details and pictures of the manager, staff and studios of the new venture.

A week later the first Sheffield edition appeared, and the following week Liverpool made its debut with BBC Radio Merseyside, whose introductory supplement on 16th November even boasted spot colour!

Innovations came thick and fast. BBC-2 started its full colour service on 2nd December, and the page heading was subtly altered to include the word 'colour' in the BBC-2 heading. Colour programmes were now prefixed by the word reversed out in a very prominent rhombus box above the programme's billing.

BBC 2

6.30 *COLOUR*

BILLY SMART'S CIRCUS
The skills, thrills, and comedy of the colourful world of circus presented under the Big Top of this great travelling show

FREE-FALL AFLAME
Stan Lindbergh, the human torch, free-falls from a great height into a blazing tank

HIGH WIRE SPECTACULAR
The seven fabulous **Rudolfo Steys**

MONKEY MAGIC
Silvano's Chimps

GIRL IN THE MOON
Ria and the Caribbean Chorus

ELEPHANT BOY
Gary Jahn and his gentle giants

MUSICAL MUSCLES
The amazing, amusing **Terry Elflett**

HIGH DRY DIVE
from the roof of the Big Top on to a cushion by **The Great Primletty**

THE CLOWNS ARE LOOSE
Maxo, Toto, and Co.
paint everything in sight

THE GREAT WHITE ARCTIC BEARS
Presented by **Sandra Shrimpton** and **Walter Milde**

SKATING HIGH
The Four Willers on twin aerial rinks

CIRCUS OF DOVES
The wire-walking, acrobatic, fluttering friends of **La Paloma**

SPRINGBOARD SENSATION
The Great Pusztai Troupe

RIDING FOR A LAUGH
Volunteers try the 'riding machine' in a Force 8 gale of laughter

FIREWORK FINALE
Circus direction,
Ronnie, David, and Billy Smart
Guest Ringmaster, **Pierre Picton**
Musical director, KEN GRIFFIN

† Produced by DEREK BURRELL-DAVIS

7.45
THE NEWS
and **SPORT**

Trade Tests for COLOUR

Since eighty per cent of BBC-2 programmes are now in colour, the colour trade test service takes on a new importance. Already a new look has been given to these tests with more colour films during the week and regular information for the television trade and for those viewers who have new colour sets.

Monday to Saturday—mornings:
10 Service information; 10.30 Colour Receiver Installation film; 10.45 Colour film; 11.30 Service information, as available; 11.35 Colour film.

Tuesday to Saturday:
12.10 p.m. Colour Receiver Installation film.

Monday to Saturday—afternoons:
2.30 Service information, as available; 2.35 Colour film; 3.10 Colour Receiver Installation film; 3.30 Colour film; 4.30 Colour film; 5.30 Colour film.

Monday to Friday:
7 p.m. Colour information and colour film.
Subject to programme commitments and engineering work.

Colour is now official!

ROUND  ABOUT

There is a fault . . .

The friendly camera

Accent on Song

by Barry Wilkinson
Christmas 1967

The *Christmas Radio Times* put most of its efforts into a colour supplement filled with photographs of the stars of the BBC's festive programmes; regular columnists were given the week off.

On the same page that carried details of the order of service for the Christmas Eve Radio 4 transmission of the *Festival of Nine Lessons and Carols* from Kings College Chapel Cambridge, a gaudy third page banner announced:

> An exciting Radio Times free competition
> * Win a Colour Television Set with free installation and licence for one year (or £300 in cash)
> * Open to all readers of Radio Times
> * Cut this coupon out and keep it. You will need further coupons which will appear in the next five issues of Radio Times
> * Full details and the second coupon in next week's issue

Reith would undoubtedly have viewed this blatant piece of marketing as a criminal intrusion on what he would have regarded as a religious page.

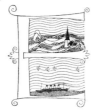

CHAPTER EIGHT
The Cannon Years

arly in 1968 Douglas Graeme Williams retired through ill health. His place was taken by C. J. Campbell Nairne, promoted from his role as Deputy and Literary Editor. Close to retirement himself Nairne edited the paper for less than two years.

Nairne's period of editorship was essentially a caretaking exercise whilst a younger successor could be found to take over upon his retiral. Even so, the paper continued to evolve under his experienced eye. The Winter Olympics in Grenoble in February 1968 were afforded a colour supplement of their own compiled by *Radio Times* stalwart Russell Twisk.

*   *   *   *   *

Radio Times - although never yet in direct competition with the ITV publications - generally found itself occupying the same corner of the nation's living-rooms week by week. As part of the ITV franchise renewals of 1968 the Independent Broadcasting Authority had insisted on a single programme journal for the whole of the ITV network.

Last issues
**The Viewer
&
Look Westward**
14 Sept 1968

Last issue
TV World
14 Sept 1968

This was, in part, because of the very mixed bag that had made up ITV's local publications. Up to September 1968, *TV Times* had appeared in 8 regional editions - Grampian, Scottish, Border, Lancashire, Yorkshire, Anglia, London and Southern. *The Viewer* appeared in the north-east of England and also the south-west where it appeared under the title *Look Westward* (the Scottish edition having been replaced by *TV Times* in 1966). Odhams Press published *TV World* in the Midlands where *TV Times* had lost its contract to print ITV programmes in 1964. All of these appeared in colour and were printed on paper with a light gloss finish.

Television Weekly *14 Sept 1968*

Last issues
TV Post *11 Sept 1968*

Channel Viewer *17 Sept 1968*

In Wales and the West, Berrows Newspapers published *Television Weekly*, which was a broadsheet monochrome newspaper-style paper, as was *TV Post* published by Century Newspapers in Belfast. the *Channel Viewer* was published in Jersey and was a web-offset magazine with spot (and sometimes full) colour.

TV Times 19 Sept 1968

On September 19th 1968, the new *TV Times* made its first appearance. Its pages were now the same size as *Radio Times* but the 80-page offset-printed magazine had colour throughout the glossy pages of its 13 editions and looked altogether superior on the bookstalls.

5.45

THE MAGIC ROUNDABOUT

Created by SERGE DANOT

English version
written and told by
ERIC THOMPSON

by Burrell
Issue 2308   1 Feb 1968

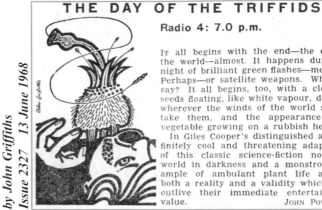

THE DAY OF THE TRIFFIDS

Radio 4: 7.0 p.m.

IT all begins with the end—the end of the world—almost. It happens during a night of brilliant green flashes—meteors? Perhaps—or satellite weapons. Who can say? It all begins, too, with a cloud of seeds floating, like white vapour, drifting wherever the winds of the world should take them, and the appearance of a vegetable growing on a rubbish heap.

In Giles Cooper's distinguished and infinitely cool and threatening adaptation of this classic science-fiction novel, a world in darkness and a monstrous example of ambulant plant life assume both a reality and a validity which long outlive their immediate entertainment value.   JOHN POWELL

by John Griffiths   13 June 1968
Issue 2327

A few weeks before the launch of the new *TV Times*, Nairne made some further changes to the layout of *Radio Times* to coincide with a circulation push to compete with the new rival. Radio billings were further diminished in order to fit them once again into a double page spread, with the "Other Home Services" element - increasingly irrelevant with the proliferation in VHF listening - exiled to the inside back page.

Television page headings were reduced in size to leave more space for billings.

by Victor Reinganum
Issue 2343
3 Oct 1968

Cooking, Gardening and Motoring were moved from the centre section to the main body of the paper (and joined a few weeks later by a regular *Blue Peter* feature and a Radio 1 Club news page); the colour pages in the centre were unashamedly used to promote the autumn programmes of BBC Television; and instead of a daily editorial segment preceding the programme pages these features were now clustered together with radio before, and television after, the colour pages.

Points from the Post was stabilised as the inside back feature - with a new heading designed by Bruce Angrave who had produced a variety of designs for the page over the years. And the crossword was placed nearer the front. A contents panel was also introduced on page three to allow readers to navigate the increasingly large publication.

by Bruce Angrave
Issue 2343

by Bruce Angrave
Issue 2309   8 Feb 1968

REPORTING TOMORROW'S NEWS TODAY

They've dumped him in a mud bath, swung him in a bucket over Glasgow and sent him down the deepest hole in the world—it's all part of JAMES BURKE's job as a member of the Tomorrow's World team

by Bruce Angrave
Issue 2313
7 March 1968

by Gerald Scarfe
Issue 2336
15 Aug 1968

Some copies of this redesigned 64-page issue were set aside for promotion and overprinted FREE SPECIMEN COPY above the masthead.

The 'Your Autumn Viewing' theme and design continued in the following issue with the 'Autumn Viewing' colour pages interrupted for the annual adult education supplement *Look Listen Learn* which still injuncted readers to pull sharply....

The Olympics Number in October 1968 was 104 pages - easily the largest since the heyday of the thirties. It contained extensive colour pages with pictures of Britain's top athletes and even an eight-page chart which allowed space for viewers to write down the results - a trick carried forward from General Election coverage in past issues. The colour features were interspersed with full-page advertising by the manufacturers of colour television sets (who saw the Olympics televised in colour as a major sales attraction) as well as the inevitable colour ads for cigarettes and whisky; perhaps equal attractions for the couch potatoes who were intent on shutting themselves away for the duration of the Games.

Regional editorial was now given a regular weekly page of its own and the Birdwatching feature quietly disappeared. In comparison with its counterparts in the mid 60s, the *Radio Times* of 1968 was over-stuffed with editorial features.

Issue 2339   5 Sept 1968
Free Specimen Copy

by Burrell
Issue 2336
15 Aug 1968

*　　*　　*　　*　　*

125

For the 1968 *Christmas Radio Times* Barry Wilkinson created a huge Christmas tree bauble which contained pictures of some of the stars appearing in festive programmes. There was even a little space for veteran Radio 2 presenter Sam Costa.

Inside: an introductory feature by an eminent churchman (who varied regionally), colour pictures of assorted stars of television and radio, and even the return of the short story.

by Barry Wilkinson Issue 2334 19 Dec 1968

Elwyn Jones was one of the writers of BBC1's popular police series *Softly Softly* and used its characters in his tale *A Gift of Murder*. This naturally was carried on in the following week's issue, which concentrated heavily on summer holidays in line with the heavy advertising that accompanied it. The seasonal number ended with a *Radio Times Christmas Quiz*.

The arrangements for printing the colour cover and pages had their downside in lack of flexibility - the colour material had to go to press several weeks before the letterpress elements, and sometimes text on colour pages had to be e m b a r r a s s i n g l y contradicted elsewhere. It was a costly and complex business to produce regional covers, and so by and large these were eliminated except where they were unavoidable.

The cover of 24th April promoting that week's FA Cup Final had to be replaced in Scotland because the Scottish Football Association would not allow the BBC to show live pictures of the English match. (Instead Scottish viewers were treated to three hours of a rather blurred black and white test card, but curiously that didn't appear on the cover of the local *Radio Times*.)

Sometimes a colour cover was amended by the addition of a letterpress overprint - the above mentioned Cup Final cover had a reference to the new Radio 2 serial *Waggoners' Walk* added at the bottom of the page, but this didn't register accurately with the colour material and was obviously a (squint) afterthought.

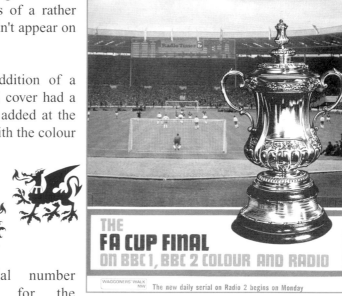

*Issue 2372
24 April 1969
London &
South East*

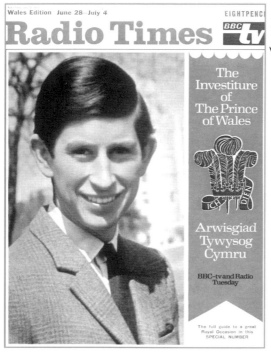

Issue 2381   26 June 1969   Wales edition

A special number appeared for the Investiture of the Prince of Wales in July, and for the first time part of the national cover was printed in the language of Wales.

Inside on three of the colour pages devoted to the occasion, the Wales Herald Extraordinary, Francie Jones, wrote of the age-old tradition of the Investiture. There were colour pictures of Caernarvon Castle (with a colour map from the pen of Lawrence Bradbury who also provided the graphics of the Prince's coat-of-arms for the cover and programme pages) and colour pictures of Prince Charles at various stages of his young life.

In the Wales edition a page was devoted to a special poem in Welsh by E. Gwyfad Evans, and a feature on *A Setting fit for a Prince* by Bowen Griffith, the Mayor of Caernarvon. This was printed entirely in the Welsh language in the Wales edition.

*by Jim Russell
Issue 2381*

TARGET MOON

The astronauts: Neil Armstrong, Michael Collins and Edwin Aldrin. Armstrong, the mission commander, and Aldrin, the lunar module pilot, will drop to the moon's surface. Armstrong will be the first man to step on to the moon. Command module pilot Collins will stay in lunar orbit. If one of the team goes sick —then all three astronauts will be replaced by another trio. NASA officials claim they could replace six teams—if they had to.

Original Issue 2383 10 July 1969
Plate 5a

Issue 2383

A fortnight later a Saturn V rocket was launched from Cape Kennedy with three men on board. Their mission was to land on the moon. The world's imagination captured, *Radio Times* carried a striking colour picture of a similar rocket launching on its cover with the simple words 'Target Moon' - supplemented by the grey letterpress (obvious) addition "Follow this week's historic adventure on BBC-tv and Radio" in a space clearly left to allow the editor to hedge his bets on the launch date. Most of the colour pages and associated editorial was taken up with astronauts and moon facts.

by Reinganum

by A. Knight

Above issue

Reinganum.

COOKING

with ZENA SKINNER

Strawberry and Apple Flan

INGREDIENTS

7-in. cooked sponge flan
¼ lb. fresh strawberries
Sugar to taste
1 lb. cooking apples
Few drops orange juice

METHOD

Cook the apples in a very little water until pulped, then add sugar to taste and allow mixture to get cold. Fill the flan case with the apple, top with a layer of whole strawberries that have been tossed in sugar. Sprinkle with orange juice and serve with cream.

Why not try this? Sounds yummy!

9.0 COLOUR
APOLLO 11
Target Moon
James Burke
looks at the 'How, where, and when' of the flight to put two American astronauts on the moon

APOLLO 11

MAN ON THE MOON

Ironically, it was in that issue that in a feature by Michael Williams, viewers were also introduced to American space series *Star Trek* which for the summer took over the 5.15pm Saturday BBC1 slot normally reserved for *Dr Who*. (*Star Trek* earned itself a full colour feature three weeks later.)

Thirty years on, *Radio Times* reprinted this entire issue and offered it for sale as an historic souvenir.

The following week a colour map of the moon's surface continued the theme as the astronauts prepared for their historic landing. Although this was the issue which included programme details for the actual moon landing, the cover picture of *The Royal International Horseshow* was rather more earthbound.

* * * * *

EIGHTPENCE

Radio Times BBC tv

TARGET MOON

Follow this week's historic adventure on BBC-tv and Radio

5a   *Target Moon 1969*

Scottish Edition
Bill McLaren – Local Encyclopaedia
Radio 4: Sunday
Just Perfick ' by H. E. Bates
Radio 1 & 2: Tues & Thurs
Nigel Dennis story
Radio 3: Friday

Programmes for 1-7 November: Ninepence
Return of Quizburgh
BBC1: Tuesday
Peter Grimes – Opera
BBC2: Sunday
Kenneth McKellar sings
BBC1: Monday

Radio Times

Faithful Sons and Big Daddies
James Drury as The Virginian, Friday BBC1
Leif Erickson, who plays John Cannon
in The High Chaparral, which returns
on Monday BBC2 Colour

5b   *The Virginian 1969   by Brian Love*

North of England Edition
International Rugby
Radio 3, BBC1 & 2: Saturday
Portrait of Glenn Miller
Radio 4: Thursday
Eugene O'Neill play
Radio 3: Friday

Programmes for 6-12 December: Ninepence
Cameron goes Back to Bikini
BBC2: Saturday
Morecambe and Wise
BBC1: Saturday
Sports Review of 1969
BBC1: Thursday

Radio Times

In Colour on BBC1 and BBC2 And on Radio

'The world has treated me very well – but then I haven't treated it so badly either'

Noël Coward
is 70 on 16 December.
The BBC starts
celebrating this week
with his plays, films,
songs and stories

5c   *Noel Coward 1969   by Charles Raymond*

Two weeks of BBC programmes 1s 6d   20 December – 2 January

Radio Times

Radio Nottingham
details on pages 94 and 95

Merry Christmas & a Happy New Year

108 pages!
24 pages in colour!
and what else is in store?
Turn to page 96

See the 1960s
out... with the BBC
Christmas
and New Year stars

5d   *First Christmas double issue 1969*

6a   Dr Who *cover 1971*   *by Frank Bellamy*

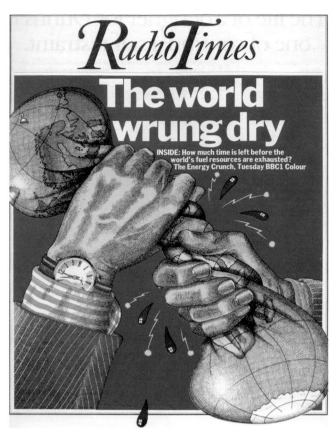

6b   The Energy Crunch *1973*   *by Peter Brookes*

6d   *The Queen 1976*   *by Dmitri Kasterine*

6d   *Christmas 1976*   *by Peter Brookes*

The moon landing issues were his swansong. On his retiral, Campbell Nairne handed over the editorial office to the youngest person ever to sit in that chair. Geoffrey Cannon was twenty-nine and did not in any way fit into the mould of *Radio Times* editors past.

The son of a tax inspector, his mother had died when he was twelve. He described himself as a "sixteen-hour-a-day swot" at school at Christ's Hospital, and he'd won a scholarship to Balliol, Oxford where he disappointed friends by getting a third in philosophy. This was perhaps because he had spent all his time editing and publishing a magazine called *Oxford Opinion* for which he even sold the advertising.

He graduated to *New Society,* then IPC Magazines women's division where he saw the demise of *Women's Mirror*. His most recent commission had been to redesign the graphic image of *The Listener* for Karl Miller.

With his square glasses, black tie, black shirt and black suit, he was seen as 'cool'. In the basement office of his home in Bayswater the ceiling and walls were covered in black cork, and he was reputed to play Rock music with the volume full on. Rock was his inspiration.

> I call it Rock, but I don't mean Bill Haley. You have to call it rock to distinguish it from pop. You don't imagine I like Englebert Humperdinck, do you? It's called Rock in America. Rock is the most efficient and potent means of communication that exists. Number one - Rock. Number two - TV. Number three - telephone. Number four - Newspapers. Number five - Radio. Number six - the Train. You could include Electric Light. There are only about half a dozen guys in Europe who are as attentive as me, there ought to be other writers more attentive. It sounds terribly arrogant, as if I'm the only guy around. Whenever I've been busy and unconnected with Rock for long stretches I've felt so deprived. If I let up for a fortnight, it's like an irretrievable situation.

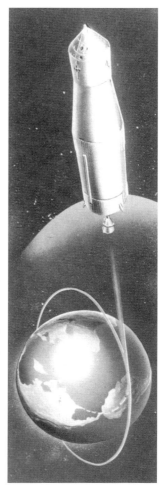

Issue 2383

How did this young man take to the staff at Marylebone High Street?

> It was as if they belonged to another race. I'd never met people like this before. I'd been warned that I'd find the civil servants very stuffy but I found them completely honourable. I've found a particular warmth for the older people. I don't want to come on too strong, but these are people who've been dedicated thirty years to an ideal. Tears come into my eyes. They are better people than I am. You couldn't think of producing the Radio Times without Hilary Cope Morgan who's been there a score of years. If I'm the icing on the cake, she's the cake. She's responsible for programme accuracy and she's indefatigable.

Surprisingly, the indefatigable Ms Morgan took equally to the cool new editor. Their working relationship remained good, despite the one occasion upon which she challenged one of his decisions - to use a page heading for Good Friday which had been decorated with secular images of holiday makers. Hilary felt this would upset many of the paper's Christian readers and told the editor so.

After a pause - during which Hilary wondered if she was about to receive a rocketing - Cannon gave the order to "stop the presses" and had the page header at once replaced by a more conventional one of thorns and nails which had been used the year before.

*   *   *   *   *

Rolf Harris – back on the box at 7.30

by Bruce Angrave   Issue 2386   31 July 1969   by Anthony Cobb   Issue 2395   2 Oct 1969

Geoffrey Cannon spoke in August 1969 about his plans for the new-look *Radio Times* which was to be launched in the autumn. He'd had clear views about the magazine long before his appointment, going as far as to produce a dummy issue for his job interview.

He inherited a publication that was selling just under four million copies a week. He fearlessly announced that if getting the paper right meant losing some of its circulation then so be it. The non programme-related features introduced with the revamp in October 1967 were all to go - Cookery, Gardening, and Travel. And the crossword had had its day.

> I feel adamant about this. The Radio Times is a programme sheet, I thought out
> the correct solution and it also happens to be the one I wanted, I'll argue with or
> against anyone over it, or if he's working for me, tell them to drop dead. Mind
> you they are equally entitled to tell me to get lost.

Around him Cannon built a team of like-minded young men - David Driver as Art Editor, Peter Gillman as Features Editor. Art remained a central element of the weekly paper - Driver adding to the established roster of artists like Eric Fraser or Robin Jacques by bringing in newcomers like Peter Brookes.

*   *   *   *   *

The new paper appeared on newsstands on 4th September. It bore few similarities to the *Radio Times* of the week before. For a start the letters R and T on the masthead were greatly enlarged. Cannon's intention had been to gently phase out the rest of the words leaving the magazine title as RT - standing not for *Radio Times* but for Radio-Television.

Gone was the coloured typography leaving teasers of the week's programme highlights on either side of the masthead, and a heavily-posed studio portrait of three of BBC-tv's top fictional policemen (Barlow, Dixon and Stone) with the provocative footer *Which one do the real coppers love?*

Inside, the first three pages were devoted to an abbreviated listing of all the week's Television and Radio programmes for those who wished them in simple, condensed form. Times and titles. Major changes in the typography were immediately noticeable on the feature pages, and the colour pages were now spread out to accompany the lead features rather than occupy a centre-page ghetto of their own.

As he had promised, the unconnected features had gone - as had the crossword - leaving longer and more thoughtful feature articles about the programmes themselves. And most of what appeared did so under the by-line of the writer. There was still room for a regional page, but this conformed to the style of the rest of the journal and so did not stick out like a sore thumb as being "regional". (Nairne had headed it with a map of the UK showing the region shaded-in.)

The programme pages adopted the new typeface and style, with as little space as possible wasted by page headings. The general layout of programmes was unchanged. At the back of the book was a lengthy feature piece, illustrated with a colour page or two and at the very back were the Letters and - where appropriate - the BBC Local Radio listings.

Circulation dropped by about a quarter-of-a-million.

* * * * *

Soon after Geoffrey Cannon took over the price was increased to Ninepence. And colour came to BBC1.

Characteristically, Cannon avoided loading the cover of this specially enlarged 88 page issue with promotion for the start of colour on the majority channel, and filled the page instead with images of helmet-clad riot police in Tokyo to accompany a documentary on BBC1 about everyday life in Japan's turbulent capital city.

Inside, enormous full-page portraits of the five leading characters in the new BBC1 'soap' *The Doctors* appeared before a regionalised page showing maps of the coverage area of the new BBC1 UHF transmitters. And Cannon's inspired *Radio Times A-Z of BBC Television* had reached the letter 'K' - for *Dr Kildare*. Four colour pages loaded entirely with tinted monochrome photographs took us through Mary Malcolm, Cliff Michelmore, Muffin the Mule, the moon landing and Orwell's *1984* to Sylvia Peters.

10.30 *Colour*
Line-Up: Monday
Introduced by MEL OXLEY
with

Cannon's first Christmas was also the first 'double issue' with two weeks' worth of programme details covering Christmas and New Year week with 108 pages for only one shilling and sixpence. Subsequent Double Issues followed the same formula - as many colour photos of the stars as possible, lots of small page decorations and as many stars as possible together on the cover. But they lacked the sense of occasion of their predecessors.

* * * * *

JAMES CAMERON, WILLIAM RUSHTON
and talk of this and that

by William Rushton
Issue 2403   27 Nov 1969

Plate 5b
Cover by Brian Love
Issue 2399
30 Oct 1969

Issue 2401   13 Nov 1969
North of England edition

Plate 5c
Cover by Charles Raymond
Issue 2404
4 Dec 1969

Christmas cover
Issue 2406
18 Dec 1969
Plate 5d

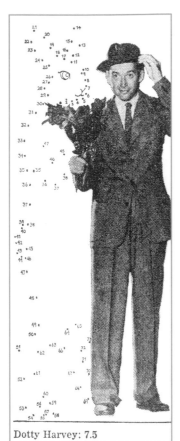

Dotty Harvey: 7.5

Issue 2412   29 Jan 1970

Some of Cannon's ideas were certainly fresh. Instead of a tired photograph of the film's star, the illustration that accompanied BBC1 transmission of James Stewart's film *Harvey* about an invisible rabbit, showed Stewart beside a join-the-dots bunny.

Regional covers had not quite been abandoned. BBC Scotland's ubiquitous (always pretty) newscaster Mary Marquis made yet another cover appearance in a special Scottish edition in which Alasdair Milne, Controller of BBC Scotland, was interviewed (in April 1970) about the future of Scottish broadcasting, while England and Wales looked forward to Chelsea playing Leeds United in the FA Cup Final.

In August 1970 more work was apparently piled on to the staff by the BBC's insistence that the *Radio Times* regional pattern should now exactly match that of BBC television. From the issue of 27th August 1970, *Radio Times* was no longer published in seven basic editions but thirteen, plus local radio editions.

With this issue, more feature material replaced the three-page listing of all the week's programmes. "After careful study and research we are sure that it has not proved sufficiently attractive," wrote Cannon.

By the end of 1970 there were 33 variants rolling off the presses:

Issue 2422   9 April 1970   Scottish edition

SCOTTISH	
CUMBERLAND AND WESTMORLAND	
NORTH EAST	
NORTH EAST	*(BBC Radio Teesside)*
NORTH EAST	*(BBC Radio Durham)*
NORTH EAST	*(BBC Radio Newcastle)*
NORTH WEST	
NORTH WEST	*(BBC Radio Manchester)*
NORTH WEST	*(BBC Radio Merseyside)*
NORTH WEST	*(BBC Radio Blackburn)*
NORTH	
NORTH	*(BBC Radio Sheffield)*
NORTH	*(BBC Radio Leeds)*
NORTH	*(BBC Radio Humberside)*
NORTHERN IRELAND	
MIDLANDS	
MIDLANDS	*(BBC Radio Birmingham)*
MIDLANDS	*(BBC Radio Stoke-on-Trent)*
MIDLANDS	*(BBC Radio Leicester)*
MIDLANDS	*(BBC Radio Nottingham)*
MIDLANDS	*(BBC Radio Derby)*
EAST ANGLIA	
WALES	
WEST	
WEST	*(BBC Radio Bristol)*
SOUTH WEST	
SOUTH	
SOUTH	*(BBC Radio Brighton)*
SOUTH	*(BBC Radio Solent)*
LONDON	
LONDON	*(BBC Radio Oxford)*
LONDON	*(BBC Radio Medway)*
LONDON	*(BBC Radio London) from 1st Oct 1970*

This number of regional editions was impressive to say the least. Yet the television pages surprisingly failed to reflect the new improved regionalisation, billing the 6pm BBC1 news programme as...

Your Region Tonight

...in all but the National regions. For the reality of all these changes was that there were now just *four* basic editions - England, Wales, Scotland and Northern Ireland. The regional programming on the former Home Service - now Radio 4 - in England had been reduced to a minimum with the introduction of Local Radio, so little variation was necessary on the radio pages; and with a specific BBC1 regional 'opt-out' slot on Tuesday night, only one page needed adjustment.

The box, which detailed local TV channels and radio transmitters in the inside back page, was the only other item that truly required 'regionalising'.

Some editions were just a facade - the CUMBERLAND AND WESTMORLAND edition (later badged as CUMBRIA) was really the NORTH-EAST edition with a different heading on the front cover, although it did merit a Local Radio edition with the start of BBC Radio Cumbria some years later.

As the new editions found their way into people's homes one BBC Local was just about to go on the air. BBC Radio Bristol made its debut on Friday 4 September 1970. Its page in the new 'West' (Bristol) edition included a feature on its women's programme by the newly recruited presenter/producer of *Womanwise* - young Kathryn Adie.

Kate Adie's RT debut
Issue 2442
27 Aug 1970
West (Bristol) edition

*   *   *   *   *

Former Art Editor Ralph Usherwood received a rare by-line when the BBC opened their 'Local' radio station in London. 'Ush' conducted an interview with station manager Peter Redhouse for the Radio London edition of 1st October 1970 headed "Radio London: the voice of 10 million". Interestingly, nowhere in the interview was there any mention of the fact that the name had previously been used by the most successful (both in audience and financial terms) of the ship borne "pirates".

"Ush" conducted similar interviews with a number of Station managers as new Local Radio stations were launched in the pages of *Radio Times* - like BBC Radio Medway on 18th December 1970. In most cases, the *Radio Times* coverage of the opening was also reprinted as a four-page supplement which the station itself would hand out as publicity material. They also acted as publicity for *Radio Times* itself as this Medway example shows.

'Introducing BBC Radio Medway'
leaflet - back page

11.15 *New series*
Week Ending . . .

Issue 2447   3 Oct 1970

One of Cannon's most far-reaching innovations was to introduce a column previewing *This Week's Films*. When it first appeared, in 1970, it was less than half a page except in the Christmas double issue when it ran to two pages. The BBC's resident movie expert Philip Jenkinson, along with Tony Bilbow (presenter of BBC-2's *Film Night)*, compiled it.

Another regular column to appear was *This Week's Sounds* dedicated to major pop and jazz events. This was written by Richard Williams of *Old Grey Whistle Test* fame.

Michael Aspel holds the reins to a global network linking Australia, Singapore, Gibraltar and Canada in Sunday's noonday 'Family Favourites.' Hurtling 23,000 miles above the Indian Ocean Intelsat III scoops the greetings from ground stations in Australia and Singapore, while from Gibraltar and Toronto landlines snake their way to Faraday Exchange, London's international clearing point for overseas communications. Messages finally meet in Broadcasting House, nerve centre of the whole operation.

by Frank Bellamy
Issue 2458/9
17 Dec 1970

Amongst the contributions to the Christmas 1970 double issue was artist Frank Bellamy (of *Dan Dare* fame) who contributed this coloured cartoon of Michael Aspel linking up world-wide for *Family Favourites.*

8.30
Famine

by THOMAS MURPHY: adapted for radio by ERIC EWENS
with Denys Hawthorne
Pauline Letts, Peter Jeffrey
Allan Cuthbertson
Geoffrey Matthews, Isobel Black
A Sunday afternoon in the autumn of 1846 in the Irish village of Glenconor. The potato crop has failed. The villagers are gathered to mourn the daughter of John Connor who has died of starvation.

by Adrian
George
Issue 2477
29 April 1971

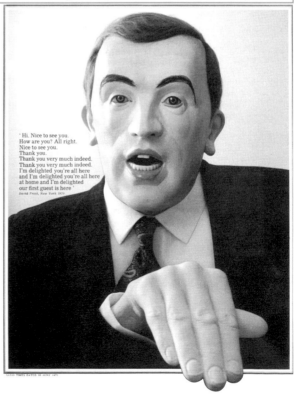

David Frost
by Peter Fluck
Issue 2483 page 7
10 Jun 1971

Before his first redesigned issue had appeared, Cannon had paid tribute to the accuracy of work from his Billings Editor, Hilary Cope Morgan. *Radio Times* still enjoyed a reputation for accuracy, but sometimes things could go awry. FA Cup Final Day in 1971 was an example.....

BBC1   Sunday *tv*

Ee-ay-addio! Who'll win the Cup?

George Armstrong
Arsenal

" He's a tremendous little fighter – he never stops working for 90 minutes. We'll have to cut out his service to the big men "
RAY CLEMENCE

John Toshack
Liverpool

" He's Liverpool's big danger in the air – he'll certainly need watching. He's scored some very good goals "
BOB WILSON

These are the men the goalies fear. See Cup Final Grandstand from 11.45, Arsenal and Liverpool kick-off at 3.0

12.55
It's a Cup Final Knock-Out

Arsenal v Liverpool
All the skills and excitement of *It's a Knock-Out* as teams from the supporters' clubs of Arsenal and Liverpool meet in this special contest for Cup Final day. Featuring celebrity supporters **Pete Murray** (Arsenal) and **Anthony Booth** (Liverpool) and personalities from the 1950 Cup Final between Arsenal and Liverpool
Joe Mercer, Reg Lewis and **Walley Barnes** of Arsenal
Phil Taylor, Billy Liddell and **Albert Stubbins** of Liverpool
Introduced by **David Vine** and **Eddie Waring**
Referee ARTHUR ELLIS
Designer STUART FURBER
Directed by IAN SMITH
Produced by BARNEY COLEHAN

1.40
Inside Wembley

All the pre-match build-up to the 1971 Cup Final, as the crowd begins to fill the Stadium: the two teams arrive and inspect Wembley's famous turf.
And as the atmosphere builds up at Wembley *Grandstand* brings you outstanding FA Cup action, with expert analysis and comment. *Action highlights* of the finalists' progress to the Cup Final, from Arsenal's trip in January to the famous Yeovil slope, to Liverpool's epic semi-final with Everton.
Expert analysis and comment by *Grandstand's* top team JOE MERCER, DON REVIE, BOBBY CHARLTON, all of whom have played in FA Cup Finals at Wembley.
Meet the Teams Arsenal goalkeeper BOB WILSON, whose analysis and comments on BBC Television have entertained and informed millions over the past season, introduces action profiles of his Arsenal colleagues and of the Liverpool players he'll be facing this afternoon.

2.25

Community Singing
Conducted by FRANK REA, with THE BAND OF THE COLDSTREAM GUARDS

2.55

Presentation of the Teams to
HRH The Duke of Kent

3.0

The FA Cup Final
Arsenal
v Liverpool

4.45

Presentation of the FA Cup and Medals by
HRH THE DUKE OF KENT

4.50*
Meet the Winners
DAVID COLEMAN talks to the men of the match, with action replay of the great moments.

Also in *Grandstand*:
12.5
International
Fight of the Week
John Kellie (Glasgow) (Number one challenger for Alan Rudkin's British and Commonwealth Bantamweight Title)
v **Claude Lapinte** (Bantamweight Champion of France)
Highlights of this important fight at York Hall, Bethnal Green, and another top contest from the week's outstanding promotion.
Commentator HARRY CARPENTER

5.5*
Results Service
including news of the Scottish Cup Final and today's racing.
Grandstand presented by BRIAN VENNER and ALAN CHIVERS
Editors ALAN HART and SAM LEITCH
(see page 3 and colour feature pp 52-55)

5.15 *Colour*
Walt Disney's
Wonderful World of Colour
Solomon, the Sea Turtle
An account of the efforts of a scientist to solve the mystery of the sea turtles' ability to navigate vast distances without landmarks.

BBC1 Variations
WALES
10.30-10.50 Cadi Ha! for the young
5.15-5.35 Television Top of the Form
5.35-6.0 Disc a Dawn Welsh Pop show
SCOTLAND
12.45-12.47 News Headlines and Weather
12.47-2.30 The Season of the 'Centenary'
2.30-4.40 Film Matinee: Union Pacific
4.40-5.15 Cup Final News

6.0 *Colour*
The News
Weatherman BERT FOORD

6.10 *Colour*
Dr Who
starring **Jon Pertwee**
Colony in Space
by MALCOLM HULKE
Part 5
The Doctor and Jo try to learn the Master's reason for visiting the planet, and fall into a deadly trap. Dent and IMC men plan a terrible revenge on the Colonists.

Winton............NICHOLAS PENNELL
Dr Who...............JON PERTWEE
Jo Grant.............KATY MANNING
Master................ROGER DELGADO
Ashe.................JOHN RINGHAM
Mary Ashe............HELEN WORTH
Dent.................MORRIS PERRY
Morgan................TONY CAUNTER
Caldwell.............BERNARD KAY
Colonist..............PAT GORMAN
Title music by RON GRAINER and the BBC RADIOPHONIC WORKSHOP
Incidental music by DUDLEY SIMPSON
Script editor TERRANCE DICKS
Designer TIM GLEESON
Producer BARRY LETTS
Directed by MICHAEL BRIANT †

6.35 *Colour*
Tom and Jerry
playing cat and mouse in an award-winning cartoon film starring Tom the cat and a far-from-underdog mouse called Jerry.
Downhearted Duckling
Created by WILLIAM HANNA, JOE BARBERA

No - the Cup Final wasn't played on a Sunday - Radio Times just lost track!
Page 15 of issue 2478   8 May 1971

Some of the older ideas from *Radio Times* past had now begun to filter back into the magazine. The anonymous (and regionalised) gossip on pages 4 and 5 under the heading *Radio Times People* seemed familiar - surely it was a reincarnation of *Both Sides of the Microphone* or *Round & About?*

Monty Python *by Keith McMillan*
Issue 2491   5 Aug 1971

And *Radio Times* under Cannon had no difficulty in getting silly when necessary. A full-page colour picture by Keith McMillan of the Monty Python team in 1971 was certainly not something of which Reith (who had died two months before) would have approved.

One sure way to sell extra copies was to find the right subject for the cover. Successive editors had realised what Cannon was acutely aware of - the cover could make a significant difference to sales, both positive and negative.

5.20 *Colour*
The Pink Panther Show
A cartoon film series presenting the optimistic, indestructible panther who is permanently in-the-pink and The Inspector with unquenchable joie de vivre who hardly ever gets his man

Issue 2491

The Christmas and New Year Double Number was always guaranteed major sales, but these were not maintained for the following week. So for the first issue of 1972 (after a Double Issue fronted by the Two Ronnies) Frank Bellamy was pressed into service for a comic-book-style cover

Dr Who *cover*
by Frank Bellamy
Issue 2521
30 Dec 1971
Plate 6a

featuring *Doctor Who and the Daleks*. Not only did this pay off in terms of circulation, but it created another collector's item since such issues now fetch high prices (up to several hundred pounds each) amongst *Dr Who* fans.

The horror of printing problems - mercifully absent for some years - reared its ugly head once more in the spring of 1972. This time it was nothing to do with trade unions. Government power restrictions had reduced the availability of electricity supplies to industry and the number of days available in which to print *Radio Times* had been restricted.

Rather than risk some areas losing their local editions and others getting the wrong one, the only solution during this crisis was once again to print just a single edition for the whole of the UK.

The first of these appeared on 24th February 1972. In the 68 pages, all the TV regional variations were included along with Radio 4 National and Regional listings. But Cannon accepted defeat when it came to Local Radio, and a single page merely gave the frequencies, addresses and telephone numbers of the 20 BBC Local Radio Stations along with a summary of some of their regular programmes. It was May before the normal service of 33 editions was restored.

Cannon cannot have made too many friends amongst traditional *Radio Times* readers, for his Easter cover in 1972 was a large photo of Liverpudlian comedian Jimmy Tarbuck with his mouth wide open. A far cry from the daffodils and churchyards of years past. In 1976 he pictured Tom Courtney as Christ - another controversial decision.

Later that year the text on either side of the masthead was eliminated and Cannon gave up trying to reduce the title to *RT*, instead expanding it back to a more widely spaced *Radio Times*.

The introduction of BBC Local Radio on medium wave as well as the existing VHF (alongside some minor changes to national wavelengths) allowed the *Radio Times,* in September 1972, to indulge in another of its regional edition-justifiers when it printed maps of the local areas with details of where stations could now be found.

Issue 2525   30 March 1972

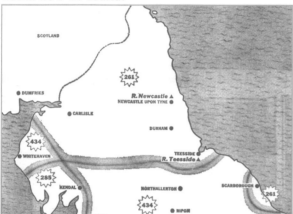

Issue 2547
31 Aug 1972
Page 68
North East/Newcastle

Issue 2551   28 Sept 1972

Sometimes the covers still reflected little bits of broadcasting history. For the first time since the 50s, the Goons found themselves back on the front in October 1972 as they performed *The Last Goon Show of All* for Radio 4. It was part of the celebration of 50 years of BBC Radio, which included a colour portrait of bandleader Henry Hall taken in Broadcasting House, London by Penny Tweedie, showing the now silver- haired man clutching the score of *Here's to the Next Time* and a 1930s issue of *Radio Times*.

Also in this (mildly) celebratory issue were Sir Adrian Boult, Jimmy Young and the Goons.

The celebrations continued for several weeks. "The BBC is 50" hailed the cover of the issue of 26th October with The Queen on the cover. Inside was a single-page history of the BBC, and scattered throughout the issue were little 'Flashback' features reflecting on people and programmes of the past half-century. But there was little of real celebration in the Organ of the BBC.

'The Champion'

A new comedy for television by
Donal Giltinan

✦

Saturday Playhouse at 9.0

A Comedy for Women
by John Van Druten

'THE
DISTAFF SIDE'

***Above illustrations
by George Mackie***

Plate 6b

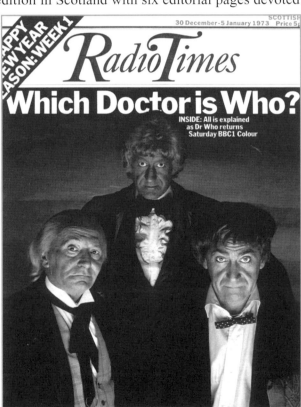

Cover by
Peter Brookes
Issue 2587
7 June 1973

The seventies continued. Each week the glossy colour pages would underline the drab, greyness of the newsprint pages, but with Waterlows geared up to produce by this method nothing short of a major plant replacement at huge cost could improve the overall appearance of the bulk of the magazine. Indeed reliance on one print firm - a substantial advantage in the fifties - would prove to be an increasing problem for the publication in the eighties.

Another personality-led cover for Christmas as Lulu, Morecambe and Wise, and Bruce Forsyth dressed as circus performers shared the cover with a rather inanimate- looking lion (perhaps it was just tired) to celebrate Christmas 1972. Inside, writer Robert Ottaway contributed a thoughtful colour feature on *Hosts of Christmas Past* tracking the BBC's fifty festive seasons. But no New Year programmes as it had been decided to cover the weekend before Christmas this time, and run from 16th to 29th December. And of course, no crossword.

This allowed for a New Year edition as well, and it was one of the rare occasions when *RT* got psyched-up for a Hogmanay edition in Scotland with six editorial pages devoted to Scottish Hogmanay matters in the Scottish edition. But not on the cover which, as in the previous year, was devoted to *Dr Who*. Not one but three of the good doctors. This presumably relied on the principle that if it worked once it would work again.

Geoffrey Cannon ensured a consistency within the pages of his paper - it had few peaks but rather continued to provide its enhanced listings service week in, week out. Graphically illustrated covers were the exception, but now and again the usual large photographs of some topical television presenter would be forsaken for a bit of art. Peter Brookes created a suitably attention-grabbing cover for the BBC1 documentary *The Energy Crunch*, which considered the possibility that the world's fuel resources might be running out.

Issue 2564   28 Dec 1972

* * * * *

It was considered that the fiftieth birthday issue of *Radio Times* did not warrant any mention on the cover, where Michael Jayston and Sorcha Cusack instead appeared in period costume to promote the new BBC-2 dramatisation of *Jane Eyre*. Inside were little snatches of old billings with brief caption commentaries that had been running throughout the month's issues, and the programme pages for 18th September were headed with a neat little row of *Radio Times* mastheads from 1923 to 1973. There was also the announcement of the *Radio Times* Drama Awards with £2000 bursaries for new writers.

The commemoration of the journal's half-century was contained in a large format softback *Radio Times 50th Anniversary Souvenir*, edited not by Cannon but by Russell Twisk assisted by Art Editor, David Driver. Ralph Usherwood carried out the research for an exceptional publication which neatly told much of the story in its well-designed 100 pages. Page 99 was cheekily reserved for some classic advertisements for corsets and garden sheds which had been pushed off the back page with the introduction of colour.

For reasons now lost in the mists of time Bruce Forsyth and *The Generation Game* devoted their top-rated BBC1 show that week to celebrating *RT*'s birthday as well.....perhaps this was in some way connected with the paper's new advertising slogan, "*Radio Times* - first choice for all the family" which appeared, somewhat apologetically, at the very bottom of the last column on the inside back page.

by Eric Fraser

50th Anniversary Souvenir 1923-1973

Gradually, the radio pages evolved, as did that senior broadcasting service. The Independent Broadcasting Authority launched the first licensed land-based commercial radio stations in Great Britain, and in order to make room for these new stations there was a general rearrangement of the UK's internationally-allocated medium wave frequencies.

This resulted in a rationalisation of Radio 4. With more and more local stations opening up in England, there was little need any more for regional opt-outs on the scale that had existed in the 50s. So Radio 4 was trimmed down to a national network with opt-outs usually confined to Scotland, Northern Ireland and Wales. In England, Radio 4 was generally transmitted on three wavelengths although those places with no local radio (the south-west and East Anglia) continued to have some local programming on VHF and - in the case of the former - on medium wave as well.

In Scotland, the Radio 4 service was renamed Radio Scotland to coincide with the launch of commercial station Radio Clyde on 1st January 1974. Later, Wales and Northern Ireland followed with Radio Wales, Welsh-language service Radio Cymru, and Radio Ulster. Later still, some regional opt-outs were introduced in Scotland and Northern Ireland causing their radio pages to become ever more fragmented as we shall see later.

All of these changes were duly reflected in the programme pages of *Radio Times*, which even under Cannon's confident leadership occasionally underwent minor changes. The first few pages were the chief recipients of regular facelifts. The chatty *Radio Times People* feature gave way to an extended contents and melange of short newsy features with various known writers brought in to contribute both preview and review columns as appropriate.

This in turn gave way to a 'week's highlights' page (suspicious overtones of the 60s in evidence) the main features starting on page 4 rather than page 6, and the review column extended to fill the inside back page. Readers in Scotland, Wales and Northern Ireland found themselves with two preview columns - one for the whole of the UK and one for their own area.

The *Letters* Pages - varying in number depending on whether you got a Local Radio edition or not - moved from the inside back to the start of the back section. And in 1975 the issue number - cunningly buried in the midst of the small print of the inside back page for several Cannon years - was reinstated in its proper position at the top of page 3.

Behind
the Palace walls
by Dmitri Kasterine
Issue 2748
10 July 1976
Plate 6c

A sure sign of changing times and attitudes was the photograph of Her Majesty the Queen on the cover in July 1976. In past issues portrayed as a revered and distant monarch, she was this time photographed in the garden of Buckingham Palace wearing a green coat and walking six Palace dogs.

And, paradoxically, some of the traditions of the 30s were revived. In particular the 'Fireside Issue', heralding the start of winter programmes. Peter Brookes drew a classic cover for the 1976 issue - and, although, sticking rigidly to his 'programme sheet' remit, Cannon merely previewed new programme series inside rather than include any 'special' features.

Straightforward colour photographs for the Christmas covers did not remain the norm forever. In 1976 readers were surprised by a stained-glass illustration of the carol *Good King Wenceslas* by Peter Brookes. (But still no crossword...)

Radio Times and *TV Times* came in for some flack when the Committee on the Future of Broadcasting, chaired by Lord Annan, reported in March. The report wondered whether the high

by Peter Brookes   Issue 2763   23 Oct 1976

by Peter Brookes
Issue 2771/2
18 Dec 1976
Plate 6d

circulations of the two papers were achieved because of their protected monopolies, as neither would allow any outside party the right to print the programmes in advance.

The Annan Committee felt the two journals had become 'flabby' and questioned that their continuance could be in the public interest, as they concluded that having to buy two programme journals to find out what was on TV was an "unnecessary and unfair imposition on the public."

However these comments might have been true, they were ignored by the government and did not find their way into legislation.... for the time being.

* * * * *

*by Nicola
Griffin
(aged 5)
Issue 2794
28 May 1977
Plate 7a*

*by Ralph
Steadman
Issue 2796
11 Jun 1977
Plate 7b*

Radio Times covers remained the only area of the paper with scope for artistic experiment. Fluck and Law's rubber models of David Frost and Richard Nixon, rather than the real people, made for an irreverent cover in 1977, one of a cluster of highly original front pages that summer. *Blue Peter* and *Radio Times* held a joint competition for a child to design a cover for the Queen's Silver Jubilee, and so at the age of 5, Nicola Griffin became the youngest-ever artist to see her work on the front cover. (The runners-up were printed inside, some in colour, some not.) And after the Jubilee, the unique style of Ralph Steadman was put to memorable use with his cricket cover.

But perhaps one of the most original covers from David Driver's period as Art Editor was for the Jubilee Souvenir Issue itself on 4th June 1977 when rather than commission an artist, he commissioned Candace Bahouth to design a tapestry of the Queen.

And, for once forsaking its pure 'programme sheet' function, this 80-page special *Radio Times* was permitted the luxury of a series of vivid features, interviews and illustrations spanning the years from 1952 to 1977. Adrian George was commissioned to paint portraits of some of those who contributed prose - including Bishop Ramsey, Sir Norman Hartnell, Lord Hunt, Sir John Betjeman and Malcolm Williamson.

At the back of the paper, the BBC's official historian, Asa Briggs and his writer wife, Susan, considered the varying styles of Royal Broadcasts over the 25 year period, with beautiful specially-commissioned colour illustrations by Eric Fraser, Victor Reinganum, Robin Jacques, Peter Brookes and Nigel Holmes. Each - probably for the first time - had a postage-stamp sized photograph of himself sitting alongside his work. Fraser's drawing revived the lion and unicorn that had originally graced the Coronation cover.

Reinganum - in that issue - described Maurice Gorham as "a ruthless perfectionist".

*   *   *   *   *

***Tapestry by Candace Bahouth
Issue 2795   4 June 1977
Below: by Eric Fraser Page 67***

In the late summer BBC Television celebrated the Queen's Jubilee year with a 'Festival 77', mostly of repeats of old programmes. The *Radio Times* cover was also a series of repeats.

A special issue celebrated Radio One's tenth anniversary in October 1977 with a baker's dozen deejays on the cover and a series of features about and by them inside. Notable was a lengthy (i.e. spread over three pages) article by John Peel, *Electric Folk to Punk Rock*. There would be more where that came from.

There was also the inevitable price increase - this one was given official sanction..

> From this week the price of Radio Times is 13p. This increase, which has been cleared by the price commission is caused by a general, unavoidable rise in costs this year.

Plate 7c

Researched by Wallace Grevatt Issue 2803 30 July 1977

And what (let us now remind ourselves) did the reader get for their thirteen pee? 80 pages; 12 in colour of which generally four were editorial pages and 8 were advertisements. Regular features: *This Week, The Week's Films, Preview, Letters* and *Review.* Programme pages: 4 for TV, 2 for radio each day. And still no crossword.

After having attempted to extend the appeal of the Christmas Double number by publishing it a week earlier (thereby missing New Year) a different scheme was introduced with the 'The Week Before Christmas' issue - a festive edition which acted as a curtain raiser to the following week's Bumper number.

by Eric Fraser Issue 2823

by Robin Jacques Issue 2823 17 Dec 1977

Robin Jacques contributed the traditional-style cover for the 1977 issue into which he even managed to incorporate his namesake. Delia Smith made an appearance with her recipe for *Ginger Oat Crunchies* and there were features on Hornby trains and Alison Uttley, creator of *Little Grey Rabbit*, with a total of 24 colour pages.

The following week's proper 120-page Christmas number had Pauline Ellison's Christmas-tree-village on the cover, and this was also used for the annual *Radio Times* Christmas card.

Perhaps Cannon's desire to produce a programme sheet free of 'women's magazine' overtones was dented a little when Esther Rantzen appeared on the cover in May 1978 clutching her firstborn, Emily Alice, and surrounded by the team of her popular BBC1 series *That's Life.*

It became the norm around this time to devote a handful of summer issues to the great God of Sport - possibly because the television and radio schedules tended to be dominated by sporting events - Ascot, cricket and tennis - across the traditional summer holiday period.

In 1978 there was also a World Cup to contend with, one for which England did not qualify and for which British interest centred on Scotland. Successive *RT* covers portrayed the World Cup; Scottish supporters; Sue Lawley in a suitable Ascot hat; tennis stars Björn Borg, Virginia Wade (both portraits by Dmitri Kasterine); golfer Tom Watson; cricket's Mike Brearley; Commonwealth Games hopefuls Tessa Sanderson, Sharon Colyear and Sonia Lannaman frolicking on a Jamaican beach; and Jamaican athlete Don Quarrie.

RT Christmas card from cover by Pauline Ellison
Issue 2824   24 Dec 1977

But in the midst of all this sport came The Proms, and the BBC's continued commitment to the annual music festival was illustrated by one of Peter Brookes' more inventive covers.

Cover
and illustration
by Peter Brookes
Issue 2853
15 July 1978

With the 'Fireside Issue' of 1978 there was the usual seasonal smartening-up with a little tweaking of the makeup. A detailed 'Contents' column was introduced on page three along with a greatly diminished summary of the week's highlights and - rather oddly perhaps - a glimpse of the following week's cover.

Delia Smith made her debut as a regular contributor as she embarked on a three-year television cookery course with a weekly recipe feature in *RT*. At long last, the archives of *Radio Times* were plundered for a new weekly "Fifty Years Ago" feature.

And Roger Woddis penned a weekly poem - his first, *Making Waves* - dealt with the impending radio wavelength changes which were of course bound to bring a string of complaints from those listeners whose radio dials had seized up, welded to the same frequency for years. The last stanza was a desperate attempt at a mnemonic. ➤

> *Radio 1's two-eight-five metres,*
> *Not forgetting ten below;*
> *Radio 2 will mode to medium,*
> *Four-three-three and three-three-o;*
> *3 moves down to two-four-seven,*
> *4's on fifteen hundred long;*
> *And to drown the howls of anguish*
> *Aubrey Singer strikes a gong.*

Despite this unpromising start, *Woddis on...* survived for quite a time.

On the inside back page, cartoonist Marc Boxer was invited to make a weekly observation. His first parodied the ubiquitous science presenter James Burke. ➤

MARC'S VIEW

Why were the pyramids invented? What is the connection with the clip-on microphone? Both were necessary for James Burke to make a TV series . . .

by Marc Boxer   Issue 2868   28 Oct 1978

Two weeks into the new look and the old "printing difficulties" popped up again: this time an unspecified problem with the colour pages. For three weeks *RT* suddenly donned its old-fashioned garb to appear on the news-stands in all its grey-and-off-white pulp glory. The portrait of *Reginald Perrin* comedy star, Leonard Rossiter (shot against a very dark background) was particularly horrid in letterpress monochrome.

Issues   2870   11 Nov
2871   18 Nov
2872   25 Nov 1978

7a   *Cover design 1977   by Nicola Griffin, aged 5*

7b   *Cricket 1977   by Ralph Steadman*

7c   *25 Years of BBCtv - Festival 77*

7d   *Michael Crawford 1978   Unpublished cover*

8a *Remembrance 1980 by Gerald Minott*

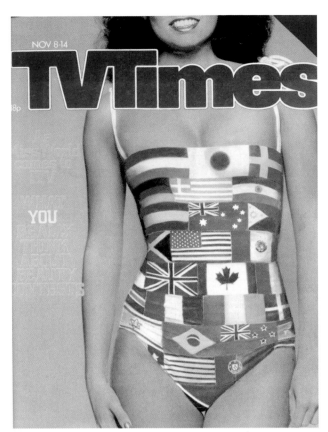

8b *Miss World Contest 1980 TV Times*

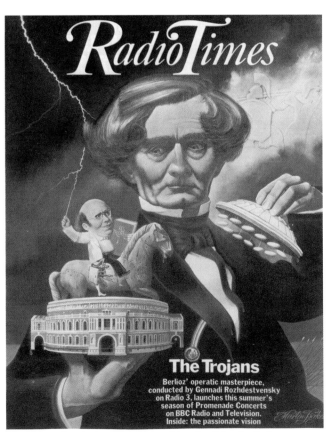

8c *Berlioz'* The Trojans *1982 by Martin Baker*

8d *Unpublished Easter cover 1983 by Penelope Wilton*

Humorist Richard Stilgoe was - at this time - hosting a weekly BBC-2 programme of gentle satire with the title *And Now the Good News....* The black and white *Radio Times* became the butt of Stilgoe's wit as he explained to viewers that the paper was now - in common with airlines, railways and the postal system - produced in three ever-diminishing versions:

> Colour - for the First Class viewers.....
>
> Black-and-white for the ordinary viewer...
>
> And for the real cheapskates, a painting-by-numbers version...

Issue 2870
painting-by-numbers version
With thanks to producer
Ken Stephinson
for allowing us to share the joke

Unpublished colour proof of issue 2870 Plate 7d

Although they never saw the light of day, colour covers for issues 2870, 2871 and 2872 had in fact been produced.

For the complicated (thanks to Roger Woddis) wavelength changes, *Radio Times* produced a series of four-page supplements (no mention of staples, alas) with maps of each edition's local area showing what to tune in to receive the BBC's national radio services.

To add to the demands on radio space, from 23rd November, Radio 4 was once again available throughout the British Isles. In the English editions this made no difference - it still got a whole page to itself. In Northern Ireland, it had to share with Radio Ulster and Radio Ulster VHF. In Scotland, this page had to accommodate Radio 4, Radio Scotland, Radio Scotland VHF, and the four regional opt-out services for Highland, Aberdeen, Orkney and Shetland. In Wales, Radio 4, Radio Wales and Radio Cymru indulged in an undignified battle for column inches.

Colour pages resumed with the issue of 2nd December 1978, mercifully in time for Christmas. For the double issue a portrait photograph of Santa Claus unmasked as Mike Yarwood adorned the front. It was Philip Jenkinson's swan song as Film Critic, as he handed over to Bryan Forbes who set out his stall for readers.

> I shall not be posing as a critic of my colleagues, but as a lifelong film buff and somebody who owes much to the industry. My personal views on these films shown on TV may be of more than passing interest to readers.

But although *Radio Times*' problems were over - temporarily - the BBC in general was suffering a 'season of discontent' as plans for Radio 2 to become a 24-hour network, and for BBC-2 to open up earlier in the evening were disrupted by increasingly effective trade union action, leading to the unprecedented step of acknowledging such problems in the pages of *RT*.

> The BBC regrets that, during the current difficult period of industrial relations some programme transmissions may be liable to change or interruption.

The dispute was settled in January 1978, but things were to get worse for *Radio Times* .....

CHAPTER NINE
Diminished Form

As *Radio Times* entered 1979 - its final year under Geoffrey Cannon - all was not well. Having just suffered the loss of colour pages in three successive issues, a lorry drivers' strike in January meant that in order to simplify the pattern of distribution, the paper appeared in just four editions - Scotland, Wales, Northern Ireland and England.

> We apologise to readers that *Radio Times* this week appears in a diminished edition. This is due to the industrial situation at the time of going to press.

In practice, many readers would have failed to notice just what exactly had been 'diminished'. The only clues were a complicated list of nine different regional programmes in the 6.50 Tuesday timeslot on BBC1, and a Local Radio page that just showed outline details of the programmes on 20 BBC stations.

VIEW
Peter Brookes on Fellini's Roma

by Peter Brookes   ***Issue 2882   3 Feb 1979***

On 3rd February, Marc Boxer handed over the back page cartoon slot to well-established *RT* illustrator Peter Brookes.

Brookes' debut as a regular was itself 'diminished' by the distribution problems caused by the lorry strike which meant that in some parts of the country *Radio Times* was not to be found. On 10th February, Cannon apologised:

> ..to readers in certain areas who will not receive their appropriate edition. Normal service will be resumed as soon as possible.

The paper had also been reduced in size to 68 pages to alleviate the problem somewhat. The following week, 'normal' service was indeed resumed and the paper returned to 80 pages with all editions blazing!

In March 1979, Sheridan Morley took over from Bryan Forbes as the film previewer. He had co-presented BBC2's *Film Night* programme with former columnist Philip Jenkinson and was an obvious choice for the role.

*   *   *   *   *

This was not a comfortable time for *Radio Times*. The print unions were under pressure to reform the somewhat inflexible practices that led to over-manning. And the entire newspaper and magazine industry was about to face the revolution of first computerised typesetting and then direct keyboard input by the journalists themselves, making the compositor and his craft a thing of the past.

By the late '70s many publications were using up to date methods, while *Radio Times* was still stuck in the Caxton days of hot metal - with each letter painstakingly inserted in a giant version of the familiar children's *John Bull Printing Outfit.*

Minor irritations on the shop floor could lead to major incidents. One such involving a dispute between one of the print unions - the National Graphical Association - and the company of T. Bailey Foreman Ltd in Nottingham, resulted for the first time in blank pages appearing in the Journal of the BBC.

In the issue of 31st March, two pages (58 and 66) appeared virgin white save for the words...

THIS SPACE WAS RESERVED FOR ADVERTISING

...in the centre. The missing advertisements appeared instead the following week.

*   *   *   *   *

At Easter, Cannon again took a risk with the cover by printing a full-sized picture of the 'Turin shroud', which purported to be the image of Jesus Christ himself. It was a far cry from the days of churchyards and daffodils.

by Clino Trini Castelli
Issue 2891
7 April 1979

But although the cover might not have been adorned by seasonal blooms, they found their way into the feature pages as Peter Seabrook began a weekly gardening page, with readers' problems dealt with by Bill Sowerbutts from the long-running Radio 4 programme *Gardeners' Question Time.*

A General Election on 3rd May earned itself scant recognition on the cover. This was due to both the lead-time for colour pages and the unexpected haste with which the election had been called. Just a small overprint beneath the name of the regional edition informed readers that this was a 'General Election Issue'. (The main cover star was - ironically - a little pussycat!) But inside the 104 pages there was plenty of political coverage including a map showing all of the constituencies, and a detailed list of the 'marginals'.

VIEW

Peter Brookes on a question of values

A fetching little piece...

Fetching how much exactly, Mr Negus?

Issue 2891

by Mick
Brownfield
Issue 2907
28 July 1979

One performer destined to have a starring role in the cast of future *Radio Times* popped up on the cover in the summer of 1979. Barry Norman hosted a weekly movie programme, which had started as a low-budget local filler in the south-east of England and risen to national status. At this particular point it bore the title *Film '79*.

Norman was fronting a series of profiles of *Hollywood Greats* and was invited to pen an article for *Radio Times* on the subject. This was the beginning of a long-standing association, which led to his later role as regular film reviewer.

Mick Brownfield created an imaginative cover in which Norman appeared as if himself on the cover of an old-fashioned film magazine, complete with frayed edges and a staple sticking out at the edge!

A few weeks later the complete ITV Network (with the sole exception of Channel Television in Jersey) was closed down for ten weeks as a result of a technician's strike.

From teatime on 17th August until teatime on 24th October those viewers north of Guernsey who tuned to the commercial channel had nothing but a caption and classical music for entertainment. *Radio Times* which had, for so many years, avoided acknowledging the existence of another channel, used the strike as the basis for a Peter Brookes cartoon...

VIEW

Peter Brookes on Blankety Blank

* Q. Can you supply the missing invective?

by Peter Brookes   Issue 2917   6 Oct 1979

The *Letters* page - under the headline...

When ITV's off, can't the BBC do better?

...was dominated by ITV fans, 'forced' to watch the BBC and clearly unimpressed with its output.

We have been without ITV for a few days now, and believe me, what a boring time it has been......

But the following week came the backlash:

How dare ITV aficionados criticise the 'drivel' BBC transmits? How can Crossroads addicts claim the BBC programmes are boring?...

It was one of the first instances of ITV programmes actually being openly discussed in the *Letters* pages of the BBC's own journal. (A journal whose competition packed up and went home, incidentally, for *TV Times* suspended publication from September 1st until several days after programmes had resumed at the end of October. Only the locally produced *Channel TV Times,* which at least had some programmes to advertise, stayed the course.)

As the seventies came to an end *Radio Times* provided a useful review of the decade in the Christmas Double Issue, illustrated with a handful of what were considered significant *RT* covers from throughout the Cannon era.

Indeed, it marked the end of that era, for not only was the decade over, but Geoffrey Cannon left for *The Sunday Times,* handing over editorial office to Brian Gearing in March 1980.

Gearing's was to be a markedly less stable era.

It began comfortably enough, with a new regular cookery feature by Delia Smith, and an Indoor Gardening column from Geoffrey Smith (no relation). Both were trailblazing their BBC books - his was *Mr Smith's Indoor Garden* and hers was *Delia Smith's Cookery Course*. The continuing integration of the BBC's publications operation meant that it was now incumbent upon *Radio Times* to promote publications from its stable whenever possible.

Also new was a regular *Help!* consumer feature that included a section in which readers could write for all sorts of consumer advice.

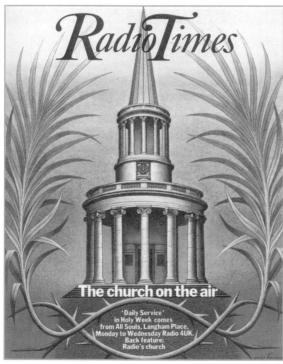

by Eric Fraser
Issue 2942   29 March 1980

A now rare Eric Fraser illustration appeared at Easter. After Cannon having done his best to shock readers with a whole series of Easter and Holy Week covers bearing assorted (and sometimes scary) images of Christ, the new editor made his mark immediately by providing comfort to the traditional readers with Fraser's delightful colour illustration of All Souls' Church in Langham Place, adjacent to London's Broadcasting House.

by Chuck Jones
Issue 2934
5 April 1980

The following week *Radio Times* readers may have been forgiven for wondering if the price increase (to 17p) had gone to the editor's head, as Hollywood animator Chuck Jones' audaciously cheeky cover illustration depicted his famous cartoon character Bugs Bunny reading *RT,* with a caption which mercilessly took the piss out of *TV Times* own advertising slogan 'I never knew there was so much in it':

Probably the first sign of humour on a *Radio Times* cover for several decades, but not the last under Gearing.

* * * * *

Bugs Bunny © Warner Brothers Inc.

7.0 Bugs Bunny
in *The Iceman Ducketh*

7.5-7.35
LONDON Sykes: A comedy series with
ERIC SYKES and HATTIE JACQUES. Eric and
Hat decide to go on a camping holiday
to the south coast. After a series of
incidents, the insurance money comes
in very handy. (*Repeat*)

SOUTH WEST Avocet Cruise: TONY SOPER
leads an expedition up the River Tamar
in search of the rare bird the avocet,
which winters in the South West. (*Rpt*)

WEST Razzmatazz: This week, GWYN
RICHARDS presents the best in music and
dance from the youngsters of GLOUCESTER-
SHIRE.

SOUTH The Getaways: The second of
two films about The King's Army who
re-create a battle of the English Civil
War period, and everyone has a wonderful time!

MIDLANDS The Garden Makers: In the
recent series of *The Garden Game*,
NORMAN PAINTING visited four autumn
gardens. Now all the gardens, and the
people who created them, can be seen
again in one programme.

EAST Quidnunc: ROBERT BATHURST presents more items showing the enterprising young in action, including collectors'
corner, music and a touch of fashion.

NORTH Beneath the Pennines: Another
chance to see this series in which SID
PEROU explores the world beneath the
Pennines. In this programme, he joins
rescue team leader HARRY LONG in the
hazardous Dow Cave. (*Repeat*)

NORTH EAST Spike's Night: The first of
three programmes in which North East
comedian SPIKE RAWLINGS plays host to
some friends from the worlds of sport
and entertainment.

NORTH WEST Contrasts: JACQUI SCOTT,
BERNI FLINT, RICHIE CLOSE and friends
present music with contrasts of mood,
colour and style.

BBC 1 Variations
WALES
10.38-10.58 Hyn o Fyd: for schools
5.10-5.40 Bilidowcar: children's magazine
7.5-7.35 Heddiw: topical items
SCOTLAND
12.40-12.45 The Scottish News
7.5-7.35 Sykes: as London

Page 47 Issue 2948 10 May 1970

A few weeks later, those dreaded words ...

> We apologise to readers that some copies
> of *Radio Times* this week appear in
> diminished form...

...once more appeared on page three, signalling the continuation of this period of industrial unrest. Again, for several issues, the number of editions was dramatically reduced, and although the various English regional editions continued to be badged on their front covers as 'London', 'West', 'North West' etc, inside they were editorially all the same with details of all the local radio stations confined to a single page and regional TV billings clustered together. Only regional advertising was maintained.

One dispute solved, another began - a problem with the Musicians' Union affected some live music and *Radio Times* once more had to step forward with an apology:

> As RADIO TIMES went to press, the
> Musicians' Union dispute had not been
> resolved. Some programmes - in
> particular the Promenade Concerts on
> Radio 3 - may not be broadcast as billed
> in our programme pages.

The issue this appeared in was a special edition celebrating the Queen Mother's 80th Birthday, to which celebration Gearing had devoted the entire issue, apart from the *Letters* pages and Sheridan Morley's film previews. There was even a full colour centrefold of the Queen Mother with a Royal corgi alongside.

Issue 2955
26 Jan 1980

Denis Norden, Frank Muir, Ian Wallace, Steve Race and John Amis: My Music – *300th edition: 6.30*

Gearing's first opportunity to stamp his own individual style on the paper came with the 1980 Autumn Season, when *RT* underwent yet another revamp, although not a total makeover.

Subtle changes included the return of the cheerful diary-style 'news and gossip' feature, now headed simply *Radio & Television* and edited by Robert Ottaway. This digest of snippets about assorted BBC programmes appeared on pages 4 and 5 and clearly was the grandson of *Both Sides of the Microphone*.

The views of BBC Symphony players interwoven with Bartok's music in Concerto for Orchestra: 8.6

by Ellis Nadler
Issue 2971
18-24 Oct 1980

Gone was Peter Brookes' cartoon, but John Craven - familiar to all younger viewers as the bejumpered anchor of BBC1's daily *Newsround* programme - now edited an inside back page feature for youngsters which included the return of a cartoon strip. This featured *Morph* the popular clay-modelled character of a thousand Tony Hart shows, replicated in just pen-and-ink by Peter Lord. And although there was *still* no crossword, Clive Doig produced a variety of weekly puzzles on this page, including *Trackword* a classic nine letter square from which readers were invited to find as many words as they could. And there was even a new weekly *Embroidery* feature!

Issue 2964
28 Aug 1980

The changes resulted in a *Radio Times* which had more comforting echoes from the past than in the Cannon years. Gearing's style was less provocative and more inclined to the traditional. As with his Holy Week cover by Eric Fraser, the Remembrance Day cover by Gerald Mynott presented a stylised impression of St Luke's Parish Church in Cannock, complete with poppies, butterflies and even a rainbow over the church tower.

Plate 8a

by Gerald Mynott
RT issue 2974
8 Nov 1980

TV Times
Vol.101
No.46
8 Nov 1980
Plate 8b

On the news-stands this cosy reminder of an age long past presented a ludicrous contrast with *TV Times* in a week when that publication devoted its cover to the *Miss World* contest with an anonymous model whose curves were accentuated by a bathing suit made from the flags of the Nations.

In November the dreaded words 'diminished form' appeared yet again as another printing dispute affected *RT* with its usual casualties - local radio pages and regional TV billings.

This dispute lasted over Christmas, although the 'D-word' did not appear in the "England" edition of the Double Issue, which was the last to suffer diminution for now. But a few months of normality ensued during which Eric Fraser penned what was to be his last cover highlighting J.R.R. Tolkien's epic work *The Lord of the Rings* serialised on Radio 4. Fraser died not long afterwards.

Carrying on in the comic tradition where Bugs Bunny had left off the year before, Easter 1981 saw America's number one comic book hero, *Superman*, doing a quick-change out of his Clark Kent outfit, thus providing artist Mick Brownfield with a rare opportunity to legitimately draw the highly-protected trademark of D. C. Comics Inc.

(A strong desire not to pursue a protracted legal battle with the good folk at D. C. Comics sadly leads the author to omit this Krypton-shattering illustration from the pages of this book....)

But undoubtedly the highlight of the Easter issue (aside from an undignified number of egg puns in a feature about Pam Ayres) was.....**a crossword!!!!**

True, it was an egg-shaped puzzle without any printed clues, since it was intended for use by listeners to Terry Wogan's radio show, but it was the first crossword puzzle to darken the door of 35 Marylebone High Street since being banished in 1969 by Geoffrey Cannon.

by Heath   January 1981

You know what you like, but is it art? Six decades of Radio Times ill-ustrations and 20 years of offerings from the 'Eye' in Arena: 10.0

*　　*　　*　　*　　*

On those occasions when *Radio Times* failed to appear, or did so in 'diminished form', the causes had always been external. The General Strike, national economic difficulties, rail strikes, and the industrial squabbles between Waterlows and its employees were all factors well beyond the control of those at 35 Marylebone High Street.

But for the first time the Journal of the BBC had to face an enemy within. Its own staff - journalist members of the NUJ - briefly withdrew their labour in the summer of 1981 leading to further 'diminished form'.

The regular 76-page issue of 6th June appeared as normal, but the following week, 13th June 1981, a 60-page 'National edition' was published. Television programme pages were normal but radio was reduced to a single page of truncated billings for Radios 1, 2, 3 and 4 - with no details for Radios Scotland, Wales, Cymru or Ulster, and a scant page of local radio information.

Although some programme features appeared, Robert Ottaway's *Radio & Television* feature was absent, as were the *Letters, Help!* Delia Smith, Roger Woddis, Peter Brookes, and *John Craven's Back Page* feature including *Morph* and Clive Doig's puzzles.

The next week, Sheridan Morley's name was missing atop the film previews, and *Radio Times* was down to 56 pages.

The regular features all returned in the subsequent 76-page issue (27th June) but this still appeared in a single National edition. By the careful use of very small type it nevertheless managed to incorporate all of each day's detailed billings for Radio 4, Radio Scotland and its five opt-outs, Radio Ulster, Radio Foyle, Radio Wales and Radio Cymru on the single page normally devoted exclusively to Radio 4! Normal Service resumed with the issue of 4th July. It was to be a very brief burst of normality. The journalists may have been placated, but the printers were about to create the biggest problems.

*   *   *   *   *

In the summer of 1981 one major public event was uppermost in British consciousness - the pending wedding of the heir to the throne. Prince Charles was to wed Lady Diana Spencer on the 29th of July. It was to be accorded the biggest television and radio coverage of any Royal event to date. Naturally, this included a bumper celebratory issue of *Radio Times* which, under Brian Gearing, could undoubtedly be relied upon to strike a suitable tone. When the special issue hit the streets it certainly did the young couple proud. Adorning the cover of the 'Royal Wedding Souvenir Issue' was an embroidered design specially produced for *RT* by the Royal School of Needlework, and within the special issue's 84 pages were all the elements you would have expected.

An exclusive and profusely illustrated eight-page interview between the young Prince and *RT*'s Tim Heald began the proceedings. Indeed, it was page 14 before Robert Ottaway's pages put in their appearance.

Design by the Royal School of Needlework

Issue 3011
25 July 1981

A centrefold of the young couple was preceded by colour pictures of Royal Weddings past. There were colour features on the cake, the rings, and a detailed Order of Service. At the back of the book (after the *Letters*) a detailed family tree traced Diana's antecedents to King Charles II as the history of her life. Family and work were detailed in a further six-and-a-half pages, leaving just enough space for Sheridan Morley's film page.

A splendid effort. But.....

Readers might just have noticed something odd on the front cover. Above the needlework were the date and price. But, although some copies were labelled ENGLAND, others bore no mention of the edition. Inside, the programme pages seemed normal enough. However, readers in Scotland, Wales and Northern Ireland would have - by page 21 - noticed that their usual radio billings were absent. By page 28 readers in much of England would have become puzzled by the references to 'Look North' and 'Look North West' as the local news magazines on BBC1. And where were the Local Radio details?

In fact, what on earth was going on?

Unpublished Issue 3012 1 Aug 1981

At precisely the wrong moment, a dispute had led to the plate-makers refusal to work on the makeup of the special issue. The first edition to be printed - the North-West of England - had been made up in East Kilbride, and so the entire print run was produced from just one set of plates, with no chance even to insert an apology or explanation.

The following week, for only the sixth time in its history, *Radio Times* failed to appear. An extension to the number of colour pages had been planned to include programme page colour features on the Welsh National Eisteddfod and the Berlin wall. But these and the rest of issue 3012 never saw the light of day.

On 8th August issue number 3013 was published as one National edition in the now-familiar truncated form, with the Radio 4 and 'National Regions' billings again squashed unhappily together, and Local Radio yet again reduced to a generic page. It was 22nd August before the full complement of regional editions returned.

Two weeks later *Radio Times* was given a very modest autumn makeover. For the first time the page 3 heading included a 'cast list' of the paper's leading figures.

Roger Woddis now found himself with a smaller space for his poetry, which appeared as an item in Robert Ottaway's pages. Sheridan Morley had bowed out of the film previews the previous week "after writing almost 130 of these columns

RadioTimes

35 MARYLEBONE HIGH STREET, LONDON W1M 4AA. TEL 01-580 5577. PUBLISHED ON THURSDAY BY BBC PUBLICATIONS: VOL 232 No 3017 © BBC 1981

Editor BRIAN GEARING
Features & Deputy Editor DAVID DRIVER
Art Editor BRIAN THOMAS
Programme Editor HUGO MARTIN
Planning Editor MATTHEW SALWAY

and notes, therefore, on over 1300 films" and handed over to Geoff Brown "before too many of the titles start coming round again" with a reminder that "Mr Brown will not be choosing the ones you see any more than I ever did - we only get to write about them."

More space was provided for the Friday billings, and more details of the following week's issue were given. But, by and large, things remained the same.

*   *   *   *   *

'National teletext month' was celebrated in October 1981 with a special colour CEEFAX index appearing in *Radio Times*, thus giving this new form of technology the official seal of approval. The issue in which it appeared featured on its cover Oliver Cotton, Adolfo Celi and Anne Louise Lambert as stars of the new BBC2 costume drama *The Borgias* set in Renaissance Italy.

by Ric Gemmell   Issue 3022   10 Oct 1981

In a rare burst of self-mockery, *Radio Times* satirised Ric Gemmell's *Borgias* cover in early 1982 for its *Not the Nine o'Clock News* cover....

Issue 3038   30 Jan 1982

...the fake 'turned page' must have driven newsagents mad! (Careful perusal of the billings on the 'turned pages' is recommended - the jokes therein are mostly at the expense of Terry Wogan.)

Issue 3025   31 Oct 1981

Another excellent piece of self-parody appeared in October 1981, with the Mona Lisa appearing as a sales tool on everything from wine to clocks and sweetie tins, but the *pièce de résistance* on this uncredited cover is the leather *Radio Times* reading case which da Vinci's inscrutable lady is holding!

Issue 3029   26 Nov 1981

Since the '50s many homes had used sturdy reading-cases just like Mona Lisa's to protect their precious copy of the current *Radio Times,* but curiously, the BBC had not been enterprising in their production. Various small private firms had seized upon the opportunity to produce these folders, which could be obtained in a variety of forms - leather, card, adorned with irrelevant colour pictures of flowers, kittens or other designs. Some would bear the words '*Radio Times*' others would be stamped '*Radio & TV Times*' or simply '*Radio & TV*'.

It was later in the '80s before the BBC's commercial arm at last decided to produce official fireside binders, stamped with the proper logo.

*   *   *   *   *

155

For Christmas '81, Tony Meeuwissen crafted a dove of peace in a belfry, both of which did their best to distract the purchaser from the price increase! (The normal weekly issue was now raised to 25p - or 36p if you lived in the Irish Republic, where the Northern Ireland edition was now sold with its price in both sterling and punts).

In January came a subtle change to the internal appearance of *RT*. The feature pages and programme pages both appeared with their heading printed in straight black on white where previously they had been white on grey. Given the general sludgy appearance of most of the paper's pages, this did have the effect of making the pages look a little crisper.

In fact the changes had been made for a specific reason. The following week, the last copies to be produced by the hot metal process were printed, and the first to be made with polymer plates produced. The changeover was made during the run of the paper, thus some editions (Scotland for example) were hot metal and others (such as Northern Ireland) polymer.

The new process made production easier, although there was no perceptible improvement in the actual print quality. It was, however, blamed for a protracted period of 'diminished form'. From early spring the various English regional editions continued to appear with the correct regional name above the masthead. Inside they were (regional advertising apart) identical with the billings for the weekly BBC1 opt-out slot containing brief details for all of the English regions, and Local Radio details reduced once more to a single page.

We are sorry that we have had to combine some regional broadcasting details on our programme pages this week. This is due to technical problems related to new equipment at our printers.

This official explanation (which didn't really explain anything) continued to appear for several months and it was the 15th of May before regional editions resumed.

Local Radio Page   Issue 3044   13 March 1982

With their resumption there was a substantial reduction in the number of editions being printed. Individual editions for each BBC Local Radio station were eliminated, and instead the programmes of all local stations in each editorial area were printed together in a new double-page local radio spread at the back of the paper.

For example, where before there had been a LONDON (BBC Radio London), LONDON (BBC Radio Medway) and LONDON (BBC Radio Oxford) edition, there was now just a single LONDON edition, which contained the programmes for all three stations.

In a few areas where there were an unmanageable number of stations, more than one edition would still be produced but with the programmes of several stations in each one. These would result in editions bearing names like NORTH 1, NORTH 2, etc.

This had the added advantage of providing a pair of local editorial pages in each of what the BBC was wont to call the 'National Regions' and so a new feature - *Seen and Heard* appeared in the Scotland, Wales and Northern Ireland editions, each with features about prominent local programmes.

Plate 8c

Cover by Martin Baker Issue 3061 10 July 1982

*   *   *   *   *

Peter Brookes designed a striking cover for Easter 1982 - he even managed to bring back the humble daffodil.

by Roy Knipe   Issue 3073   2 Oct 1982

by Peter Brookes Issue 3048 10 April 1982

The obligatory "redesign" in the autumn of 1982 went almost unnoticed - larger type for the table of contents on page 3 being probably the only visible improvement.

In October BBC Radio celebrated 60 years of broadcasting, and *Radio Times* was allowed to celebrate with all the stops out starting with an ingenious cover designed by Roy Knipe, which depicted one half of Broadcasting House in London as a giant Bakelite wireless and the other as a modern music centre.

But most surprisingly, after a page three feature on a children's programme, the first colour feature dealt, not with BBC radio, but was instead a (belated) tribute to the Corporation's commercial rivals in the '30s - stations like Radio Normandie and others belonging to the International Broadcasting Company.

After 60 years of studiously ignoring their existence, *Radio Times* now printed glossy colour pictures of IBC's various studios scattered across France in the pre-war period. Reith would undoubtedly have had a fit.

But times were changing, and the whole broadcasting ecology was undergoing massive shifts. The Journal of the BBC had avoided acknowledging the existence of its commercial radio rivals for sound reasons - it didn't want to alert its listeners to the fact that they might prefer to tune away from the BBC's own programmes. Similarly in the early '50s, there had never been any question that *Radio Times* might print the ITV programmes for the same reason.

Radio Times had, for many years, included a brief summary of radio programmes "From the Continent" that might be of interest - most of them concerts of classical music. But that was partly a result of the amalgamation of *World-Radio* with *Radio Times* in 1939, and partly because Gorham had been so bored with the dull fare offered by the BBC in the first weeks of the war that he had actively encouraged the promotion of alternatives.

It was not until 1982, however, that *Radio Times* listed television programmes other than the BBC's.

3 no. 1
October 1982

Since the beginning of the 70s there had been sustained pressure on the government to force broadcasters to make their schedules available to independent publishers so that they could produce their own listings magazines.

As far back as 1972, the *New Statesman* had called for a joint BBC/ITV programme guide with an independent editor. Both organisations had looked at the possibility - dummies had even been produced - but in 1974 they had ruled out the idea.

Now there were signs that things were changing. In October BBC Publications joined forces with major magazine publisher IPC to produce *3 The Radio Three Magazine* which included some listings of major programmes for the month ahead as well as a variety of features on Radio 3 and its programmes.

Radio 1

Martin Honeysett

In the air, on the ground and on the road: Radio 1's weekend in Newcastle: 8.0

by Martin Honeysett
Issue 3056
5 June 1982

3 THE RADIO THREE MAGAZINE 85p

BAYREUTH CENTENARY RING

SIX BRITISH ARTISTS

SAMUEL BECKETT PREMIERE

NEW RAPHAEL CARTOONS

PRITCHARD TAKES OVER

OCTOBER ON RADIO THREE

It was the first time that a major BBC programme service had been given its own magazine but the poor circulation did not justify the venture and it was quickly abandoned.

But at the same time the BBC was faced with the anomaly that all of its Welsh-language programmes were to be moved to the new Welsh Fourth Channel - Sianel Pedwar Cymru - which was a commercial channel outwith the BBC's immediate control.

The bold decision was taken to include details of all Welsh-language programming on S4C in *Radio Times* even though the programmes would also be printed in a new journal *SBEC* which was issued free inside Welsh copies of *TV Times*.

The Wales edition of 30th October was an historic one. For a start it bore its own distinctive colour cover - a pinup of Welsh megastar Tom Jones - and it had four more pages than other editions. This led to a magnificently eccentric page numbering with pages 18a, 18b, 19a, 19b, 78a, 78b, 79a and 79b! The S4C programmes appeared immediately after Friday's radio billings and included both the BBC's and HTV's Welsh language programmes, although the latter had no acknowledgement as to their origin whereas the former were all credited as BBC Cymru.

As a reciprocal, *SBEC* later printed the daily programmes of the BBC's Welsh- language radio service Radio Cymru.

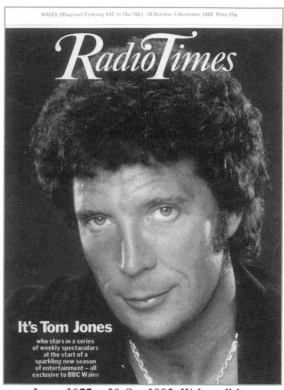

Issue 3077   30 Oct 1982 Wales edition

Page 79a of above issue

S4C did not just broadcast programmes in the Welsh language of course. Its remit was to provide Welsh language programmes in peaktime. But outside peak hours it broadcast English language programming, most of which was rescheduled material from Channel Four.

Radio Times appeared to draw the line at inviting its readers to tune in to commercial alternatives in the Anglo-Saxon tongue, so whenever these appeared in the schedule, they were simply billed as....

Rhaglenni Saesneg

- in other words, 'Programmes in English'!

Radio Times may have been shy about presenting its competitors' programmes - but at the same time it was facing direct competition on the news-stands for the first time. Previous attempts to compete in the listings market had failed as a result of the BBC's carefully controlled copyright in its programme schedules. Thus magazines like *TV Mirror* in the '50s had been reduced to printing 'selected highlights' (usually just one or two programmes from each day) and gossip about the BBC programmes.

Issue 1
TV Choice
5 Nov 1982

Then along came *TV Choice*. Launched in November '82, it claimed to be the first magazine to provide the whole week's listings for all four channels.

In reality it circumvented the copyright problem by using guesswork to predict the programmes that each of the channels would show - with the exception of Channel Four who had made their first week's listings available free to anyone who wanted them on the simple principle that as a newcomer they needed all the publicity they could get.

TV Choice was not the first attempt at such a ruse - *Time-vue* also tried to break into the market in 1974 but was scared off by lawyers representing the BBC and *TV Times* publishers ITP.

TV Choice added a very strange rider to its listings:

**Whilst every care is taken
in compiling programme details
any inaccuracies are the responsibility of TV Choice Ltd.**

There certainly were inaccuracies. There were also blank spaces in the listings grids where guesswork couldn't come up with the titles of the movies that were to be shown. In future issues they added the line ...

Approximate time. Check press.

... which made their programme guide about as useful as a chocolate teapot.

And in spite of the bravado it exhibited on its first leader page ("this publication must be an independent publication, free to praise the best and slate the worst...") it wasn't quite brave enough in the first issue to publish the name of its editor, publisher or printer, although it did so the next week. It clearly expected a battle - and it got one.

Independent Television Publications Ltd - owners of *TV Times* - took *TV Choice* to court, as did BBC Publications. *TV Choice* printed a vigorous defence of its position in its leader on 1st January 1983, along with revamped and more detailed programme billings. And with this bizarre disclaimer:

> The details of forthcoming BBC television programme titles and timings which appear in TV Choice have been prepared by the magazine's publishers, TV Choice Ltd. TV Choice wish to make it clear that the BBC has not approved such details, and the publishers accept full responsibility for any and all inaccuracies in the details of BBC programme titles and times appearing in the magazine.

TV Choice then vanished without trace. Evidently the legal action had put paid to the plans of the publishing executives the magazine named as Chris Barnard and Norman Thomas. (In 1999 German publisher H. Bauer revived the title, using it for a low-price listings magazine from its own stable.)

But by now, London listings magazine *Time Out* had taken up the battle by publishing brief TV listings in October. Anthony Elliott - *Time Out* proprietor was unmoved by legal threats:

> We have every intention of carrying on as we are, barring being put out of business by a legal suit. What we did this week was not a bit of fun. It was carefully thought out and stimulated by the arrival of Channel Four.

But *Time Out* lost its case - the judge ruled that it had published more programme details than it should under an earlier agreement - and it was ordered to pay court costs.

Time Out did not give up the battle, as we shall see later.

Play Away Joke

Q: *What do punks learn at school?*

A: *Punktuation!*

Another anniversary was celebrated in 1982 - fifty years of the BBC's External Services. This naturally received optimum coverage in *London Calling* but surprisingly it also merited a *Radio Times* cover - tied to a BBC1 documentary in celebration.

Frances Donnelly's *Radio Times* colour feature on the BBC World Service included illustrations showing covers of the current *London Calling* as well as an early *World Radio* Empire Programme Supplement and a stereotypical photograph of a group of Africans sitting around a radio set outside a straw hut.

Christmas 1982 was one of those years when the planners were faced with the dilemma which came around roughly every seven years: Christmas Eve was on a Friday. Should the Double Issue start with the Saturday before Christmas and therefore miss New Year's Eve? Or should it begin with December 25th and miss Christmas Eve?

by Space Frontiers   Issue 3082   4 Dec 1982

This time Gearing decided to have his cake and eat it, and went for a Double Issue with fifteen days of programmes, starting with Friday December 24th and ending on Friday January 7th. The resulting 120 pages made it one of the biggest issues to date. Peter Brookes and Roger Woddis (aka 'Agatha' Woddis) joined forces once more for the annual illustrated spoof story and there was a Christmas Back Page quiz as well as the *Willo the Wisp* cartoon strip by Nicholas Spargo which had replaced Peter Lord's *Morph* strip in October.

WILLO THE WISP by Nicholas Spargo

Issue 3088   15 Jan 1983

Another broadcasting revolution was dealt with in January 1983 when the BBC began its regular national breakfast time service on BBC1, following earlier experiments in Scotland in December 1980. *Breakfast Time* naturally earned its place on the cover.

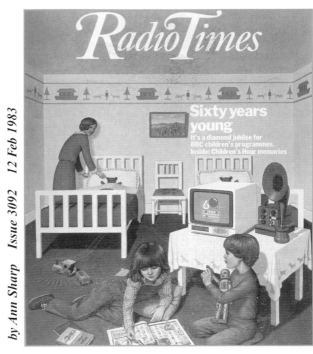

by Ann Sharp   Issue 3092   12 Feb 1983

And as anniversaries continued to pile up, the BBC celebrated sixty years of children's programmes in February with Ann Sharp's rather bizarre cover illustrating two children whose bedroom appeared to be suffering what Star Trek's Captain James T. Kirk would no doubt recognise as breaches of the time-space continuum.

*Issue 3098
26 March
1983
North East
edition*

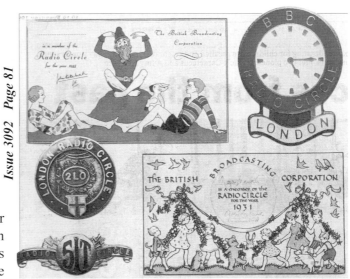

Issue 3092   Page 81

The Holy Week issue (its cover depicted the crucifixion in a detail from Norwich Cathedral) had just got into its print run (with the first editions to be printed on their way to newsagents at the extremities of the British Isles) when the printers struck again and once more much of country found itself without copies of their favourite magazine.

*Unpublished
cover by
Penelope Wilton
Issue 3099
2 April 1983*
Plate 8d

The printing dispute of 1956 had not prevented publication of an Easter Issue, but in 1983 that special edition fell victim to a strike of members of the union Sogat 82, and the cover illustrating Penelope Wilton as author Beatrix Potter surrounded by some of her creations was never published.

Neither was the issue for the following week.

Radio Times resumed on 16th April with a single National edition all copies of which were printed at East Kilbride. It contained the tediously inevitable reference to 'diminished form', cramped radio pages and squashed up regional TV opt-out billings. Local Radio got two pages at the expense of any editorial for Scotland, Wales or Northern Ireland, and this time even the S4C programmes found their way into the National edition.

By now, Waterlows was part of the giant BPCC - presided over by Robert Maxwell - which was in the process of 'tackling' the trade unions in order to modernise procedures in the print industry. *Radio Times* was up to this point still printed in Twyford Abbey Road and East Kilbride, with the colour pages printed at Purnell's in Paulton - also part of BPCC.

The National edition of 16th April was typeset at Park Royal but the giant presses there remained silent.

The following week, a printing revolution took place unannounced, as London copies of what was still a "National edition" were printed in web offset at Petty & Sons in Leeds while issues for the rest of the British Isles were again printed in East Kilbride.

The resulting offset issue - with slightly smaller pages - was a revelation for readers accustomed to grey print on grey paper. Sparkling black on clean white paper, and integrated colour pages printed on the same presses.

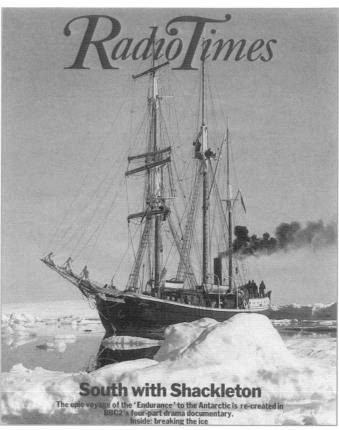

South with Shackleton
The epic voyage of the 'Endurance' to the Antarctic is re-created in BBC2's four-part drama documentary. Inside: breaking the ice

Unpublished
Issue 3100   9 April 1983

NATIONAL EDITION · 23-29 April 1983   Price 25p

THAT MODERN DECADE

People and events in 'Britain in the Thirties' are remembered in BBC2's new series. Inside: mutiny, movies and moving out

by Ian Beck
Issue 3102   23 April 1983   London offset edition

The dispute plodded on with London copies continuing to be printed at Petty's in Leeds and the rest in East Kilbride, and all copies containing the same pages with no regional editions.

But as the FA Cup Final and Scottish Cup Final loomed, it was essential that at least Scotland should have its own edition that week. So on 21st May, two editions appeared - a "National edition" in its familiar form, printed this time in both Twyford Abbey Road and East Kilbride, and a Scotland edition.

This singular curiosity bore a different cover, and a different lead article about the Scottish Cup Final. The television programme pages for Saturday had been regionalised, but that was all - the rest of the Scotland edition contained the same pages as the National edition complete with billings for Radios Wales, Ulster and S4C. This compromise issue understandably confused Scottish readers (including the author)!

Another compromise was required for the General Election, and so the 4th June issue appeared in similar form with editorial matter relating to the political situation in Scotland, but with the 'national' programme pages.

The problems at Park Royal did not go away, and *Radio Times* carried on as one single edition through the summer. The launch of a new BBC local station - Radio York - in July was dealt with by producing a feature highlighting BBC local stations across Britain (thus justifying Brian Grimwood's inventive cover based on a radio circuit diagram) which allowed Radio York its first (and only) country-wide cover appearance.

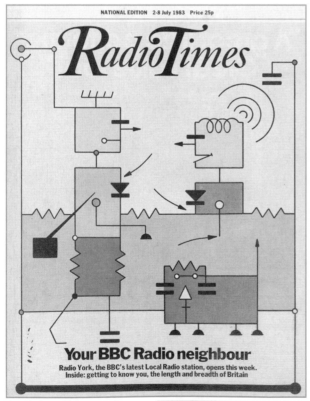

by Brian Grimwood
Issue 3112
2 July 1983

by Gray Jolliffe

The confusion between love and sex examined by Laurie Taylor in 'This Thing Called Love' (Radio 4)

Issue 3112

BRAINBOX
by Clive Doig
page 70

Play Away Joke

Q: *How many skunks does it take to make a big stink?*

A: *Only a phew!*

Dog Show
Three gentlemen from different places took their dogs to the dog show. ALBERT, BERNARD and COLIN did not live in places that started with the same letters as their names, nor own dogs whose names did. The man from ALGERIA's dog was not a BEAGLE. The man from COLOMBIA went into the ring first. The CORGI belonged to ALBERT. The man from BELGIUM went into the ring before the ALSATIAN.
In what order did the dogs enter the ring?

As a concession, Radio York was given half a page all to itself for its first week's programmes.

It was the 16th of July before *Radio Times* resumed its complement of a dozen regional editions - after fifteen weeks of disruption, the longest period of printing difficulties in its history.

The London edition continued to be printed web offset in Leeds, and it was clear that the old-fashioned polymer process was doomed.

*   *   *   *   *

Circulation at this point - despite the travails of printing problems - was still good, with an average of 3,400,000 copies sold each week. A breakdown of the population served by the twelve regional editions at this point makes interesting reading, as it shows the differences in potential profitability of the individual editions as they were - at that time - arranged.

With a potential readership of 43.4 million, the percentage of this 'universe' that each edition had the possibility of reaching is shown in this table. ➤

LONDON	*26.5%*
MIDLANDS	*14.4%*
NORTH WEST	*12.7%*
NORTH	*9.6%*
SCOTLAND	*9.3%*
SOUTH	*5.6%*
NORTH EAST*	*5.6%*
WEST	*5.3%*
EAST	*5.0%*
SOUTH WEST	*3.0%*
WALES	*2.9%*
N. IRELAND**	*n/a*

*It served the BBC's purposes for Cumbria and the Isle of Man to defy geography, and be included as part of north-east England!!

**No regional circulation figures were issued for the NI Edition.

(Source: National Readership Survey, July '82 - June '83)

The low percentage of potential readers in the Principality was undoubtedly the starting point for the eventual absorption of the Wales edition into that covering the West of England, which had always included a summary of the programmes of the English-language Radio Wales. As there were only two local radio stations in the area it nicely filled up the space on the local radio pages.

A variety of statistics were produced at the time to entice potential advertisers. 4.5 million of *RT* readers were in the upper social classes - known as ABC1s in the marketing business - making it the leading means of reaching the managerial and prosperous classes. *RT* also boasted that more businessmen (a quarter of a million) read it than any other magazine.

*   *   *   *   *

Soon after the printing dispute went off the boil the price was again increased. From 13th August *Radio Times* cost 28 pence.

The magazine celebrated its Diamond Jubilee early (in September) to avoid clashing with television's new season.

In the issue of 10th September, a neat 12-page supplement appeared with its own cover showing 16 classic *RT* covers over the years. Inside: a full size reproduction of the front page of issue number one; a brief history written by Brian Gearing; a neat chronology of the paper's life and times with short recollections of broadcasting history by some of its pioneers.

At the same time the BBC, in partnership with European Illustration, published a large hardback book *The Art of Radio Times* which celebrated sixty years of fine illustrations including interviews with, and biographies of some of the artists themselves.

Supplement   Issue 3122   10 Sept 1983

With an eye to increased sales just before Christmas, the 19th November issue incorporated all five incarnations of Doctor Who in a front page designed by Andrew Skilleter. Inside, readers were treated to a profusely illustrated "Who Who's Who"!

by Andrew Skilleter Issue 3132 19 Nov 1983

by John Jefford Issue 3133 26 Nov 1983

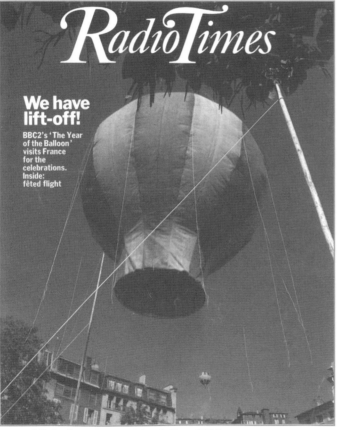

Unpublished   Issue 3134   3 Dec 1983

The following week's issue (picturing Alan Bates) appeared as normal - but its historic significance would soon be understood as the printers at Twyford Abbey Road walked out on strike just three weeks before Christmas.

Consequently, the issue of 3rd December failed to appear.

The words 'diminished form' do not adequately describe the issue of 10th December, which appeared as a single National edition.

Brian Gearing explained the problem:

For the second time this year unofficial action by print union Sogat 82 is disrupting *Radio Times*. In recent weeks copies have not been available in some areas and last week's issue was not printed. This week's *Radio Times* is produced as one national edition. Unfortunately, it is not possible to show details of Radio Scotland, Radio Wales/Cymru and Radio Ulster, but we do include a summary of BBC Local Radio. We hope to be back to normal as soon as possible.

At the races with Julia Booth and a special steeplechase: Wed 12.3 pm

by Sally Lecky-Thompson
Issue 3133
26 Nov 1983

32

SUNDAY Radio

Radio 1

1053kHz/285m
1089kHz/275m

News on the half hour until 11.30 am, then 2.30, 3.30, 5.0, 7.30, 10.0 and at 12 midnight

6.0 am
Mark Page
eases you gently into Sunday
Sunday

8.0 Tony Blackburn's Sunday Show
Keith Chegwin is let loose with Tony Blackburn for two hours of music and fun. Your requests, dedications and a few surprises. Producer TED BESTON

10.0 Adrian Juste
Producer PHIL WARD-LARGE

12.0
Jimmy Savile's 'Old Record' Club
featuring
The Double Top Ten Show
This week 1970 and 1982
Producer DON GEORGE

2.0 pm
Steve Wright
Producer MALCOLM BROWN

4.30 The Great Rock 'n' Roll Trivia Quiz
Quizmaster David Jensen introduces two celebrity teams.

Andy Partridge of XTC, Julian Cope of Tears For Fears and Colin Irwin pit their wits against Tom Robinson, Gary Davies and David Knopfler
Producer JOHN LEONARD
BBC Manchester

5.0 Stereo
Top 40
with Tommy Vance
Producer DON GEORGE

7.0 Stereo
Anne Nightingale
with your rock requests
Producer PETE RITZEMA

9.0 Stereo
Alexis Korner
Producer JEFF GRIFFIN

10.0-12.0 Stereo
Sounds of Jazz
Peter Clayton
with The Ian Henry Trio and The Pete Beachill/Rick Taylor Quintet
Producer LAWRIE MONK

R1/2VHF:
88-91

5.0 am-5.0 pm
with Radio 2

5.0-12.0
with Radio 1

12.0-5.0 am
with Radio 2

Radio 2

693kHz/433m
909kHz/330m

News: 6.30 am and on the hour (except 8.0 pm)

5.0 am Stereo
Tony Brandon
The Sunday Early Show
Producer DAVID WELSBY
BBC Birmingham

7.30 Stereo
Paul McDowell
says Good Morning Sunday including at 7.45
Bishop Bill Westwood
Research ALISON BURNETT
Producer CHRIS REES

9.0 Stereo
David Jacobs
with Melodies for You
BBC CONCERT ORCHESTRA
REGINALD LEOPOLD ORCHESTRA
with Marie Hayward Segal
Producer ROBERT BOWMAN

11.0 Stereo
Desmond Carrington
Radio 2 All-Time Greats
Producer SANDRA BLACK
12.2 Sports Desk

12.30 pm Stereo
Ed Stewart with Two's Best
Written by JOHN THOMPSON
Producer BARBARA PAGE
(Repeated: Mon 1.0 am)

1.30 Stereo
It Sticks Out Half a Mile
(Details: Friday 10.0 pm)

2.0 Stereo
Benny Green
Producer KEITH STEWART

3.0 Stereo
Alan Dell
with Sounds Easy
Producer KEN EVANS

4.0 Stereo
Sing Something Simple
THE CLIFF ADAMS SINGERS and THE JACK EMBLOW QUARTET
Producer TIM McDONALD
(Repeat)

4.30 Stereo
String Sound
Presented by Jean Challis
Producer CHRISTOPHER VEZEY
(Repeated: Tues 1.30 am)

5.0 The Fosdyke Saga
in 13 programmes
11: 'Ditchley's found the Schmidt contracts, and he's blackmailing me. We're done for.'
starring Stephanie Turner as Rebecca
Philip Lowrie as Jos
Miriam Margolyes as Victoria
David Threlfall as Tom
Enn Reitel as Albert
Christian Rodska as Roger Ditchley
Larry Lamb as Von Richtofen
Other parts played by TREVOR COOPER,
DAVID ENGLISH, NICK MALONEY and NICK REVELL

Page 32   Issue 3135   10 Dec 1983

Once more, the entire run was printed at East Kilbride, since the situation at Twyford Abbey Road had reached crisis point in the battle between Maxwell's management and Sogat. With Park Royal out of action, the *Radio Times* was hastily typeset "by a member of BPCC group" (the credits were intentionally vague). As a result much of the paper - especially the programme pages - appeared in unfamiliar fonts. As Maxwell - in a fit of rage at the print workers - demolished the presses at Twyford Abbey Road *RT* staff had rushed aboard a plane and set off for a 'secret' BPCC location to set issue 3135. Some illustrations were mislaid en route leaving odd spaces in the paper. *Radio Times* was left as a homeless child, reliant for its print facilities on BPCC under the quixotic and unstable Maxwell. What fate would befall the 120-page Christmas Double Issue (on a year when it had been decided to start on the week before Christmas leaving New Year programmes to an issue of their own)?

In England it made it to the bookstalls - just - with a more consistent (if still slightly eccentric) set of fonts but predictably in a single edition with just four pages in which to detail all the Christmas programmes on the BBC's 31 local stations. London readers received their usual web offset copies - the Christmas issue particularly benefiting from this enhanced printing process. The Scotland, Wales and Northern Ireland editions appeared as normal. The four pages devoted to local radio in England provided Wales with the space for S4C's Christmas fare, and for Scotland and Northern Ireland four pages for their *Seen and Heard* features.

The printing credits for all copies of this issue were given simply a "Typeset and printed by members of BPCC Group". But the following week all except the Petty & Sons copies were again credited as having been printed in East Kilbride where the presses were being pushed to their limits.

Thus 1984 - a year with rather negative associations thanks to George Orwell - began badly for *Radio Times*. The Winter Olympics in February allowed Torvill and Dean to appear on the cover, as they Boleroed on ice for gold in Sarajevo, but in England as far as programme pages (but not advertising) went there was still a single edition with all that entailed. Worse still, even some of the London copies were being printed using the old polymer process at East Kilbride.

In January Robert Ottaway ceased to be responsible for the chatty Radio and Television pages. These passed first to David Gillard (who managed to sneak the Radio 1 crossword in at the end of the month) - then *Radio Times'* US correspondent Henry Fenwick (on a sojourn to London) in February with Madeline Kingsley taking over in March before Gillard returned at Easter.

Regional TV details resumed, and a hopeful note was struck in March when the (by now) weekly announcement of troubled times on page 3 told readers that..

> The industrial action by SOGAT 82 is now over and we will carry fully regionalised programme details as soon as possible.

Local Radio - the Cinderella of *Radio Times* - got its two pages back soon afterwards.

The Holy Week issue had Tom Fleming on the cover exploring Jerusalem. But the cover of the Easter Holiday issue bore nothing seasonal, instead featuring stills from the British film *Chariots of Fire* which was being shown on BBC1 on Easter Day.

As usual the Cup Final meant different covers for Scotland and the rest of the UK. In 1984 Mark Thomas came up with a design that required little alteration: in the Scottish version the prominent football in the foreground bore the coat of arms of the SFA, and Wembley's twin towers were gently airbrushed out!

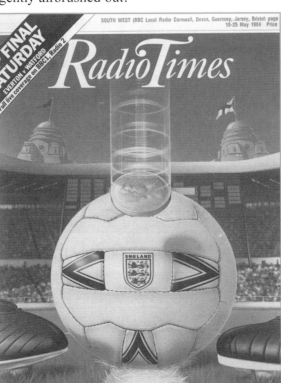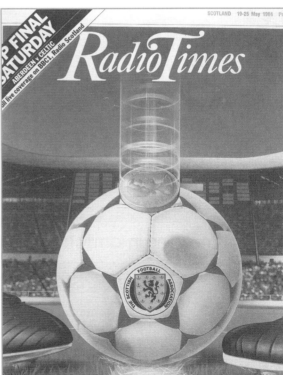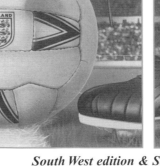

by Mark Thomas   ***South West edition & Scotland edition***   ***Issue 3158   19 May 1984***

With the issue of 16th June, printing arrangements were clarified for the reader. Typesetting was being undertaken by A. Wheaton & Co Ltd in Exeter, and as well as being printed by Petty & Sons in Leeds and Waterlows in East Kilbride, Chromoworks Ltd in Nottingham were now producing some copies while Purnells in Paulton continued to produce colour pages for those issues printed from polymer plates.

Also that week, the Radio and Television highlights pages continued their unexplained turnover of editors, with Programme Editor Hugo Martin doubling up as editor of the double page feature.

The following week, Brian Gearing wrote about a number of impending changes:

> Radio Times is, proudly, 61 years old - but, in production terms, we will soon be among the most modern magazines in the world. We are changing our printing method to web offset; some copies are already printed by this process - readers receiving them will have noticed whiter paper and sharper, clearer type and illustrations.
>
> All copies of *Radio Times* will be printed like this from the issue covering programmes for 1-7 September. That issue will see *Radio Times* take advantage of the design opportunities and flexibility that web offset allows and there will be other changes that will enhance our editorial service to readers.
>
> Not all the improvements must wait until then. This week sees an important advance on our Radio programme pages. We have redesigned these pages to improve their legibility. We hope that readers will agree that the new Radio programme pages are more attractive to look at, easier to read and to follow.

This is the rate card of the mainly black and white publication, with limited colour pages, which stays in people's homes nine days, arrives every Thursday, has twelve regional editions, and is Britain's largest-selling magazine.

Radio Times
advertising rate card
January 1984

Where hitherto Radio 1 occupied a single column; Radio 2 two columns; Radio 3 three columns; and Radio 4 either six or three depending on whether or not it shared the page with a National Region; the radio pages were now made up of five columns. Each station now occupied part columns, and its heading was a clear and large number (or letter in the cases of S for Radio Scotland and so forth).

One result of this changed arrangement was that both Radio pages had to be completely reset to create space where it was necessary for Radios Scotland, Wales, Cymru and Ulster - and so while the English editions carried quite a lot of illustrations on the radio pages the National Regions with their different layout did not.

As the Olympic Games got underway in Los Angeles, in August, *Radio Times* provided readers with a 24-page Olympics Supplement with profiles of British athletes and charts to fill in results. The 120-page Olympics edition coincided (!) with a price increase to 30p.

The very last, grey-and-sludge polymer issue to be printed was issue 3172, dated 25-31 August 1984. 72 pages, of which 12 were in colour. It was the last such issue to roll off the much-lauded Crabtree presses at East Kilbride.

Goodbye to grey
Issue 3172   25 August 1984

CHAPTER TEN
The Listings War

onning its new clothes *Radio Times* appeared on 1st September, as Brian Gearing had promised, in glorious web offset with more colour pages than before. In the first of the new-look issues, 21 pages were in colour.

The paper was considerably revamped. Page headings (including the TV programme pages) were redesigned to match the new radio page headings that had already been introduced. This resulted in the TV pages losing the clear dividing rules between BBC1, BBC2 and the advertisements. The page 3 feature was now in colour, as was John Craven's *Children's Section*. David Gillard's *Highlights* section was now exclusively devoted to radio, and renamed *Hear This!* Geoff Brown's films page was revamped and for the first time all editorial pages had the ability to 'bleed' - that is occupy the entire space of the page without being obliged by the technical process to stick to a frame within the page surrounded by a white margin. This was used to effect with some of the new page headings.

A new cartoon strip featuring the children's character *SuperTed* was introduced (although not in the relaunch issue), and at the back, alongside Delia's cookery and Roger's poetry was....**a crossword!!!!**

Brian Gearing's new-look *Radio Times* washed away much of the Cannon image, and restored a balanced magazine that could have broad appeal across the family.

It continued to be typeset in Exeter by Wheaton & Co, and the now large group of seven printers producing it were Petty & Sons in Leeds, Chromoworks in Nottingham, Carlisle Web Offset, and Nickeloid Litho in London - all part of BPCC - plus independent printers McCorquodale Varnicoat Ltd in Pershore, East Midland Allied Printers in Peterborough (albeit briefly) and Alabaster Passmore & Sons in Maidstone.

The changes did not all meet with enthusiasm. A few weeks later, the *Letters* pages - headed "Editor under fire" - caught the mood of those for whom the changes were unwanted.

"...I wondered what on earth was happening to my eyes; they could not focus properly - the printing and layout were so confusing."

"...the paper itself has no body and rolls up into permanent waves when put through the letter box or in the magazine rack..."

"The new Radio Times is an impregnable mess....."

"....for sheer messiness, confusion and what I can only describe as a vulgar attempt to look like TV Times the new television pages would take a lot of beating..."

"I cannot describe my horror at this week's issue...."

"Your layout people seem to have been given the go ahead for an almighty ego trip."

"It looks cheap and nasty; how will I ever find out what programmes are on?"

There were a few readers who applauded the improved print quality, and at least one who was delighted at the return of the crossword.

The beleaguered Gearing answered his critics:

> Not so long ago readers were writing to me to say that they didn't like the way the ink used in Radio Times came off on their fingers and the reproduction was so bad that they couldn't see what was supposed to be in the illustrations. We've tried to change all that by moving to the modern print process known as web offset. This method offers all sorts of flexible facilities that Radio Times didn't have before. It could be that we embraced them with an excess of enthusiasm!
>
> Our readers have shown tremendous loyalty to Radio Times during our difficulties of recent years, and I willingly acknowledge the need to take seriously the comments they now make over our new look. We have changed our format with an eye to the future. Television goes on expanding and the new print process - which offers clearer reproduction on whiter paper - presented the opportunity to make more efficient use of the available space.
>
> Any new design takes time to settle down, and adjustments are always made. Having listened to your comments, we have made some adjustments this week. I hope readers find them effective.

At this point the correspondence was, as they say, 'closed'.

*   *   *   *   *

It was still possible to produce regional covers. Within a few weeks of the relaunch, BBC Northern Ireland celebrated its Diamond Jubilee with a special issue - while the rest of the UK had a machine-gun totin' Michael Caine on the front, the Northern Ireland edition had a simple piece of blue silk with an invitation to viewers to join BBC1's gala programme in celebration of 60 years of broadcasting in the province.

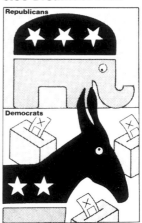

BBC 1

6.0 Ceefax AM

6.30 Breakfast Time

BBC Northern Ireland celebrates its Diamond Jubilee

*Issue 3180
20 Oct 1984
Northern
Ireland
edition*

Inserted into all the editions of that issue was a glossy 16-page colour supplement heralding the launch of the Vauxhall Astra car. It was the first in a long line of bound-in advertising supplements. (The inserts that obey the laws of gravity and fall out as you pick up the paper were still a few years away.)

Comedy on a grand scale leaps from some unexpected sources
Radio 4, 3.0 pm Humour in Music

by Jean Christian Knaff   Issue 3180

*   *   *   *   *

The Queen Mother made another appearance on the cover in November 1984 (she was attending a Royal Variety performance) fronting what was described in a cover flash as the 'Royal Baby Souvenir Issue'. This 120-page special contained no less than nineteen pages of pictures and features by Madeline Kingsley celebrating the birth of Prince Henry.

As midnight approaches join a galaxy of stars in the Gleneagles Hotel for their Hogmanay celebrations.
BBC1, 11.40 Live into 85

The Christmas Double issue for 1984 was a gigantic 160 pages, with a cute winking wreath cover designed by Roy Knipe. The unwieldy size of issue was not matched by an increase in the weight of the paper's cover - which was likely to tear away sharply from the staples before many readers had even got it home.

Much of the issue was in colour, and now traditional features (like the 'Agatha Woddis' story with Peter Brookes' illustration) were to be found inside. And for the very first time colour pictures appeared on the programme pages: the Queen, and Julie Andrews as *Mary Poppins* on the BBC1 Christmas Day page; Joan Hickson as *Miss Marple* on the Boxing Day BBC1 page.

by Terry Kennett

by Roy Knipe
Issue 3189
22 Dec 1984

The BBC still used its journal as a mouthpiece when it suited. In the issue of 19th January 1985 the Corporation's chairman Stuart Young argued for an increase in the licence fee in a carefully worded exchange with "interviewer" Chris Dunkley, television critic of the *Financial Times*. This assault on readers continued the following week when Dunkley interviewed Bill Cotton (Managing Director - BBC TV) and Richard Francis (Managing Director - BBC Radio) under the unbiased heading "The BBC - the best bargain in Britain." And the following week Director-General, Alasdair Milne, completed the series.

With hindsight, the funniest juxtaposition of this piece of corporate propaganda (even its layout and typesetting made it look like an advertisement) was that the following pair of pages were devoted to advertising the Sinclair C5, probably the greatest turkey in the history of powered transport!

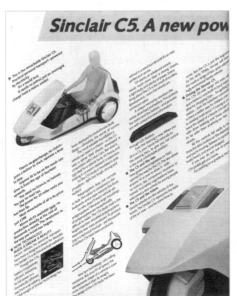

Sinclair C5 advertisement   Issue 3193

Inevitably, these articles provoked replies from readers, most of whom were far from convinced by the arguments for an increase in the licence fee. But the BBC used the dozen or so letters (which occupied just over a page) as the hook upon which to hang a lengthy reply from the Controller of Information Services, Michael Bunce. He was allowed almost half a page to respond, in contrast to the usual three or four lines when *RT* thought a managerial response appropriate.

The cover for the issue of 16th February illustrated BBC1's new twice-weekly serial, *EastEnders,* and inside introduced viewers to a new-look BBC1 globe, and Terry Wogan's three nights-a-week show, as well as providing a helpful plan of Albert Square and profiles of its inhabitants. This was all part of a new image introduced by the new BBC1 controller, Michael Grade.

Issue 3196   16 Feb 1985

by Ian Dicks   Issue 3196

Those readers who longed for a reprise of the Golden Age of *RT* in the '50s (perhaps spurred by the lack of an Easter cover) must have been heartened by Don Smith's cover which rolled back the years to publicise an *Omnibus* documentary about Tony Hancock.

For the first time the *Radio Times* masthead was obscured by a segment of the original '50s masthead, and most of the cover was 'borrowed' from that of 28th February 1960.

The anniversary of VE day was commemorated in May with a special issue (Churchill was on the cover) including a 20-page supplement recalling the war years in pictures, including four pages of classic wartime *Radio Times* covers, illustrations and even advertisements. It was one of the few occasions when *Radio Times* acknowledged its past achievements.

by Don Smith   Issue 3205   20 April 1985

173

In July *Live Aid* - a unique global pop concert to raise cash for famine relief in Africa that had been masterminded by Bob Geldof - featured on the cover and inside. The concert occupied ten hours on BBC2 and switched over for a further six hours on BBC1.

Once again *Radio Times* cashed in on the public affection for the Queen Mother with a birthday special - celebrating her 85th - and offering more tributes to the former Lady Elizabeth Bowes-Lyon. Gearing's *Radio Times* - unlike Cannon's - led the British public in celebrating major events, especially Royal ones.

*   *   *   *   *

In September 1985, the Monopolies and Mergers Commission published their report "on the policies and practices of the British Broadcasting Corporation and Independent Television Publications Ltd of limiting the publication by others of advance programme information...." In other words: should the listings monopoly be broken?

The six-person group found in favour of the existing BBC/ITP arrangements but added the rider:

> We are unanimous in the view that the present arrangements are not necessarily the best that can be devised, and we considered the extent of the obligation of the BBC and the IBA to the public in connection with the provision of programme information.....In our view both organisations should make it their objective to provide programme information in a way which is responsive to the requirements of the public.

In fact it had been a close call, for three of the six members of the group were less convinced, and it took the casting vote of the chairman to find in the broadcasters' favour. The three dissenters published their own view:

> Our conclusion is that the referred practice of the BBC and ITP operates and may be expected to operate against the public interest.

Powerful publishing forces wanted their bite of the lucrative listings cherry, and *Radio Times* and *TV Times* had won this first round by the skin of their teeth. They could not expect the outcome of the war to be in their favour.

*   *   *   *   *

Christmas 1985 was not celebrated with an illustrated cover, but in *TV Times* style, the stars of *Only Fools and Horses* were pictured in a characteristically vulgar celebration of the Festive Season. 160 pages for 34p (the price had gone up again) and for the first time a full colour decorative border for the Christmas Day, Boxing Day, New Year's Eve/Hogmanay and New Year's Day TV billings and more colour pictures on other billings pages.

A name from the past began to appear in the small print that detailed printing arrangements. Waterlow and Sons (1984) Ltd, East Kilbride were again printing the magazine in Scotland.

*   *   *   *   *

The paper had slipped into a new pattern of publication. From time to time, a special issue - often with a large supplement - would be used as much to boost circulation as to complement the Corporation's programmes. *EastEnders* celebrated its first birthday with a 12-page supplement including a pin-up of actress Anita Dobson and a competition to win a colour TV, video recorder <u>and</u> (sic) a trip to Albert Square.

The Queen's 60th Birthday warranted a "Special 16 page Pull-Out Colour Souvenir" which managed to squeeze in the Coronation front cover once more. The Mexico World Cup occupied 33 pages of the 112-page World Cup Issue ("win a Florida holiday that's truly out of this world...")

*　*　*　*　*

The battle to break the BBC/ITV listings monopoly was still simmering, but in May 1986, there was another sign that the status quo was not to be an option.

As the fledgling cable television companies began to dig up the pavements of Britain, more new television channels were appearing on the horizon. Would the viewer need to subscribe to a different magazine for each one? Early experiments with multichannel TV over existing TV relay systems had been supported by a variety of under-funded, over-glossy programme sheets.

But - in a clear case of history repeating itself - just as the first ITV contractor, Associated-Rediffusion, had itself found it necessary to take on the task of publishing *TV Times*, so one of the first cable licensees, Croydon Cable, took on the task of producing a full-scale listings magazine for its fledgling industry.

Cable Guide first saw the light of day as a confidential dummy issue produced for the cable industry's approval, in June 1986. It proposed a glossy, perfect-bound guide with regional editions for each operator.

When it was launched in September the first issue contained an impressive six-page movie guide, and listings for thirteen cable TV channels. But there was a glaring omission as publisher Robert Stiby observed:

Cable Guide *dummy issue   June 1986*

> While Cable Guide is devoted to full daily listings of all the major cable and satellite channels currently available on cable TV, the only channels not listed are BBC and ITV. This is not because we choose to ignore them but quite simply because we are not allowed to carry them. And yet the only TV channels cable operators have to carry by law are - you've guessed it - BBC and ITV."

Thus in multichannel homes, the only way of getting TV programme information in advance was to purchase three different publications. Another nail in the monopoly's coffin.

*　*　*　*　*

Radio Active

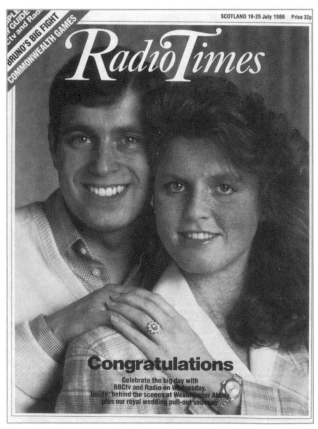

Issue 3269   19 July 1986

Curiously - in the light of its mass circulation and very high profile - *Radio Times* had rarely been the butt of any serious spoofs. A 30s student magazine had produced a passable parody, but there had been few other attempts to 'send up' the journal.

The notable exception in 1986 was Radio 4's comedy programme *Radio Active* whose Sphere Books paperback was a complete imitation of *Radio Times* right down to its crossword and 'kiddies' pages. Features, advertisements and programme pages were all faithfully copied from *RT* in font, size, style and layout.

Written by Angus Deayton and Geoffrey Perkins, *Radio Active* was a rare example of the sincere flattery of imitation.

*   *   *   *   *

Amongst the supplements and competitions, the core of *Radio Times* - its programme billings - was suffering from clutter. BBC1 and BBC2 would fight for odd-shaped spaces on the same page; both would battle it out against the paid-for and the BBC's own advertisements. Feature articles - like Henry Fenwick's *America* column - would find themselves occupying programme pages without the discretion of a few well-chosen rules which had separated the Light Programme from editorial in days past.

And programme-related photographs would lurch out across the margins, bleeding towards the edges of the page. There was a *Today at a glance* box, an idea which *TV Times* had tried - and abandoned - several years before.

In short, the programme pages were a bit of a mess.

But there were always more Royal features.

There was nothing like a Royal Wedding to warm the hearts of broadcasters and editors alike. Madeline Kingsley was sent to check out the principal players in the latest Royal nuptials - Prince Andrew and Sarah Ferguson, who naturally graced the cover. Four pages in the body of the paper *and* an eight-page pull-out supplement written by Nicki Household.

(Well, actually two of those pages were for a jolly tasteful advertisement for BMW......)

By now, readers' homes must have been awash with souvenirs. In November there was a celebration of 50 years of BBC Television (of course it wasn't really 50 years because TV had shut down for the war, but we've been through all this before, haven't we?....)

by Tony McSweeney
Souvenir Issue 3284   1 Nov 1986

Tony McSweeney's cover illustration depicted a 1930s family - living in the shadow of Alexandra Palace - somehow watching the 9 o'Clock news on a modern colour set.

The first part of the celebration inside (which had an assortment of covers passim scattered throughout) was marred by sloppy research - the cover of the October 1936 Television Number was captioned as "the first 'Radio Times' TV issue" when in fact it carried no TV programmes. The wartime closedown was alluded to as having been 'during a *Mickey Mouse* transmission'. It wasn't. The film ended, television closed down and a test pattern was shown for an hour before the switch-off came. This was all the more unfortunate since the text was credited to Nicholas Moss -

...author of the commemorative book 'BBCtv Presents - a 50th anniversary celebration' now available at bookshops.

It was a shame that the special issue got off to a weak start, because the rest incorporated some of the best features on television that the paper had printed for several years, from an impressive cast of contributors. The feature on television comedy was from the pen of comedy scriptwriter Barry Took, and therefore contained none of the errors of the Moss contribution.

Likewise Monica Sims' feature on children's television was as informative as you'd expect from the former Head of that very department; similarly one time Head of sport, Peter Dimmock, contributed a first class potted history of televised sport. Shaun Sutton - Head of Drama for twelve years - wrote an enlightened and well-illustrated piece on television plays as far back as 1930; and the BBC's Controller of Music, John Drummond dealt with music and arts programmes.

Desmond Hawkins - founder of the BBC Natural History Unit in Bristol in 1957 - took us from George Cansdale to *Life on Earth* and there was a prize (of course there was) of a reproduction 1937 television which contained a modern colour TV and video recorded inside.

The Reader Offer sold a specially designed toy *Radio Times* period Model 'A' Ford delivery van although whether such vans had ever really existed is doubtful. They certainly couldn't have had 'Fifty Years of Television' painted on the side!

The recipe later in that issue came from the late Philip Harben, TV chef *extraordinaire* in the 1940s and 50s. *Radio Times* recklessly printed his recipe for fried ice-cream, but also included the observations - *Cooking by radio waves* - which Harben wrote in 1951.➤

Fifty Years of Television was a popular theme in 1986 - it formed the basis for that year's *Royal Variety Performance* in November. Since it was once more performed in front of the Queen Mother it was another excuse to put her on the cover, just ahead of another price rise - this time to 35p.

* * * * *

BBC Publications - for so long the proprietor of *Radio Times* - had now become merged with the main commercial arm of the Corporation, BBC Enterprises Ltd, which not only sold BBC programmes abroad, but also dealt with the ever increasing stream of programme-related material including books, records, and merchandise. BBC Publications now became the Journals Division of BBC Enterprises, but otherwise *Radio Times* carried on as before from Marylebone High Street.

* * * * *

EastEnders secured for itself the hallowed Christmas cover in 1986, as well as a complete short story inside by Gerry Huxham. Again, the Christmas Day television programme pages were in colour with a delightful double-page illustration by Paul Slater of a Santa Claus (bearing a distinct similarity to character actor Buster Merryfield from *Only Fools and Horses*) flying over a town whose inhabitants apparently include Russ Abbot and Annie (from the musical of the same name) - all three of whom could be seen in BBC1's peaktime Christmas Day programmes.

Cooking by radio waves
There has been an invention recently which looked at one time as though it was going to revolutionise kitchen technique utterly and completely. *It has been found possible to cook food by high-frequency waves, which make the molecules vibrate so rapidly that heat is created.* Unfortunately, although the basic process has been well enough established, the practical application of it has proved so full of difficulties that it is extremely unlikely that the process will ever be commercially or domestically practised in this country or ever at all.

Illustration by Joe Wright

Never say never!

by Tom Johnston   Issue 3284

Hogmanay and New Year's Day were also permitted colour headings and illustrations, but although the new printing process clearly made colour programme pages possible - this was the third Christmas to have made use of the facility - it was only at this time of year that the pages had hitherto been illuminated.

But in the New Year there were several experiments with colour pictures on the programme pages - a practice that was however not continued beyond the end of January.

EastEnders got their eight-page birthday souvenir in February, and in the same month BBC Scotland's major 16-part documentary series on the future of the Scottish nation was - unusually - permitted a "regional" cover with a design by Jay Myrdal that subsequently appeared on the BBC Scotland book of the series.

by Jay Myrdal
Issue 3300
21 Feb 1987
Scotland edition

The Holy Week illustration by Ashley Potter of Christ carrying the Cross was unusually bold for a Brian Thomas commission, and sat uncomfortably on the front of a magazine now accustomed to using this page to sell competitions and souvenirs. The next week's Easter cover had an elegant (and more commercial) photograph of Prince Edward at Hampton Court Palace sitting by a window overlooking the grounds.

Many of the front pages in 1987 urged prospective purchasers to **Win!** something - in May it was a car - in June, a cruise. Clearly, there was a circulation push on. But perhaps it went too far by printing the cover price in the currency of the Irish Republic - on the front of the *Welsh* edition! (Viewers in south-east Ireland generally got their cross-channel TV pictures from transmitters in Wales, admittedly, but the circulation bosses must have been desperate to have allowed such a step to be taken.)

Plate 9a

by Ashley Potter
Issue 3307
11 April 1987

As usual Scotland got its own Cup Final cover (a big picture of the Scottish Cup itself), and the rest of the UK had for once a graphic illustration - by Paul Cox - that had an old-fashioned look to it.

The General Election in June brought out the swingometer and Peter Snow, and the usual helpful *Radio Times* list of marginals to watch out for.

The design and makeup of the paper was by now evidently to the editor's satisfaction for there was little change to *Radio Times* for the rest of the decade. Photographs of television performers generally dominated the front cover, although from time to time art editor, Brian Thomas, still commissioned graphic covers - but they were clearly something of an endangered species. Ian Beck's 'Proms' cover in July 1987 provided a rare sighting of this phenomenon.

The tenth anniversary of the death of Elvis Presley gave *RT* an excuse to produce a special edition, with seven pages in tribute to 'the King' - an extended feature which readers would have been unlikely to find in the *Radio Times* of Cannon's years.

by Ian Beck   Issue 3320   11 July 1987

The first week in September had now traditionally become the time for tinkering with the layout, and 1987 was no exception. Gearing introduced an innovative idea - devoting the first three pages to *Upfront this week*, a clutch of illustrated snippets of gossip and news about the week's programme highlights.

Did I say innovative?

In its first week, *Upfront* was anonymous, but later it was credited to staff writer Nicki Household and later Eithne Power.

A genuine innovation, however, appeared in October 1987 when for the first time gatefold front covers appeared, allowing the advertiser- in this case BMW - three pages in which to sell their wares before page 3 began. This was good news for advertisers and readers alike because in order to make the gatefold practical the front cover had to be printed on a heavier (and as it happened whiter, glossier) paper and therefore such covers were less inclined to part company with the rest of the magazine even before they were liberated from the paper boy's satchel.

by Paul Slater   Issue 3341   5 Dec 1987

Another advertising innovation - or perhaps curse? - was the development of technology that allowed 'inserts'. 'Inserts' are pieces of advertising material which are not bound in to the main body of the paper, but loosely stuffed inside - with the ability to fall out and draw attention to themselves. Well, that's the theory. In practice of course they often escape on the way home from the newsagent's.

One of the first such issues contained a 36-page HMV Christmas catalogue, a 16-page 'Toys 'R' Us" catalogue and a 16-page "Image Photovideo Store" catalogue, each of which tumbled out of the issue of 5th December 1987. Perhaps this was designed to make the issue appear bigger than its 104 pages, since this coincided with yet another price hike. 37p bought you a nice Paul Slater drawing of *Sherlock Holmes*, with some programme listings attached to all the catalogues your paper boy could carry.

It is strange to consider that a man with Holmes' observational skills has failed to notice the existence beside the news-stand of a billboard advertising a magazine that was still thirty-odd years away from being published, linked to a technological discovery that had only just been made - but we'll let Slater renew his artistic licence.

BBC 2

9.00am Laurel and Hardy's Laughing 20s

Issue 3343

by Carol Lawson Issue 3343 19 Dec 1987 Plate 9b

160 pages at Christmas as usual, and a creative cover by Carol Lawson with sixteen Christmas carols concealed in it - readers were given a fortnight to work out the answer before it was published in the first issue of 1988. Local Radio was given a whole two pages of editorial space for an extended *Yours Locally* preview of seasonal fare from the neighbourhood stations.

The seasonal combination of 'Agatha' Woddis and Brookes returned (it had been missed the previous year) with book tokens for those readers able to solve the murder mystery. And over the page from a thoughtful Mary Kenny article on the significance of the Virgin Mary, a loud and very *TV Times* pair of pages offered prizes and gifts galore...

As part of the BBC's new policy of better informing its listeners and viewers, the BBC's 24-page Annual Review for 1987 - titled *See For Yourself* was inserted into *Radio Times* for 2nd January 1988. This replaced the annual *BBC Handbook* which had been published almost every year from the late '20s and had contained summaries of the Corporation's most significant activities for the previous twelve months. This 'user-friendly' booklet clearly feared for the attention span of its readers and so provided three 'fun quizzes' to leaven the fact.

But it would take more than fun quizzes and BBC propaganda to prop up the old listings system. The real battle was about to commence. In February 1988 an MEP asked the European Parliament to look into the *Radio/TV Times* monopoly. A formal complaint was registered by the Irish Company, Magill TV Guide Ltd., against state broadcaster Radio Telefís Éireann, the BBC, and Independent Television Publications Ltd. Its wordy response cannot have encouraged the broadcasters.

> The behaviour of the BBC in relation to the product [sic] in which it is dominant, namely its weekly schedules, had the effect of excluding a competitor in a related market, namely that of periodicals in general.

The EC didn't think much of the arrangement then...

> ..the BBC, like ITP and RTÉ uses its position as a broadcaster to advertise and promote its own TV guide, thereby affording it a promotional advantage over other TV guides and other publications.

Supplement   Issue 3344   2 Jan 1988

The Commission concluded that there were grounds for considering that certain practices of the BBC infringed Article 86 of the EEC Treaty. This Treaty provided that an abuse was committed if an undertaking in a dominant position limited markets to the prejudice of consumers.

The campaign for open access to schedules was now seriously hotting up. More questions in the House, and as the Government took another look at the situation a diverse group of vested interests joined together to form the 'TV Listings Campaign' lobbying anybody and everybody with their claims to open access for listings.

Irish soap star Mary McEvoy adorns a contemporary issue of **RTÉ Guide**

It was not just *Radio Times* and *TV Times* who were under attack. The EC case had started in the Republic of Ireland, where state broadcaster *RTÉ* - heavily modelled on the BBC - had since 1961 published its own *Guide*.

Before television began in the Republic, a variety of publications had carried some sort of listings for Radio Éireann; notably *Radio Review* which had also printed the weekend's BBC radio programmes and some BBC Television listings as well as those for Radio Luxembourg.

When it began, *RTV Guide* (the name was changed later to *RTÉ Guide*) printed - under agreement - full details of the BBC radio and television programmes since those were widely available in Eire. It was only once Telefís Éireann (launched in 1961 - with more than a little help from none other than Maurice Gorham!) had reached the whole of the country that the BBC programme details were dropped from the pages of the Guide.

But - as in the UK - *RTÉ* held on to its listings copyright for a very good reason: the small and often cash-strapped state broadcaster made a substantial amount of money out of its programme journal.

RTÉ was no safer from attack than its cross-channel brethren. A MORI poll of 1993 adults (guess who commissioned it?) found that 78% of the public believed that newspapers and magazines should be allowed to publish a complete advance guide to each week's TV programmes.

Those with sharp axes took the opportunity to do some serious grinding:

> If the present copyright situation is not changed, by the mid-1990s when there are 40 or 50 channels to choose from, viewers may be forced to buy as many as a dozen separate listings magazines to find out what is showing...

...thundered the *Sunday Times* in June, with a clear eye to its own oft-stated desire to print the week's listings in advance.

The Adam Smith Institute - a public policy research unit - chucked in its tuppence worth:

> One might be rather more likely to find criticism of the Soviet government in *Pravda* than to find *Radio Times* advising viewers that a coming programme is no good.

Pointing to the publication of the BBC's schedules in a variety of Dutch listings magazines, critics argued that it was unacceptable that publications in the Netherlands could enjoy a freedom that those in the UK did not.

In July, the All-Party Home Affairs Select Committee came to the conclusion that:

> Any service operator ... should be permitted to publish details of all the programmes which he is entitled to carry ... [a reference to the status of cable operators in this debate] ... and that newspapers or magazines should be able to list all television and radio programmes regardless of copyright considerations.

Meanwhile, in July, BBC Enterprises purchased a small magazine publisher - Redwood Publishing - with the stated aim of adding more publications to its existing range. The *Clothes Show Magazine* (tied in to the television series of the same name) was an early example.

Predictably, just as in the 1920s when *The Listener* had appeared, other publishers (including ITP) cried foul. John Mellon, IPC's Managing Director, complained to the Office of Free Trading, claiming that *Clothes Show Magazine* benefitted from unfair advertising support through its "grossly unfair" free promotion on the BBC's channels.

A sign of growing unease on the part of the BBC and ITP was their unprecedented joint promotion of the August Bank Holiday issues in 1988, seen by some as a sign of future co-operation on the part of the two publishers.

Geoffrey Cannon was unable to resist the opportunity to make his views on this subject known, and on 14th September 1988, he wrote to *The Times*:

Restricted Vision
3 Nov 1988

> At its best, Radio Times complemented BBC programmes with listings and writers who did not fawn on programme makers ... and TV Times has done Channel Four a great favour by printing its listings side by side with ITV, against the wishes of Jeremy Isaacs who wanted to publish them separately in a Channel Four magazine.
>
> However, the argument for a free market of programme information is now overwhelming. We all want to know what is on a week ahead, by looking through one magazine.

It is not clear whether Cannon had always taken this view; or whether the prospect of more employment opportunities for former editors had tempered his opinion.

In November the TV Listings Campaign published its own 16-page booklet, *Restricted Vision*, putting forward the arguments for the breaking of the monopoly. The members of the Campaign were named as: *Time Out*, News International (owners of Sky TV and publishers of *The Times*), IPC, EMAP, *Daily Telegraph*, *The Independent, The Observer, The Evening Standard,* Cable Guide Ltd, Perry Publications, Ingersoll Publications, *The Birmingham Post, The Western Gazette,* Associated Magazines, *The Birmingham Daily News,* Satellite TV Publications, Hamfield Publications, *The Guardian* and *Manchester Evening News.*

Formidable foes.

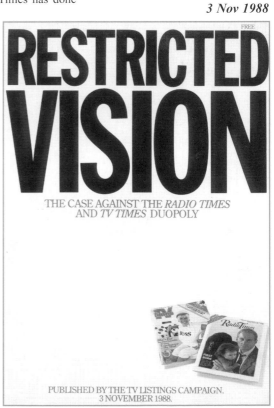

PUBLISHED BY THE TV LISTINGS CAMPAIGN.
3 NOVEMBER 1988.

On page 3 of this booklet, the Campaign headlined unequivocally

THE BRITISH PUBLIC IS BEING RIPPED OFF EVERY WEEK OF THE YEAR

and went on to exercise the familiar arguments that viewers had to spend nearly £40 a year on listings magazines that provided uncritical and biased information.

Some of its arguments - like the one that *Radio Times* short-changed radio enthusiasts by not listing independent radio programmes despite its title - were somewhat specious. No market for commercial radio listings had ever been proved.

* * * * *

Most commercial stations - both offshore and, after 1974, onshore - played records all day. The names of the five or six disc jockeys that took it in turns to do so hardly constituted 'listings' with the result that after the demise of Radio Luxembourg no serious attempts had been made to publish periodicals focussed on commercial radio.

In the case of Luxembourg, its pre-war programmes had been published in *Radio Pictorial* and after the war Charles Graves had edited the monthly *208 and View* for most of the '50s. In 1968 pop magazine *Fabulous* had tied up with Luxy and was renamed *Fabulous 208* complete with detailed listings for the Station of the Stars.

242
Issue 6 Sept 1966

Both exceptions to this dearth of contemporary commercial radio publications had been in Central Scotland, where in the mid 1960s, against the trend, ship-based pirate station Radio Scotland had put out its very own modestly successful listings-and-pop- news monthly *242 Showbeat*, a publishing curiosity which survived under editor David Gibson from April 1966 until the station's demise in August 1967.

When land-based commercial radio started, it was Glasgow station Radio Clyde that produced its own listings magazine. *Clyde Guide* was launched in 1978 but after less than a year its circulation was tiny, its losses less so, and the paper folded.

Clyde Guide   *Issue 1   28 Sept 1978*

TV Times had proposed to print commercial radio programmes, and for a brief spell did carry skeleton listings for the London stations. A pirate radio magazine, *Script* transformed itself into *Radio Guide* in 1975 and printed a rather ragbag selection of ILR schedules.

In 1976, *Radio Guide* split into regional editions and did a distribution deal with *TV Times* owners ITP. It continued for a year or so before being subsumed by *TV Times* who then relaunched it in September 1977 as the quarterly *Tune-In* and published it as 'A *TV Times* Extra' with *Radio Guide* inside as a separate A5 insert. It ceased publication in 1980 without public comment.

*   *   *   *   *

As the battle for listings control raged above its head, *Radio Times* showed no signs of the conflict (although curiously the opening 'credits' listing the editorial team were dispensed with in April).

Radio Guide   *30 April 1976*

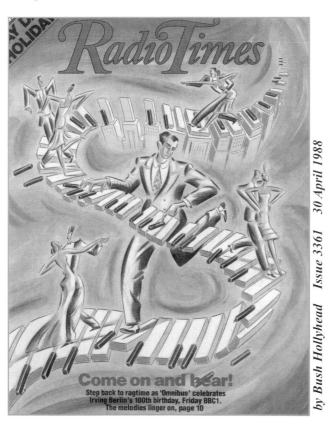

by Bush Hollyhead   Issue 3361   30 April 1988

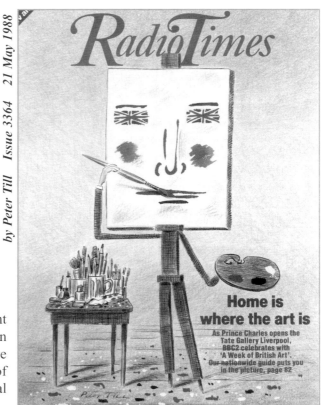

by Peter Till   Issue 3364   21 May 1988

A handful of original artworks fought their way to the front cover. Bush Hollyhead produced a nostalgic cover in celebration of Irving Berlin's centenary that wouldn't have looked out of place in the Gorham era. And BBC2's "Week of British Art" in May 1988 inspired Peter Till's highly original cover design.

All-American comic book superhero *Superman* burst forth on Radio 4 (of all places) in June (courtesy of artist Dave Gibbons) for a "Happy Birthday Superman" special issue celebrating a half-century of the Man of Steel. Uniquely, this issue contained a specially produced authentic Superman cartoon strip, which occupied two whole pages of *RT* and probably did publishers D.C. Comics no harm at all!

(Your author here confesses to being a lifelong Superman fan, and admits to being thrilled by this little piece of publishing convergence!)

by Peter Brookes   Issue 3374   30 July 1988

And Peter Brookes contributed a cover on 30th July for a pair of programmes that considered the myths surrounding England's victory over the Spanish Armada.

CHAPTER ELEVEN
Enter Nick Brett

or once, there was no 'tinkering' with the paper in September as the new Television season began. Another editor was about to be appointed to steer the magazine into the uncharted waters of multiple listings magazines that had become an inevitability.

Brian Gearing handed over to Nicholas Brett at the end of the month, and Brett allowed himself a few more weeks before his first effort at stamping his own identity on the magazine. Brian Thomas was made Deputy Editor and Jenny Fleet was put in charge of Art.

In the meantime, there were special events to consider. The 1988 Olympics in Seoul occupied most of an issue in September - and, at the beginning of October, BBC Radio celebrated 21 years of the start of Radios 1, 2, 3 and 4 with a revival of the Radio Show at Earl's Court exhibition centre in London. A special *Radio Times* featured a nicely illustrated potted history of the four networks which included a clutch of past radio covers.

* * * * *

Nicholas Brett's first issue (under his own name) was published on 12th November 1988. It featured an unremarkable cover picture taken from the Dennis Potter play, *Christabel*.

But page three immediately showed the new editor's influence. Gone was the familiar *Radio Times* masthead to be replaced by the bold letters *RT*. A full 'cast list' of editorial staff occupied the first column, along with all the small print that included issue number, printers, subscription rates, and a new bold list of BBC addresses (including the local headquarters for readers in Scotland, Wales and Northern Ireland).

Gone, too, was *Upfront* and instead a classy illustrated teaser for the magazine's main features along with a detailed table of contents and a colour preview of the following week's issue (featuring Daleks - Brett had learned *very* quickly)

The opening feature on the Potter drama didn't look much like the old *Radio Times* - stylishly set in reversed-out type (white on black) and with the background bleeding right up to the edge of the page (no margins in sight) it must have caught the attention of readers hitherto accustomed to a mess of black and white boxes.

Gillard and Brown continued their radio and films features as before, Roger Woddis continued to rhyme alongside the crossword, and beyond the first few pages all seemed much as it had been.

Brett had left his job as Features Editor of *The Times* to edit the BBC Journal. He describes his first day in the new job as traumatic. His desk was empty - it appeared that his predecessor had eschewed paperwork. All that sat on it was a copy of that week's issue of *Radio Times* which he spent the entire day studying. No one called him. Nobody came near his office.

The magazine on his desk was - in his opinion - dull, lifeless, messy, uninspired. He went home that night and told his wife that he'd made a terrible mistake giving up his job at *The Times*.

Fortunately he didn't hand in his notice - he started to reform the magazine. Recognising the value of regular 'star name' contributors, he asked Barry Norman - long-time presenter of BBC1's film programmes - to write a weekly film column. The first appeared on 3rd December, and in the same issue the *My Kind of Day* inside back feature began. A classic upmarket magazine feature, this described an average day in the life of a current BBC personality. The first to appear was *Tomorrow's World* presenter, Maggie Philbin, wife of children's TV presenter, Keith Chegwin.

And a subtle change was made to the radio pages, with the billings for each network now starting at the top of a column, allowing rules to be inserted dividing the four (or five) networks. A summary of the BBC World Service programmes also appeared in English editions.

LONDON (BBC Local Radio Bedfordshire, Essex, GLR, Oxford)
17-30 December 1988   Price 80p

by Lynda Gray   Issue 3394   17 Dec 1988

Whatever Brett's magic was, his Christmas Issue was remarkable. With an average circulation just below the three-and-a-half-million mark, issue number 3394 gained a place in the *Guinness Book of Records* as the biggest-selling edition of any magazine in British history with a staggering 11,220,666 copies sold!

Lynda Gray's striking Christmas cover was a far cry from the *EastEnders' Only Fools* designs of previous years. The opening feature echoed the *RT* of the '50s and '60s as the Archbishop of Canterbury, Dr Robert Runcie, was invited to contribute a Christmas Message.

With the aid of photographer Victor Watts, *Radio Times* staged its own elaborate paper pantomime, picturing a variety of BBC stars as its cast (aka "The *Radio Times* Players") and telling three classic fairy stories in verse, written (of course) by Roger Woddis.

The final tongue-in-cheek credit of this feature - "A *Radio Times* production, © MCMLXXXVIII" showed how far the paper had moved in just a few months. Other features in that issue included *Walford at War* - highlighting an *EastEnders* special - features on *The Goons*, Nat 'King' Cole, wildlife, and an expanded film guide including Barry Norman's *Talking Pictures* feature.

Colour on some of the festive programme pages was extended to radio as well, and Woddis/Brookes collaborated on an 'Edgar Allan Woddis' Christmas murder mystery.

Issue 3395
31 Dec 1988
Scotland edition

by Martin Baker
From page 29

Bubbling over: Carlos Kleiber (right) celebrates the New Year with Johann Strauss's flighty 'Fledermaus' overture **BBC2, 11.15am New Year's Day Concert**

The following week there was also a clear sign of Brett's change of policy. For the first time since 1949, Scottish readers had their own Hogmanay issue, with its own cover featuring comedy actor Rikki Fulton.

There was also an innovative free gift - a *Radio Times* year planner wallchart with four magical illustrations by Peter Brookes each incorporating the letters *RT* in the design, and listing significant events for the twelve months ahead.

by Peter Brookes
Spring, Summer, Autumn, Winter
illustrations from wallchart
Above issue

Plucking the heartstrings:
400 years of song and dance
9.35am Radio 3

Issue 3404

A restructuring of the chain of command meant that Brian Thomas became Managing Editor, looking after the business side, with Peter Barnard as Executive Editor.

A 'Green Issue' in March (with a baby seal on the front) took the opportunity to 'plug' the BBC *Wildlife Magazine*. And *RT* joined the ranks of magazines now printing a bar code on their covers for the convenience of supermarkets and other retailers using computerised stock control.

What price marriage? Can families of Asian women stop the horrors of increasing materialism within the dowry system?
Network East, 2.45pm BBC2

by Caroline Church
Issue 3404   4 March 1989

Brett's *Radio Times* was yet to appear in its fully revamped form. That happened with the Easter issue in 1989. The first obvious change was the loss of the white margin around the front cover - the picture of Paul McCartney that occupied it ran from edge to edge, although a discreet rule was left to show where the margins once were.

*Easter
Issue 3407
25 March 1989*

The edition name was shifted to the corner cover 'flash' and the date and price given more prominence - no longer looking like an afterthought. Page three was redesigned again with more emphasis on the leading features.

BBC2

9.00am Pages from Ceefax

**12.05pm
The Greatest Story
Ever Told**

F / I / L / M starring
Max Von Sydow
as Jesus
Dorothy McGuire
as Mary
Charlton Heston
as John the Baptist
John Wayne
as the Centurian
David McCallum as Judas
Van Heflin as Bar Amand.
Producer-director George Stevens spent more than four years preparing to make

King of Men:
*Max Von Sydow
as Jesus of Nazareth*
**The Greatest Story Ever
Told, BBC2 12.05pm**

Clocks go forward tonight

by Fiona McVicar
Easter 1989

A general overhaul of fonts, page layout and design had taken place, with a major makeover for the programme pages. The programme titles were now printed in an expanded font with the channel headings reversed out for greater clarity. BBC1 and BBC2 were once again very clearly separated, but the biggest shock of all for readers was the return to the 1950s layout, with TV at the front of the book and radio at the back. The week's Radio 1 billings occupied a single page, then Radio 2 had a facing pair. Radio 3 had five pages of daily billings and Radio 4 had six. Local Radio then followed, or the appropriate national stations in Scotland, Wales and Northern Ireland. Regional features - absent from the English editions of the paper since the late 60s - were resumed in a localised page *See Hear*.

At the back was a new regular health page, Geoff Hamilton's *Gardening* page, children's pages renamed *Switched on* (and minus John Craven) there was cookery, travel, antiques, Clive Doig's *Brainbox* feature and the crossword. Peter Brookes returned with his weekly cartoon the following week, and later *Voice Over* allowed a personality the space to give their opinions on a contentious issue. And from this issue, Sue Robinson took over as Features Editor. More of Sue in the next chapter.

VOICE OVER

Ringing the changes at *Radio Times* – the Editor explains himself

NICHOLAS BRETT

'The last time someone interfered with *Radio Times* you could feel the earth move here in Marylebone High Street. If there were not actually *RT* fundamentalists beating down the door there was a whole flood of letters from 'Yours Disgusted'.

And among the flurry of cartoons that the 1984 redesign provoked was one that is framed and hanging on the wall above this word processor. It shows an exasperated couple wrestling with *RT*. The caption reads: 'Well I'm not sure dear, but as far as I can tell there's a double-glazing ad on at 8.00...'

So, by now you are on page 116 of the 1989 redesign and you will, I hope, have noticed extensive evidence of our tinkering and tampering. If you are 'Deeply Satisfied' then all well and good. Should you be 'Deeply Concerned' then this is an attempt to head you off at the letterbox and explain the latest changes.

Our principal aim was to produce a clearer, cleaner and more classically designed magazine, one that would be easier for you to find your way around. A magazine fit for the new world of broadcasting in the 1990s. I believe we have achieved this through more disciplined design, the new typefaces for headlines, rules between columns and the creative use of white space to make the pages look more inviting.

All very well... but what about the separation of radio and television listings? Contrary to what a few of you seem to think, I don't step out of the shower in the morning exclaiming, 'We must separate radio and television!' While changes do grow out of hunches they are shaped by extensive market research among existing and potential *RT* readers.

Among those of you who buy the magazine principally for radio information we found a majority in favour of a self-contained radio section; and, that said, a majority in favour of such a section being arranged by network rather than by day.

In presentation terms, too, a self-contained radio section

Underneath a photograph of himself (we had rarely seen sight of an editor before) Nick Brett explained his changes and anticipated some of the reactions.

After describing the additions to the writing team - Anne Gregg (travel), John Tovey (antiques), Dr Barry Lynch (health) and wildlife writer Gareth Huw Davies, Brett solicited readers' opinions.

And he got them!

One reader - unhappy with the changes - had his own solution

By buying two copies of *Radio Times* cutting them up with scissors and sticking the pieces for each day together, I can get quite a useful guide to a day's radio listening. It just needs a date at the top of the page - that's all!

Another described the number of pages that had to be turned to find what was happening on a given day as 'a nightmare'. But many were happy with the new presentation and said so.

From page 216 of Easter issue 3407   25 March 1989

West Midlands & Scotland editions
Issue 3410   15 April 1989

For the next two weeks, Radio 2 is joining forces with the Health Education Authority in a nationwide campaign to increase health awareness. *Healthcheck* will underline the importance of regular medical check-ups – and give sound advice on healthy living.

There was even a return to a greater regional identity in Scotland, where a cover showing Helena Bonham-Carter as 'An English Rose' was replaced by one picturing comedy duo Jack Milroy and Rikki Fulton as 'Francie and Josie' - onetime ratings toppers for ITV and now some twenty years later returning for a special on BBC1 Scotland.

by Trevor Dunton
Above issue

Let's hear it for your rights!

Does somebody love you? Esther Rantzen from *That's Life!* thinks every child has the right to be loved. Esther's work with ChildLine (0800 1111) – the children's phone help service – has shown her the many kinds of suffering that thousands of children live with. She writes about

it on the opposite page.

Esther and her team think that all children should be healthy, safe, loved and able to love, listened to, able to play and able to do their best. What do you think? Write to tell us at My Rights, Radio Times, Room 20, 35 Marylebone High Street, London W1M 4AA.

by Joe Wright
Above issue

9a   *Easter 1987   by Ashley Potter*

9b   *Christmas 1987   by Carol Lawson*

9c   *Jack Nicholson 1989   by Herb Ritts*

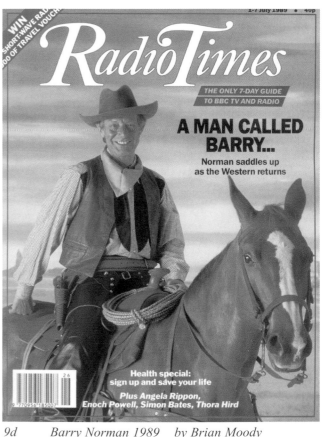

9d   *Barry Norman 1989   by Brian Moody*

by Mark Oldroyd   2 November 1991
The Father

by Paul Dickinson   12 October 1991
The Wide-Brimmed Hat

by Chris Price   The Cabaret of Dr Caligari
23 November 1991

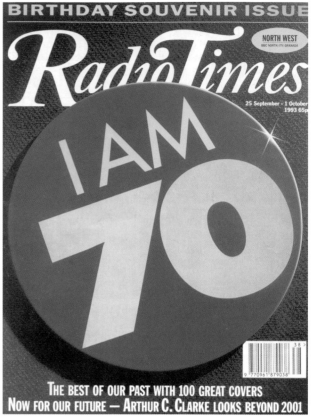

RadioTimes

NORTH WEST
BBC NORTH / ITV GRANADA

25 September - 1 October
1993 65p

I AM
70

THE BEST OF OUR PAST WITH 100 GREAT COVERS
NOW FOR OUR FUTURE — ARTHUR C. CLARKE LOOKS BEYOND 2001

9 770961 879038

10   Radio Times *70th Anniversary*   *25 Sept 1993*

by Kim Marsland
A Stone from Heaven
15 April 1995

by Michael Sheehy
All in the Mind
15 April 1995

Quiet and unassuming covers were out - exciting and eye-catching covers were in. It was a bold decision to use a large photograph of the painfully reconstructed face of Simon Weston (badly burned victim of the Falklands conflict). Politically brave was the depiction (by Victor Watts) of Margaret Thatcher as Britannia.

by Victor Watts
Issue 3412
29 April 1989

Sue Lawley
Photo by John Timbers
Photography Supplement
Issue 3414   6 May 1989

Warren Mitchell
as Alf Garnett
Don Smith's photograph

In May an *RT* Photography Special supplement celebrated 150 years of photography with 13 pages of outstanding examples from the magazine's own archives, many of them photographs commissioned for the cover but now printed without any typographical adornments. The supplement had its own cover of Sue Lawley, photographed by John Timbers.

Sue Lawley's portrait launches our celebration of 150 years of photography. From the Radio Times archives we present an album of pictures both magical and memorable

193

Now into his stride, Nicholas Brett and his team worked hard to claw back lost circulation in order to place *Radio Times* in the forefront when the listings monopoly was ended.

With new technology available, it was now possible for journalists to type their copy directly into a word processor and for those words to turn themselves into print without the intervention of another human being. This was one of the revolutions of the last decade of the century. There were many others. Databases allowed the gathering of programme listings by a central agency for onward distribution to other users - of crucial importance when BBC listings were to be made available to all who wanted them.

*Jack Nicholson
Photo by Herb Ritts
Issue 3418
10 June 1989*

Plate 9c

Brett had a policy of continuing changes, as they were possible or necessary. The issue of 10th June 1989 appeared for the first time with a glossy cover - a heavier paper was now used giving the magazine a noticeable improved appearance. The back section, now named *Life Times,* brought together the features on lifestyle issues like antiques and food.

Life Timer of the Year
Over 8,000 readers have entered our competition, and now 300 of you have been sent a Life Timer T-shirt or a *BBC Diet* or *Healthcheck* book. Keep up the good work, and in six weeks' time we'll run the final questionnaire which could be your passport to a fabulous holiday in Singapore.

12 Aug 1989

Life Times
Your weekly guide to good living starts here

Cover photography was now elevated to a higher level and leading photographers commissioned to produce the material. Columnist Barry Norman was photographed dressed as a cowboy (complete with horse) for a feature on westerns.

Fifty years after the outbreak of the Second World War, *Radio Times* produced a 17-page supplement tracing the history of those six momentous years. And in November, television cameras were allowed into the House of Commons for the first time. Speaker of the House, Bernard Weatherill was the tactful choice of cover star.

As Christmas 1989 approached, Brett succumbed to the pressures of complaints and letters from listeners: he restored the day-by-day, side-by-side radio listings, to two pages for each day - with Radios Ulster, Wales, Cymru and Scotland once again sharing the Radio 4 page. In the English editions there was space for daily editorial features on radio as well.

By now the cover price was 45p - having risen first to 40. By 1990 it was 50p. Inflation and the high costs of paper were blamed as usual.

*Barry Norman
Issue 3421
1 July 1989*
Plate 9d

194

The 1989 Christmas Double issue (164 pages, with a King's College, Cambridge, chorister on the cover) included the annual *See For Yourself* report. This issue, perhaps surprisingly, was devoid of many really special features - although the main writing team of William Greaves, Nicki Household, Roland White and David Gillard wrote much about the Christmas programmes.

The prize crossword (in colour) offered 20 volumes of the complete Oxford English Dictionary (value = £1,500) as a prize. And there was a new, cleaner font for the TV programme titles.

Not averse to a little self-promotion, *RT* carried a cover flash in February 1990 describing it as "Britain's Biggest Selling Magazine" which was now in the shops on Wednesday instead of Thursday.

A sign from the heavens (as it were) in April '90 was the launch of new British Satellite Broadcasting, licensed by the IBA (who were also responsible for ITV) and beamed to small square satellite receiving dishes known affectionately as 'squariels'.

By the time it launched, BSB unexpectedly found itself in direct competition for viewers with Sky Television (backed by Rupert Murdoch). So, as well as publishing its own magazine *TV Month*, BSB took a leaf out of Reith's book. Just as Reith had advertised the BBC programmes in the *Pall Mall Gazette*, BSB took the back four pages of *Radio Times* every week to entice viewers with the highlights from the coming week's programmes on its five channels.

*   *   *   *   *

The following week - 2nd June - *Radio Times* appeared in yet another new guise. With Kenny Everett and new columnist Gloria Hunniford together on the cover, it sported a much larger masthead, which included the slogan "The Only 7-Day Guide to BBC TV and Radio". This issue began with a lengthy editorial by Nick Brett. He described how detailed research into what readers wanted was behind the latest changes. The answers to the research had been surprisingly simple.

> "Give us a more colourful magazine and one that is easier to use but do not sacrifice any of the authority, accuracy and high level of information..." You warned us not to become cheap and gaudy. "Don't get like the other one" was how many of you expressed it.

At last this was the long awaited full-colour *Radio Times*. Monochrome pages were almost a thing of the past confined now to the Local Radio, S4C or *See Hear* pages and some regional advertising pages. Each day of the week was given its own distinctive colour and this was used both at the top and - innovatively - on the edge of the programme pages along with dark blue for television, light blue for radio and deep pink for films. Said Nick:

> I am sure in time you will become as familiar with our day colours as you are with the place colours on a Monopoly board.

But there were other even more fundamental changes. On the TV pages, after a right-hand *At A Glance* page with short features on the day's highlights, BBC1 always occupied the left-hand page and BBC2 the right-hand, with *no advertisements on programme listings pages*. The radio pages were enlivened with colour logos for each of the BBC stations at the top of the page.

Issue 3468   2 June 1990

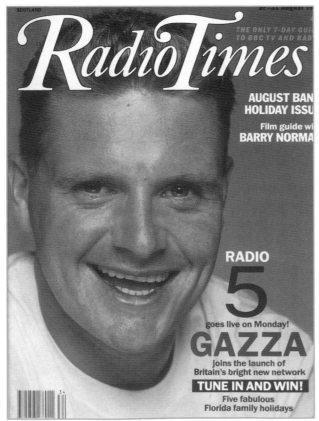

Issue 3480   25 Aug 1990...

The *Life Times* pages had an edge column on each page directing viewers and listeners to related programmes on the particular subject. For the first time, audience ratings were published for all four channels, and there was even a bunch of flowers for the best of the week's *Letters*.

In the Scotland edition there was a new feature - *A Scottish Diary* a chatty column contributed by well-known journalists. The first of these was Ruth Wishart, and in this first new-look issue the main Scottish *See Hear* full-page feature was - by sheer coincidence - devoted to a programme called *The Tony Currie Wireless Show*.

The following week, *RT* offered an eight-page World Cup pull-out and was faced with the necessity of running a separate cover and lead feature on footballer Mo Johnston in the Scotland edition, as other editions featured a cover and interview with England's Peter Shilton.

Radio Times celebrated the Queen Mother's 90th birthday with an elegant picture from the Glenn Harvey Collection and a five-page supplement that included a special poem by Roger Woddis and a feature by Godfrey Talbot, the BBC's very first Royal Correspondent.

In August 1990 the BBC launched its first new radio network since 1967. Radio 5 was to be a national station for youth, education and sport. Footballer Paul Gascoigne appeared on the cover promoting the launch. Now the right-hand radio page put Radios 4 and 5 together (and the National stations in those editions).

...in which Radio Five makes its debut

MW 693, 909 kHz
Sports Desks on the hour (not 9.00am, 8.00pm or 9.00) Including European Athletics Championships from Split

9.00am Take Five
Bruno Brookes with music, quizzes and stories. Plus Andy Crane's search for Britain's scariest white-knuckle ride. Guest: **Paul Gascoigne**.
● FEATURE: *page 4*

10.25am
1, 2, 3, 4, 5
Stories and songs for young children. Plus Andrew Sachs reading *Wiggly Park* adventures. *(Repeated at 2.00pm)*

10.45am
The Last Egg
Greg Snow's story read by Dermot Crowley *(R)*

11.00am This Family Business
Johnnie Walker with news, views and music.

12.30pm
Time Travel
1940: The Battle of Britain

1.00pm
Radio 3 on Radio 5
Lunchtime concert *(R)*

2.00pm
1, 2, 3, 4, 5
(Broadcast at 10.25am)

2.30-4.35pm
World Service
2.30 Society Today; 2.45 Personal View; 3.05 Outlook; 3.30 Stone's America; 4.05 Science in Action

4.35pm Five Aside
Reflecting life in the UK, plus athletics from Split. Presenter Martin Kelner.

7.40-11.00pm
Vox Pops
7.40 Celebrity Stories Andy Crane reads from *Truckers* by Terry Pratchett.
7.55 Orphans in Waiting
A six-part spy thriller by Wally K Daly.
8.25 Euro-Mix
Europe's youth scene with Caron Keating.

This was too cramped for comfort, and a few weeks later it was decided that the National stations would be moved. It meant the end of *See Hear* and instead the programmes of Radios Scotland, Wales, Cymru, Ulster and all their regional opt-outs would occupy the pair of pages reserved in England for Local Radio listings. This led to increasingly poor relations with Controllers of the 'National Regions' who - understandably - felt that their programming was being under-valued and under-sold by the London-controlled *Radio Times*.

*   *   *   *   *

BSB's last four-page spread appeared in the issue of 27th October 1990. On the 2nd November, BSB was merged with Sky Television to become British Sky Broadcasting, and the advertising in *Radio Times* ceased at once. So did *TV Month*.

by Mick Brownfield   Issue 3497   22 Dec 1990

The day before, the Government had published its new Broadcasting Act. Section 176 of the 1990 Broadcasting Act finally placed an obligation on broadcasters to make their programme listings available to anyone who "reasonably requires it" - but the Act made it clear that broadcasters could charge for this information. It was now enshrined in legislation that the *Radio Times'* monopoly would very soon come to an end.

The magazine carried on as before, pushing itself to the front of the news-stands wherever possible. Madonna graced the cover on 1st December; actress Wendy Richard was given the full glamorous works the next week.

Page 2

And the very last BBC-only Christmas Double Issue featured a traditional Father Christmas (complete with TV remote) drawn by Mick Brownfield.

The TV programme page headings had undergone some typographical adjustment in this special issue with a clear view to the multichannel future.
A full page advertisement gave readers plenty of advance notice of the impending changes.

1991 was going to be a momentous year for *Radio Times*.

CHAPTER TWELVE
"If it's on - it's in!"

mas was past, and for the first few weeks of 1991 it was 'business as usual' for *Radio Times* - at least on the pages. But behind the scenes everything was changing. New databases, many more sources of information, photographs and differing deadlines had to be co-ordinated in time for the relaunch.

It had been agreed by all concerned that Section 176 of the 1990 Act would be implemented as from 1st March 1991. While *Radio Times* was putting new systems into place to carry other people's listings, *TV Times* - now published by IPC who had bought the title from Independent Television Publications - was preparing to publish the BBC's programmes - television *and* radio - for the first time, and a handful of new magazines were preparing to launch.

With the issue of 9th February the *Preview* gossip pages (great-great-great grandson of *Both Sides of the Microphone*) began to run features on a few ITV and Channel 4 programmes, with the editorial tag,

ITV in *RT*? There'll be lots more from March 1st

ITV's "*Inspector Morse*" and Channel 4's *Roseanne* were amongst the first to feature in this way.

On the programme pages a diagonal 'flash' at the bottom of each right hand page featured an ITV or C4 programme with a picture - for example, on Sunday's page, Harry Secombe appeared with the line,

Harry Secombe and Highway in *RT*? Yes from March 1st!

Page 99   Issue 3504   9 Feb 1991

A full-page advertisement on the inside back page pictured *Coronation Street* actress Anne Kirkbride.

Radio Times was pulling out all the stops to generate as much excitement as possible for its new role as an all-channel listings magazine.

The following week's issue was extraordinary. A cover strap -

On the trail of Inspector Morse

- made it clear that ITV now figured in its editorials. Astrologer Patric Walker joined to the team, providing - for the very first time - horoscopes.

But the biggest surprise came on the programme pages, which had already been revamped to make space for ITV and Channel 4.

Sean Connery from front cover of issue 3505 photo by Terry O'Neill

What's on the other side tonight?
Matthew Kelly takes a gamble and
steps into Bruce Forsyth's shoes in You
Bet! Over in LA, Roxanne threatens to
quit, while Kuzack gets a new look.

Soon we'll be able to give you more than
the headlines. Watch this space: from
March 1st it will be filled with a
complete guide to ITV and Channel 4
programmes.

if it's on, it's in . . . Radio Times

Issue 3505
16 Feb 1991

Page 43
Page 94

The logos for both channels appeared in their allotted corners, and there were photographs relating to that day's programmes on both channels as well as BBC1 and BBC2. But where the listings would be there was just lots of white space - filled with brief teasers for the following week's historic issue.....

And now the new strapline was used on every one of that issue's programme pages

If it's on - it's in .....*Radio Times*

The new layout started with the *At A Glance* page; then an advertisement and, on the next right-hand page, TV daytime billings. The evening (from 5.30pm) occupied the next double-page spread with three columns for BBC1, two for BBC2, three for ITV and two for Channel 4.

Nicholas Brett's now regular weekly letter to readers was given special prominence. ➤

His strategy was brilliant. He had given existing - and more importantly potential readers - a chance to see what the new *Radio Times* looked like a good week before its rivals without breaking the rules. And he had produced a dry run like no other!

*   *   *   *   *

Letters

Nicholas Brett
Editor, Radio Times

The waiting is over. Next week I shall be able to give you the magazine that you and I have always wanted. Because of a change in the law, from Friday 1 March I can publish full weekly details of *all* programmes on radio and TV. *Radio Times* is ready. For two years we've been raising her hemline in a modern and colourful way. All that's been missing is ITV, Channel 4, and satellite details. Now that will be put right.

The changes I've made since I became Editor have been conceived and shaped in 'conversations' with you, through surveys and reader-research groups. When you've said something's not right, it's been changed. The last conversation was before Christmas in a survey on these pages and many thanks to the twenty thousand of you who took part.

Look at the television pages in this issue and you'll see that ITV and Channel 4 information is going to be presented *your* way. Three-quarters of you thought it should be given equal space and arranged in an easy-to-use format.

A minority of you (15%) wanted satellite details, but since the majority thought this information should be arranged in its own discreet section that is what I shall do from 1 March.

You've no doubts about the importance of radio (64%) and I guarantee that our coverage will remain second to none.

You told me how much you liked the film pages and TV's 'at a glance' panels, so how could they possibly be better? Well, find out next week.

Nicholas Brett

Send your letters to The Editor,
Letters, 35 Marylebone High Street,
London W1M 4AA Tel: 071 - 224 2442

Wednesday 20th February 1991.

Radio Times appears with the giant letters ITV on its cover - and the standfirst "From Friday ... if it's on it's in!"

Because 1st March fell on a Friday, both *Radio Times* and *TV Times* produced issues that only contained multichannel listings for the last of the seven days that issue covered.

Radio Times - with Arnold Schwarzenegger on the cover - featured *Coronation Street* actress Thelma Barlow in its back page *My Kind of Day* feature and trailed it on the cover, stealing a march on *TV Times* whose cover featured Peter Falk as *Columbo*, and only mentioned in comparatively small type

BBC Friday programmes in this issue

Radio Times features included one on Granada's new *Sherlock Holmes* series and an individually numbered insert allowed participants the chance to match two numbers (available in successive issues) to win £10 cash prizes.

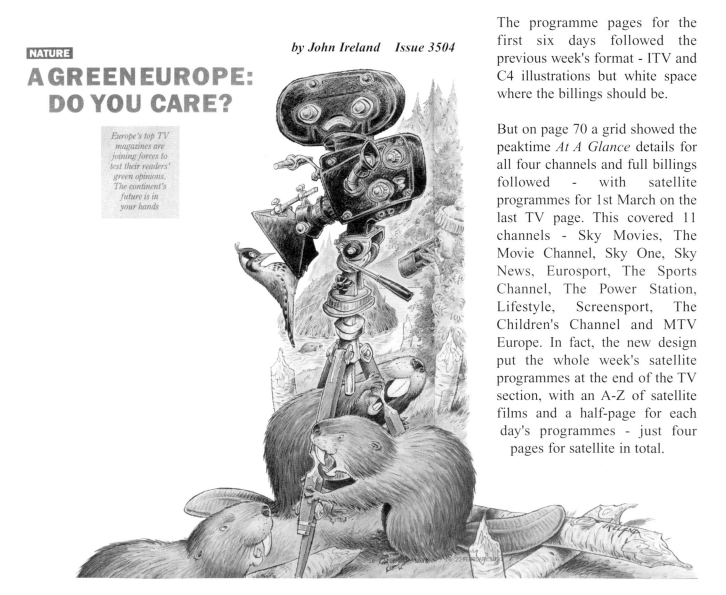

NATURE

A GREEN EUROPE: DO YOU CARE?

Europe's top TV magazines are joining forces to test their readers' green opinions. The continent's future is in your hands

by John Ireland   Issue 3504

The programme pages for the first six days followed the previous week's format - ITV and C4 illustrations but white space where the billings should be.

But on page 70 a grid showed the peaktime *At A Glance* details for all four channels and full billings followed - with satellite programmes for 1st March on the last TV page. This covered 11 channels - Sky Movies, The Movie Channel, Sky One, Sky News, Eurosport, The Sports Channel, The Power Station, Lifestyle, Screensport, The Children's Channel and MTV Europe. In fact, the new design put the whole week's satellite programmes at the end of the TV section, with an A-Z of satellite films and a half-page for each day's programmes - just four pages for satellite in total.

The Local Radio pages now included a list of all the available commercial stations in the area and their frequencies, with a couple of words describing each station's format. When the new National commercial stations, Classic FM and Virgin Radio began they were given space on the local radio pages for a brief summary of 'times and titles'.

Nick Brett's editorial letter echoed Arthur Burrows' words in the first issue: "Hello everyone! We will now give you *The Radio Times*. The good new times...."

FM 97.6-99.8 MHz

Issue 3505
23 Feb 1991

...because from now on we shall again be the complete guide to broadcasting as we were in 1923. In those days there was only radio ... and *Radio Times*. If it's on - it's in. Everything you need to know about television, satellite and radio programmes can be found in one, easy-to-use magazine: the original. These are *the good new times!*

FM 88-90.2 MHz

Below Brett's editorial was printed a letter from an indignant Mr Haime from Hawkchurch, Devon expressing his regret at:

...the Editor's encroachment on to the Letters section with his picture alongside his large-print comments denying space for the more important opinions of listeners and viewers.

...as ever proving that you can't win 'em all!

FM 90.2-92.4 MHz

From this issue *Radio Times* also had to appear with a new pattern of regional editions. These were:

London	(BBC South East & ITV Thames/LWT)
South-West	(BBC South West & ITV TSW)
West	(BBC West & ITV HTV)
South	(BBC South BBC South-East & ITV TVS)
Midlands	(BBC Midlands & ITV Central)
East Anglia	(BBC East & ITV Anglia)
North West	(BBC North [Manchester] & ITV Granada)
Yorkshire	(BBC North [Leeds] & ITV Yorkshire)
North East	(BBC North [Newcastle] & ITV Tyne Tees)
Borders	(BBC North [Manchester] & ITV Border)
Ulster	(BBC Northern Ireland & ITV Ulster)
Central Scotland	(BBC Scotland & ITV STV)
Grampian	(BBC Scotland & ITV Grampian)
Wales	(BBC Wales & ITV HTV)

FM 92.4-94.6 MHz

MW 693, 909 kHz

Strangely - considering the fact that a detailed billing for the channel had appeared in *RT* right up until the previous week, only a brief summary of S4C programmes appeared in the Wales edition - the main billings were for Channel 4.

The regional editions formed a complicated pattern, which was destined to be rationalised later, as was the almost identical pattern of *TV Times* editions. (TVT had already combined its Wales & West editions into one.)

No edition of either magazine printed detailed programme listings for Channel Television, the ITV contractor based in St Helier, Jersey. This was because Channel continued to publish its own C*TV Times*, which - from this week - also included BBC programmes.

The following week, newsagents offered for sale - for the first time in British history - a range of magazines all providing the listings for *all* the TV and many radio stations.

Alongside *Radio Times* (116 pages - 'still only 50p' - Win! ten hot hatchbacks plus a Kenyan Safari) were *TV Times* (100 pages - 'Half price - 25p') with a horrid cover mostly taken up by the names of the four channels in gigantic red type. Its strapline:

Full details of all the programmes on all the channels

...was clumsy and unmemorable.

Time Out
Issue 1071
27 Feb 91

IPC also launched a cheap 'spoiler' (designed to soak up some of the bottom end of the market) titled *What's On TV*, priced at 35p normally, but for the first 64-page issue was 'Special Price 25p' and came with a free clipboard and pen. Strapline:

The easy way to find out what's on TV

(Nine years later the free pen still works perfectly, by the way.)

Hamfield Publications issued *TV Plus* with its strapline,

It's got the lot!

(76 pages - 45p - Win a car!). *Time Out* (156 pages - £1.20 - Win An Apple Macintosh system, Win A Sony TV & Video), was jubilant at finally winning its battle to carry TV listings. It had an imaginative front cover (more so than any of its rivals) with the team from Channel Four's very popular comedy improvisation show *Whose Line Is It Anyway?* and the headline,

Whose Listings Are They Anyway?

Alongside *Time Out*, which only circulated in the south of England, several regional and national newspapers immediately produced weekend supplements with full TV listings for the week ahead. Three weeks later giant Hamburg-based publishing firm Heinrich Bauer published the first issue of their *TV Quick* (6 pages - 'starter price 10p' - Win a car a week) with the strapline...

Your EASY guide to all the week's TV radio & satellite.

Bauer - who already published the high circulation German *TV Hören und Sehen* - carefully waited a few weeks before entering the UK market, and fuelled the price war by putting *TV Quick* on the bookstands at 10p until 8th June, when it shot up to a realistic 40p.

In fact the price war did not continue for long. *TV Times* remained 'half price' for just a fortnight, but resumed the offer for the first three weeks in June. *What's On TV* reacted to the launch of *TV Quick* by dropping to 10p then returning to 25p in June, rising to 28p in November.

Of the new entrants, *TV Quick* had the best radio listings, and more satellite details than the others. But *Radio Times* had the widest and fullest range of programme details.

Most of the other magazines had gone for a layout familiar to readers of continental programme guides, most of which had for many years carried listings not only for their own country's five, six, or even seven TV channels, but also programmes from neighbouring countries.

July 1991

The common system of presenting programme details had been to eliminate all but the essential billing information (so goodbye to detailed cast lists, production credits, plot synopses) and squeeze as many channels together, side-by-side, each with a gaudy coloured background and large logos at the top of the page. The neighbouring countries' programmes, along with satellite, cable and so forth were usually printed as 'times and titles' in the smallest font available.

The new UK versions didn't carry programmes from any other country but most adapted the continental formula in some way. *Radio Times* chose a rather different route - one which, ironically, was later adopted by some continental programme guides, like *Supertelé* in Spain. (*Radio Times* was a founder member of the European Television Magazines Association - ETMA - whose members shared ideas.)

Newspaper guides grew at an alarming rate - nationals, regionals, locals and freesheets all cobbled together their own 7-day guides, of very varying quality. Once the market had settled down, most were of necessity fairly simple - rather dull- looking efforts with times and titles, synopsese of popular soaps, a few colour pictures of Carol Smillie, and film previews. The *Daily Express* was one of the few papers to study *Radio Times* very carefully, and in its *Saturday* magazine produced an acceptable clone of the original.

These developments were to come over the next few years - in March 1991 nobody knew - or could predict - how the market would swing. But there were bound to be casualties.

Spanish Guide

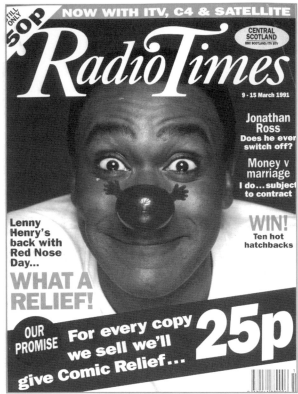

Issue 3507
9 March 1991

Radio Times' response to the price war was clever. Instead of reducing the cover price, for two weeks Brett pledged 25p to the Comic Relief charity for every copy sold - tying up nicely with the cover picture of Lenny Henry in a red nose promoting the marathon Comic Relief broadcasts on BBC-tv.

This not only raised over a million pounds for the charity, but also in December won the Magazine Publishing Award for Best Cover of the Year. The judges said:

The unquestioned winner here. The colour and cover lines were brilliant and the image was very clean. A terrific cover which really stood out."

Alone amongst the listings magazines *Radio Times* continued to print local covers where they were obviously necessary - which continued principally to mean Cup Final covers in May. Once again in 1991, Scotland (both editions) had a different front page from the rest of the UK. This ability to vary the cover would - in time - prove to be a particular strength for *Radio Times*.

The circulation battle continued in earnest. *TV Times* had developed a trick (although they probably called it a 'reader retention device') which involved printing a unique number on each cover and then by means of a premium telephone line, allowing customers to discover whether or not they had won a cash prize. The use of a premium telephone line was significant, because it probably paid for the promotion all by itself.

Radio Times had the technical ability to work the same trick, and from 23rd March to 11th May printed unique numbers on the cover. This game - 'Soundcheque' - had something of a twist, since winning numbers were read out by presenter Mark Goodier during Radio One's top-rated *UK Top 40* programme on Sunday afternoons. Additional numbers were printed in the following week's issue of *RT* thereby using the promotion to boost both the circulation of the magazine, and the audiences for Radio One.

Promoting its journal in this way led - inevitably - to loud howls of outrage from competitors. It just *wasn't fair*, they wept, the BBC *can't* use its own radio and television stations to promote its own journal.

The upshot of this was that the BBC were forced to drop their in-house 'commercials' - not just for *Radio Times* but for all their publications. They were still allowed brief (ten-second) announcements over a still picture of the cover, but these announcements had to acknowledge that "other listings magazines are available."

Radio Times responded by buying advertising time on ITV. This and other promotional activities - plus a consistently high quality magazine ensured that *RT* kept its head well above the waterline. Others didn't. The first casualty was *TV Plus* whose owners, Hamfield Publications, closed down after less than a handful of issues. Gillian de Bono thus goes into history as the unfortunate editor of the shortest-lived TV programme journal in British history!

Setting price wars aside, one of the biggest problems confronting the brand new listings industry was that of the regional editions. Put simply, many of them just weren't viable. In the golden monopoly days *TV Times* had somehow managed to sustain editions serving very small areas, but only because theirs was the sole means of obtaining advance programme information.

Now viewers in Carlisle, for example, had a choice of four magazines and probably five or six newspaper guides. This meant that any one publication had a very much smaller share of the local market - and the Border Television area covered only 170,000 homes.

Already many of the new guides had fewer editions than *Radio Times*. *What's On TV* had from the start combined STV, Grampian and Border; Wales and the West of England; the Midlands and East Anglia; Yorkshire and the North-East. *TV Plus* had even included Ulster TV in the Scottish edition, as others did later.

Radio Times reduced the number of regional editions in July. It eliminated the Grampian, Borders and Wales editions. The ITV programmes of Grampian, STV and Border now shared the Scotland edition with Border also appearing in the North-East edition. With HTV now providing similar English-language programmes in both Wales and the West of England, the new Wales/West edition made sense. It also took the opportunity to increase the billing space and details for S4C by cutting down on the detail in the Channel 4 billings in that edition, and allowing S4C to share some of its space.

The listings monopoly had also been broken in the Irish Republic, where the *RTÉ Guide* now faced competition from both sides of the Irish Sea. *Radio Times* rebadged its Ulster edition as the 'Ireland edition' and incorporated detailed billings for the Irish State broadcaster's two channels, RTÉ-1 and Network 2. These occupied the lower half of the three columns devoted to ITV billings in other editions. Since most of Northern Ireland could also receive RTÉ's transmissions this arrangement seemed a useful one. Meanwhile *RTÉ Guide* now also details all the BBC, ITV and Channel 4 programmes as well as those it was already including for cable and satellite channels.

CTV Times
Vol. 23
Issue 42
19 Oct 1991

In the Channel Islands the situation was more difficult. Some 32,000 households now had to choose whether to go on buying the 60-page black and white *CTV Times* for 50p, or one of the four major guides.... or a newspaper. It didn't seem to make much difference that only *CTV Times* gave details of local programmes, since Channel TV's local opt-outs were mainly for the news programme *Channel Report* whose start time could reliably be predicted.

It spelled the end of the last regional ITV magazine. *CTV Times* had survived the IBA's intervention in 1968 but could no longer survive without its listings monopoly. It published its last issue in October. In it Channel Television's Managing Director John Henwood wrote a brief obituary:

> We felt there would continue to be a niche for an entirely local publication but too few Channel Islanders agreed. The increased number of rival TV magazines some with heavily subsidised cover prices has damaged our circulation. This, in turn, has made it more difficult to earn advertising revenue in an already well supplied local market.
>
> In short, *CTV Times* had ceased to be profitable.
>
> It remains only for me to thank faithful subscribers and advertisers for their support over the years.

Only *Radio Times* acknowledged the existence of Channel Television by adding it to the cover flash of its South edition - although CTV's programmes were still only given in skeleton form in that edition.

The circulation figures for the first half of 1992 showed how the cake had been cut. Total average weekly sales for the 'big four' magazines were 4.7 million. *Radio Times* led the pack with 1.5 million weekly copies; *What's On TV* was close on its heels with 1.4 million; then *TV Times* with 1.1 million; Bauer's *TV Quick* with just 700,000. *RT*'s circulation may have dropped, but it was weathering the storm.

*   *   *   *   *

Gary Smith

Denis Healey
by Gary Smith
Issue 3545

More reader inducements were offered in the summer, with *Radio Times* dangling the carrot of five brand new Vauxhall Nova GSi cars as prizes - this time instead of hearing winning numbers on the radio, readers had to trot along to their local Vauxhall garage to listen to a cassette of Radio 2 presenter Derek Jameson reading the numbers out!

With the start of the new TV season in September, *Radio Times* brought the satellite listings into the main body of programme pages. These were rationalised slightly, with Children's Channel and MTV now warranting a brief mention of their general content rather than specific listings. Now the daytime pair of pages started with satellite - then BBC1 and 2, then ITV and C4 and finally the evening *At A Glance* section. The editorial features on programme pages were (temporarily) banished, but the programme billings were enhanced and a number of peak time programmes were given the kind of detail that they had enjoyed in monopoly days.

Issue 3545
30 Nov 1991

Special editions continued to exist - the Rugby World Cup in October warranted a 24- page supplement, for example.

Various printing devices were used to attract attention to the magazine on bookstalls - a small flier, stapled to the main body of the book was regularly used to point up the increasing number of prize competitions and special offers. A hatchback car was offered in October, and in November a free CD of music by Mozart. Rather than taping a disc to the cover (as many magazines now did) *RT* achieved a great deal of market research by asking readers to return a coupon containing their name and address in exchange for the disc.

Radio Times continued to pursue the high ground when it came to covers. In November it dressed TV presenter Esther Rantzen as a leather-clad punk, complete with pink hair to promote her new series *Heart of Gold*.

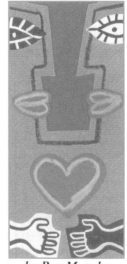

by Bee Murphy
From issue 3545

CAUGHT ON CAMERA SPECIAL

It was the *RT* party of the year, just before Christmas, when we presented the stars with the covers that featured them in 1995. Master of ceremonies Chris Barrie transformed himself into misbegotten leisure centre manager Gordon Brittas for the night, while BBC chairman Marmaduke Hussey helped *RT* editor Nicholas Brett hand out the framed covers. And businessman Stanley Silver declared it a glittering occasion after his £5,000 donation to Children in Need gained him a special invitation – watch out for his My Kind of Day in a forthcoming issue.

"I do not believe it!" Richard Wilson feigns modest surprise at gaining his second Victor Meldrew cover. Marmaduke Hussey (centre) and *RT* editor Nicholas Brett help him cope with the shock

A VE Day to remember: Patricia Garcia told *RT* of her "wonderful surprise" at recognising her sister Jeannie Lebby on *RT*'s anniversary cover. Aged four in 1945, Jeannie, sadly, died shortly after the picture was taken

Your leisure centre or mine? MC Gordon Brittas (also known as Chris Barrie) gets into a *Dangerfield* liaison with Amanda Redman

In a spirit of matrimonial reconciliation *Casualty*'s Julia Watson and Robert Duncan display matching his 'n' hers covers

They went thataway. Patricia Routledge in Hyacinth mode tastefully asks *Food and Drink*'s Oz Clarke and producer Peter Bazalgette where to find the canapes

"Thnska!" Carol Vorderman gets her vowels and consonants all mixed up in a moving but largely incomprehensible acceptance speech

"I'll show you mine if you show me yours." *EastEnders*' Patsy Palmer and Gillian Taylforth both claim, correctly, they woz framed

Is there a doctor in the house? *RT*'s Mark Porter, with his wife Ros, was on hand to provide counselling for any cases of "party tummy". It was a busy night.

Just before Christmas, the Magazine Publishing Awards named *Radio Times* as 'Magazine of the Year' saying "the quality of editorial and imaginative covers made it a popular winner." It had held on to its circulation with around six million loyal readers.

At Christmas time the Magazine of the Year held what was to become an annual party, inviting all those who had graced its front cover during the previous twelve months. Stars went home clutching a framed copy of their appearance. It became a status symbol to be invited to the *RT* covers party, and after the first couple of years the parties themselves became the subject of an annual *Radio Times* feature illustrated with lots of photographs of the stars mingling in the Sixth Floor Suite in London's Television Centre.

RadioTimes

Mr Marmaduke Hussey, Chairman of the BBC, requests the pleasure of the company of

Tony Currie

at a reception to present

RADIO TIMES COVERS

on Wednesday 13 December 1995 at 6pm in the Sixth Floor Suite, Television Centre Wood Lane, London W12

RSVP
Nicholas Brett, Radio Times, Room A1179, Woodlands, 80 Wood Lane, London W12 0TT, Tel: (0181) 576 3120

This is a personal invitation. Please bring it with you.

Christmas cover by Paul Slater   Issue 3548   21 Dec 1991

The seasonal Double Issue itself, with Paul Slater's Father Christmas on the cover, was the largest ever printed so far - 180 pages plus a 16-page Thomson Holidays brochure bound in. Radio 2's "Ideal Home" competition offered a £7,000 cash prize. The prize for completing the Christmas crossword was a camcorder.

Inside were the now familiar features - *My TV Dinner* in which each week a celebrity chose the dish they most often chomped on while watching the box - Bruce Forsyth admitted to a passion for toasted cheese. *What I Watch* was a similar feature asking stars to nominate their favourite programmes; Noel Edmonds choice was *Only Fools and Horses*. The 'A - Z of children's classics' came to an end with *Zoo Time*. Seventeen pages of film preview; 20 pages of Holidays with all that lucrative advertising; Libby Purves with a thoughtful piece on the traditions of Christmas. There was the Order of Service for Radio 4's annual broadcast of *Nine Lessons and Carols*. Scottish edition pages with their own headings for 'Hogmanay' rather than 'New Year's Eve'. And it was Audrey Hepburn's *Kind of Day*.

by Kam Tang
The Tailor of Panama
26 July 1997

by Nick Foot
BBC Proms 97
26 July 1997

by Tess Roberts
BBC Proms 97
26 July 1997

by Clifford Harper
What If?
20 June 1998

by Philip Disley
Over the Moon
4 July 1998

by Bill Sanderson
Opera on 3
11 July 1998

by Andy Bridge
Cat among the Pigeons
11 July 1998

by Geoff Grandfield
BBC Proms 98
25 July 1998

by Daniel Pudles
La Clemenza di Tito
29 May 1999

by David Junper
Devonia
5 June 1999

12a Easter cover 1999
Photograph by Sven Arnstein
Illustration by Jenny Tilden-Wright

by Brent Hardy-Smith
Albertina   12 June 1999

1970s

SPECIAL ISSUE From TV and film to fashion and food, we join
BBC2's celebration of this outrageous decade

12b   Elton's shoe from the 1970s   July 2000
Cover by James Johnson

by Caroline Thomson
The Summer of a Dormouse
12 June 1999

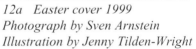

by Debbie Lush
The Green Detectives
26 June 1999

by Simon Bartram
Choice
3 December 2000

In February 1992 Britain celebrated 40 years of Queen Elizabeth II's reign, and *Radio Times* produced a Royal Souvenir Issue with its masthead printed in gold (a colour requiring a very expensive ink to reproduce) over a monochrome photograph of Her Majesty, taken by Dorothy Wilding in 1952. Eleven pages of features and photographs inside included a large picture of the Queen sitting in Buckingham Palace watching TV with a copy of *Radio Times* prominently sitting on top of the set!

Issue 3561   28 March 1992

In March *Radio Times* marked the demise of the BBC's once despised rival Radio Luxembourg with a major feature tied to a BBC2 documentary. Changed days. And Harry Enfield advised readers not to buy whatever was sitting alongside *RT* on the newsagent's counter...

A General Election in April put Peter Snow and his 'swingometer' on the cover and *RT* included a separate 16-page A4 colour *Election 92* magazine and 8 pages of summer film previews.

Photo by Dorothy Wilding
Issue 3553   1 Feb 1992

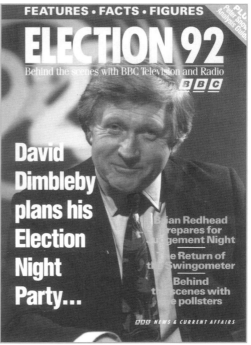

Issue 3572   13 June 1992

Paul McCartney's 50th birthday also warranted a special issue in June (Mick Jagger was similarly honoured in July 1993), and in July Nicholas Brett introduced another 'star' columnist with a page each week devoted to the opinions of the BBC's social affairs correspondent, Polly Toynbee. The new football season was marked with another 16-page A4 supplement this time produced in association with Sky Television whose deal with the BBC saw the two broadcasters sharing coverage of England's FA Premier League.

Photo by Harry Goodwin
Issue 3572   13 June 1992

Issue 3593   29 Aug 1992

by Mick Brownfield   Issue 3599   19 Dec 1992

An outrageous cover appearance by Dame Edna Everage (aka Barry Humphries) in August - the first lady of Oz sported a unique pair of *RT* spectacles.....

The vastly increased satellite and cable audience demanded more listings. So to compete better with magazines like *Cable Guide* and *Satellite TV Europe,* from 5th September, *Radio Times* devoted two pages a day to satellite listings. This meant that the TV billings were now spread over six pages - creating more space for daytime listings for the four terrestrial channels.

There was now room for detailed billings for Sky Movies, The Movie Channel, Sky Sports, Eurosport, Screensport, Sky One, The Comedy Channel, Lifestyle, and The Children's Channel. Times and Titles were given for Sky News, CNN, MTV, Bravo, Discovery, The Learning Channel and Superchannel, and brief generic descriptions of TV Asia, AsiaVision, HVC and The Adult Channel.

In the autumn, *RT* produced another 16-page booklet in conjunction with UCI cinemas, previewing the major movies of the season and incorporating a two-for-one cinema ticket offer.

A cookery promotion (for six weeks starting in October) gave away free 'wipe clean' cookery cards written by TV chef Michael Barry. And, as the cover stars swilled champagne at their annual party, another record was broken with a massive 212-page double issue. Its gatefold cover - Mick Brownfield was the artist - folded out to reveal a three-page advertisement for the new ITV breakfast company GMTV. For the first time the Christmas programme page decorations were credited - to Francesca Pelizzoni.

Seventeen pages of film previews were carefully placed with most of those pages facing advertisements, compensating for the absence of any ads on the programme pages. Satellite and cable listings had been further enhanced - they now incorporated the channel logos and proper listings for TV Asia and AsiaVision. This had been done at the expense of mention of The Adult Channel and HVC, both of which showed soft porn and were considered to be unsuitable for inclusion in *RT*.

In the new multichannel world those who controlled listings of what was available would increasingly hold the balance of power over audiences. A new channel could be guaranteed more viewers if its programmes were included in a top selling magazine - and equally could be denied viewers if they were *not* told of its existence.

Radio Times pages also bade farewell (in the appropriate editions) to ITV companies TV-am, Thames, Television SouthWest and Television South - and, on 1st January 1993, included the first programmes of GMTV, Carlton, Westcountry TV and Meridian.

1992 covers
Page 210
Issue 3599

From that day *Radio Times* billings also included "VideoPlus+™" code numbers for each programme which allowed viewers with suitably equipped video recorders to enter just the programme's number to ensure that the machine would set its timer to tape the show. There was a prize of a TV set satellite receiver and VideoPlus+™ recorder to be won in the trivia quiz, and lots of advertisements for VideoPlus+™ machines.

And for the first time a montage of all the year's covers occupied the inside back page.

Amongst the eye-catching covers the following year was the 'Love' number celebrating Valentine's Day which also had a tiny 16-page 'Comic Relief' fundraising kit attached to the outside of the magazine.

The Easter issue - although including 7 day listings as usual - added the Good Friday TV movies to its films guide and, in return for tokens collected over four issues, offered a free children's cassette with readings of extracts from classic children's books and radio programmes.

Issue 3606   13 Feb 1993

211

Issue 3617   1 May 1993

Brett's vision of *Radio Times* was not only as the superior listings magazine, but as a rounded magazine with opinionated columnists, interviews and features. He was well on his way to achieving this - but there were still some elements to come.

Delia Smith was one of them. She had appeared many times in the magazine before, and not only were her cookery books best sellers, she appeared to have almost single-handedly galvanised a lethargic nation into reaching for the seasoning and the heavy-based pan. In May '93 she began a ten-week BBC2 series, which coincided with the start of her regular recipe column in *RT*. She was also the subject - that week - of *The Andrew Duncan Interview*.

This feature had been introduced to allow veteran journalist Duncan to probe in detail the lives of the very famous, for which he generally got a page and a half plus a full-page photograph. These interviews often yielded hitherto unknown secrets about their subjects, which would be turned into press releases giving the *Radio Times* advance publicity as never before.

Photo by Cecil Beaton Issue 3621 29 May 1993

Scotland's annual cover appeared as usual at the time of the FA Cup Final - this time it wasn't football-related as BBC Scotland weren't screening the Scottish Cup Final, so actor and fisherman *extraordinaire,* Paul Young, made an appearance promoting his popular *Hooked on Scotland* series.

The 40th Anniversary of the Coronation was an obvious case for a Souvenir Issue, and the cover of this 132-page issue featured an official colour portrait of Her Majesty on the throne, by official photographer Cecil Beaton. Ten pages of special features included a chance to see the Coronation cover again, as well as Cecil W. Bacon's illustration of the procession route. He got a credit for this a mere 40 years later!

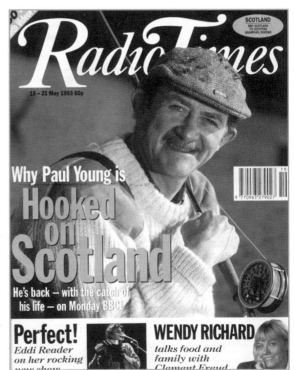

*Issue 3619
15 May 1993
Scotland
edition*

The following week it was time for the radio pages to get a makeover. The Local Radio pages incorporated the weekly 'Frequency Guide', which now included all stations available on the local dial. Virgin, Classic FM and the BBC World Service had their space on the daily pages making this the most comprehensive guide to radio listings available anywhere.

In September, *RT* celebrated its 70th Anniversary. Given that past anniversaries had often either gone unnoticed or been celebrated in a minimal way, it was all the more surprising that *RT* really pushed the boat out this time. The inside front page folded out to allow the front cover of issue 1 to sit side by side with the 70th Anniversary cover - and on the reverse side a hundred covers with a list of 'facts' about *RT* over seven decades. Jane Asher had produced an edible wireless cake in celebration, and Arthur C Clarke introduced an eight-page section looking at the future of television and the media with a handful of celebrities from Melvyn Bragg to Mary Whitehouse recalling the best and worst moments in broadcasting.

A new feature appeared - *That was the week....* which looked back at a *Radio Times* from the past, and the week of programmes it covered. Mark Lewisohn produced the weekly item, and for the illustrations the BBC often had to borrow copies of back numbers from collector Wallace Grevatt, a retired schoolteacher whose complete collection of issues had been started as research for his book on the history of the BBC's *Children's Hour*.

Back numbers were not exactly in plentiful supply. A stock of past issues had been kept by BBC Publications, but many of those had been destroyed as a result of enemy bombing during the war.

Issue 3638
25 Sept 1993
Plate 10a

However, when *Radio Times* began, John Reith had issued instructions that five copies of each issue should be preserved for posterity. And, dutifully, five copies were set aside, and wrapped by book packers in kraft paper and sealed with brown gummed tape to protect the contents from the acidity in the air. As the number of editions increased the order was interpreted to mean five copies of *each edition*, and so the number of neat brown parcels increased rapidly. *The Listener, World Radio* and *London Calling* were also wrapped and stored.

Reith left no clues as to when posterity might be deemed to have arrived, permitting the archive to be opened. The magazines were stored - along with assorted BBC books - at the BBC's enormous 150,000 square foot warehouse in Bermondsey, one of the largest in south London. The saving of these issues was not allowed during the war years but BBC staff still faithfully sent their own copies to Bermondsey when they had finished with them.

A small transport and distribution company, Longstone (set up in 1981 by Alex Taylor and his son Paul) had been doing work for the BBC for some years when in 1988 BBC Enterprises decided to dispose of the warehouse. Its upkeep was now more than the Corporation could justify. Longstone acquired the fixtures and fittings, including wonderful hand-made packing benches crafted from four-inch oak. When Taylor and his son came to remove the fittings they discovered sixty-five year stash neatly in the pigeon-hole shelving. Upon enquiring as to what should be done with this hoard he was offered the superfluous 40 tons of newsprint for a modest additional sum!

The deal was done and the back numbers moved to another warehouse in London from where many were quickly flogged to specialist dealers. The remainder were moved again, this time to Longstones's 7,000 square foot warehouse in Rochester where it took a year to re-sort and catalogue them, all spread out over the warehouse floor.

Little effort was made to market these old magazines: for the first 18 months the Taylors dealt only with customers referred by the BBC. A number of the keenest collectors became regular customers - the inevitable *Dr Who* collectors (known as Whovians) prominent among them.

Geoff Thompson with some of his 2,000 copies

Geoff Thompson was one who was prepared to risk his neck climbing ladders that didn't quite reach the top of the mountain!

Longstone needed the space at Rochester, and so the peripatetic *Radio Times* (and their cousins) journeyed again - this time to Bristol where they spent a year before moving back to Rochester.

The Taylors advertised the back issues as birthday and anniversary souvenirs. They did a respectable amount of business for a while but lacked the enthusiasm necessary to seriously market the stock, and ultimately decided that there was insufficient return to justify the cost of the space they occupied.

Photo by Norman Young

Len Kelly

In the Spring of 1999 second-hand book dealer Len Kelly, together with collector David Bishop, purchased the lot from Paul Taylor and his father. Bishop kept a near complete set, and Len Kelly (specialist in publications in broadcasting and mass media) set about making the stock available once more to the wider public. Len's illustrated catalogues of *Radio Times* (two so far) are already collectors items in their own right!

*   *   *   *   *

There are a number of us enthusiasts, dedicated to the pursuit of aging bundles of newsprint.

Wallace Grevatt has devoted many years to a serious study of the BBC's Children's hour culminating in the publication of a definitive book on the subject, *BBC Children's Hour* (published by The Book Guild Ltd, Lewes, Sussex). Along the way Wallace, who lives in Brighton, has built up a complete collection of all the issues ever published and has contributeed to many works on the subject, notably the book *The Art of Radio Times*.

Other collectors are spread across Britain. Amongst the most dedicated are: Robert Barr in Kilwinning; Roger Bickerton in Harrogate; David Bishop in Llanwarne, Herefordshire; Penny Fabb in Maidenhead; Norman Graham in Limerick; Christopher Hill in Norwich; Peter Lord in Hull; Jim Palm in Salisbury; Vic Pickard in Burnley; Michael Rounce in Norwich; Edward Rowlinson in Blackpool; David Ryder in Aldershot; Les Sheehan in Lincoln; Geoff Thompson in Birmingham.

*   *   *   *   *

In the Autumn, veteran DJ John Peel joined the *Radio Times* writing team to contribute a quirky weekly column titled *Family Album*, illustrated by a cartoon from Kipper Williams. Brett's pride in his star 'team' led him to list them on the cover of 9th October. They were: Sue Arnold (who wrote general features from time to time) - Clement Freud (who entertained a star to a meal once a week and wrote of the conversation that ensued) - Geoff Hamilton (Gardening) - Barry Norman (Films) - John Peel (*Family Album*) - Libby Purves (another regular feature writer) - Delia Smith (Cookery) - Polly Toynbee (controversial columnist) - Patric Walker (Astrologer).

Still to join were Dr Mark Porter (of Classic FM) with his weekly health column, children's presenter Andi Peters with pages for young readers and Alan Hansen's sports column.

A special edition of *Dr Who* produced in 3D for the annual *Children in Need* charity broadcasts gave *Radio Times* the excuse it needed to once more run a *Dr Who* cover. This one featured all the Doctors with the exception of the original - William Hartnell - who had died.

Issue 3646   20 Nov 1993

Nicholas Brett's efforts were recognised not only by the readers, but by his peers - he was voted 'Editor of the Year' by the British Society of Magazine Editors.

Mick Brownfield's gap-toothed carol singer on the Christmas cover was not to everyone's taste but the issue sold its usual numbers. The 220 pages included 18 pages of films, and Jilly Goolden's advice on which bottles of bubbly to buy. Sue Townsend wrote a new *Adrian Mole* story and for the second year the issue ended with a montage of that year's covers.

by Mick Brownfield From cover of issue 3650 18 Dec 1993

1993 covers Page 219 Above issue

In January a new cover idea received its first tryout - a half-page was folded to form a flap over the front cover which could be used to promote a special offer and then removed to reveal a different picture below.

Issue 3652
8 Jan 1994
With & without
front flap

Other original ideas included Dawn French stealing the letter 'm' from Times for the *M is for Murder Most Horrid* cover, and a 50th Birthday portrait of New Zealand born opera singer Kiri te Kanawa. But possibly one of the most original (and daring) covers ever created was produced to celebrate the relaunch of Radio 5 as "5 Live" the new rolling news-and-sport radio channel. Using modern technology, Nelson Mandela, Bill and Hilary Clinton, Boris Yeltsin, John Major and Benazir Bhutto appeared to be photographed as a group, all wearing nice new '5 Live' t-shirts.

The cover was the work of Sven Arnstein, with Jones Bloom's electronic retouching. Once upon a time even this information would have been considered unnecessary to pass on to the reader, but we were also told that the sportswear came from Lilywhites and the footwear courtesy of John Lewis. (What would Reith have said? He'd probably have considered the Easter cover - with comedy actor Leslie Nielsen perched on the back of a motorcycle being driven by a giant chicken - as tasteless.)

by Sven Arnstein   *5 Live is live!*
Issue 3663   26 March 1994

Issue 3663

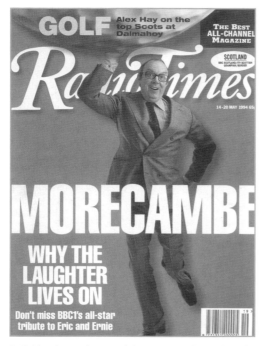

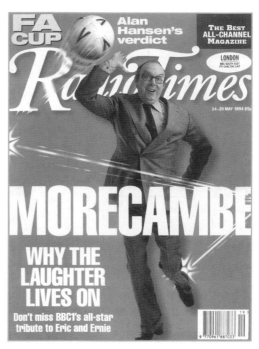

The use of electronic trickery to manipulate images was by now extremely sophisticated. So much so that, as you will see from the two covers below, it was possible to move the arm of the late Eric Morecambe to suit his pose when adapting the cover design for the Scottish edition....

Issue 3670
London & Scotland
editions

While the other guides now often duplicated each other's covers - simply because they all relied on the same press releases from TV companies, and the plot lines of current 'soaps' often dictated what would be on the cover - *Radio Times* maintained its tradition of surprising readers from time to time. Two rather contrasting examples from 1994 were the D-Day cover in June with the prominent words of Churchill printed in white on a red background; and the "Horror Special" cover in August by Ian McKinnell.

D-Day remembered   Issue 3673   4 June 1994

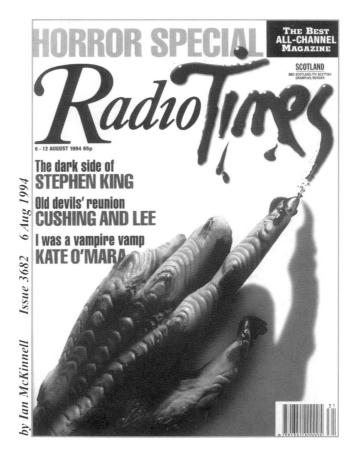

Issue 3682   6 Aug 1994
by Ian McKinnell

Radio Times received a revamp in September 1994. Using as little hyperbole as possible, Nicholas Brett described the changes:

> By increasing our TV coverage by 20%, I've been able to give each of the television days an extra page. No other UK newspaper or magazine has more width and depth. *Radio Times* is the broadcasting magazine.
>
> Yet at the same time we've made the magazine easier to use. We've removed the single-page advertisements from the listings section signposted the days more boldly and generally tidied up.
>
> Similarly for the many of you who are 'light' viewers and listeners because of your busy lifestyles we've picked out more prominently the day's 'choices'. We've even provided you with a one-page snapshot of the week's best terrestrial TV, satellite films and radio where you want it - up-front on page 3.

(Just a smattering of hyperbole, would you agree?)

The free *Radio Times* BT phonecard (with six tokens - four Kipper Williams designs to choose from) was the seasonal bribe to new readers. And the masthead was given a 'tidying-up' by squashing the lettering slightly and adding a drop shadow.

The redesign was - with just a few adjustments - to survive beyond the century. The '*today's choices*' section at the start of the TV billings for each day highlighted a small handful of programmes genuinely recommended by the *RT* writers, still anonymous. Later they would be allowed to attach their initials to the paragraphs.

A brief satellite 'choice' followed on the two pages devoted to those listings, with a chronological movie planner detailing hour-by-hour all the movies available on cable & satellite channels. This resulted in yet another size increase. From 20 pages in 1944, to 164 pages in 1994.

And a truly nostalgic Christmas cover in 1994 as Bob Venables redrew the cover by artist 'Abbey' from 70 years earlier. Changes in fashion demanded only a couple of alterations to the original.

by Abbey
Issue 65
19 Dec 1924

by Bob Venables
Issue 3701
17 Dec 1994

From Valentine's Day 1995, another national radio station was added to the daily radio pages with the launch of *Talk Radio*. And in March Carol Vorderman joined the ranks of *RT* star writers with her weekly science column.

The daffodils were back at last - the Easter cover 1995 had plenty of yellow blooms as it advertised Geoff Hamilton's 16-page Gardening Supplement.

Issue 3717   15 April 1995

Having celebrated the anniversary of D-Day the previous year, *RT* recalled VE Day in a souvenir issue in May 95. There was a sad story about the little four-year-old girl on the cover. She had died of meningitis just five days after the photograph was taken by a passing American serviceman who later sold it to a photo library.

VJ Day was also commemorated in August.

VE Day Souvenir
Issue 3720   6 May 1995

A rare opportunity to change the strapline regionally came in May (Cup Final time as you must be well aware) when the edition north of Hadrian's Wall carried the strap...

Although purchased primarily for its content, *Radio Times* was still able to use the magic touch of its Art Editor, Mike Clowes, to sell extra copies on the strength of its cover alone. *RT* had exploited the immense popularity of television's soap operas since the days of *The Grove Family* in 1955. *Compact*, *The Newcomers*, *United*, and even the short-lived *Eldorado* had all received their fair share of front-page pictures.

But under Clowes' direction, these were elevated to an art form. Some of Britain's greatest photographers were commissioned to make the soap stars look like top models. Following the 'glamorisation' of *EastEnders'* actress, Wendy Richard, there were two memorable covers featuring her colleagues - Patsy Palmer (who played Bianca) was photographed in a seductive pose by David Bailey, and Gillian Taylforth (in the role of Kathy Mitchell) was photographed by Patrick Lichfield.

Photograph by David Bailey
Issue 3735   19 Aug 1995

Photograph by Patrick Lichfield
Issue 3765   23 March 1996

Issue 3773   2 Sept 1995

The printers had obviously laid in enormous stocks of gold ink, because following the impact of the gold-topped Royal Souvenir Issue in 1992, *RT* used gold as a background for the New Season issue in September 1995, featuring Patricia Routledge in character as Hyacinth Bucket.

RT readers now had the opportunity to put a face to the star features writer who - despite protests - found her picture now adorning the assorted features she wrote under the umbrella *Alison Graham at Large*.

RT also made the most of its cookery columnist, Delia Smith. When Delia's *Winter Collection* of recipes appeared, Delia was given the cover for the start of the series, and then occupied a third of the front cover every week for the next five weeks, returning after Christmas for a further appearance. Nobody had ever appeared on six consecutive covers before!

1995 was, apparently, the last Christmas issue to be edited by Nick Brett - 220 pages and even Mick Brownfield's Father Christmas cover had a reference to Delia on it. Note the ring that the old guy is wearing....

Issue 3752
Page 219

Left: (top to bottom)
John Peel,
Geoff Hamilton,
Polly Toynbee,
Barry Norman,
Emma Norman

Right: (left to right)
Dr Mark Porter,
Andi Peters,
Alan Hansen,
Delia Smith

[Notably missing:
Andrew Duncan,
Alison Graham]

by Mick Brownfield
Issue 3752   16 Dec 1995

On its inside back page, instead of a montage of covers, readers were treated to the sight of the magazine's star writers (well, most of them) dressed immaculately, and toasting the New Year. It was probably the first time in the 70-year history that the writers had been pictured together in this way.

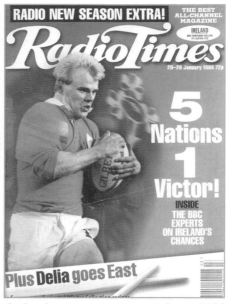

West/Wales	*Scotland*	*Ireland*	**Issue 3756** **20 Jan 1996**

In January, the first batch of regional covers for many years came with the Five Nations Rugby tournament. Separate covers were produced for the English editions, the Wales/West edition, the Ireland edition and the Scotland edition.

Another excuse to put the Queen on the cover came with a Royal Birthday Souvenir issue in April 1996. Her Majesty was 70 - so out came the gold again for the masthead. Inside *Radio Times* continued its serialised adaptation of Catrine Clay's book *Princess to Queen*, and of course there was *another* chance to reprint the Coronation Cover!

Issue 3771
4 May 1996

Issue 3769   20 April 1996

An imaginative use of archives was made in May when Carla Lane's situation comedy *The Liver Birds* returned to BBC1 for the first time since 1978. On the cover the show's stars - Polly James and Nerys Hughes - were pictured looking at the first *RT* cover they had appeared on in February 1972. Inside, Gordon Burn, who had interviewed them for that '70s issue, talked to the pair once again.

Doctor Who not only got back on the cover a fortnight later (in the guise of Paul McGann who appeared in the new feature-length episode) but earned himself a 16- page A4 pull-out souvenir which traced the show's history and included illustrations of all the *Radio Times* covers that had ever featured the Time Lord. The following week, *RT* began a weekly strip cartoon featuring the nemesis of the Daleks on its brand-new *Science Fiction* page. It was written by Gary Russell (who wrote the novel of the film) and drawn by Lee Sullivan, who also drew for the *Doctor Who Magazine*.

From this issue, the programmes of *Virgin Radio* and *Talk Radio* no longer appeared in the radio pages. The width of the Radio 3 columns was increased to mirror that of Radio 4, and thus the width of the Radios 1 and 2 columns (and Classic FM) was reduced. Nick Brett described altering the radio pages as "like handling gelignite".

Issue 3774
25 May 1996
16-page **Time Lord**
souvenir inside

As usual, sport figured largely in the summer issues, with a 16-page guide to the Euro 96 football in June and lots more gold for the Olympics cover. But perhaps one of the riskiest covers appeared at the end of July - commemorating 15 years since the wedding of Prince Charles and Lady Diana Spencer. The cover appeared to show Princess Diana reading the *RT* Royal Wedding Issue from 1981.

But of course it was a lookalike - model Christine Hance, who herself was the subject of a BBC2 documentary, talked inside to Alison Graham.

Princess Diana lookalike - Christine Hance
Issue 3783   27 July 1996

Geoff Hamilton's last Gardening page appeared on 10th August 1996. The following week, readers were stunned to read of his sudden death at the age of 60. He had been taking part in a charity cycle ride and had suffered a heart attack. The BBC2 programme *Gardeners' World* which he'd presented for seventeen years had been hugely popular. Its producer, Gay Search, wrote in the *RT* tribute the following week of the many letters, faxes and phone calls the production company had received, including a call from an 85-year old man in tears.

Hamilton had been a full time nurseryman and landscape gardener until a chance meeting with the editor of *Garden News* in 1970 had given him the opportunity to write about his passion. He became a weekly columnist for that paper before joining *RT* in 1989 as the first of Brett's new team of star writers.

Nick Brett wrote:

Geoffrey Hamilton
Issue 3786
17 Aug 1996

Geoff encouraged millions of us with just the faintest streak of green on our fingers to get outside and have a go. We achieved things we never dreamed possible. He made gardening accessible. He was simply the best.

*   *   *   *   *

In September, eight years to the day since he first became editor, Nicholas Brett bade readers farewell as he vacated his office (clutching his second 'Editor of the Year' award - this time from the PPA).

This is the last time I'll get up at dawn on Friday to write the editor's letter. I'm moving upstairs - well, down the corridor actually - to become publisher of *Radio Times*.

My first task as publisher has proved remarkably easy - finding the new editor. Sue Robinson, my deputy for six years, will be only the magazine's twelfth editor in nearly 73 years and the first woman to get the job.

What's she like? She's a brilliant journalist and a fan of quality television and radio. She helped me design and build the new, all-channel *RT* to weather the competition that arrived when the Government removed our exclusive right to publish the BBC's weekly schedule of programmes in March 1991. And she's been a key part of the magazine's success ever since.

At the same time Brett announced the departure of award-winning Art Director, Mike Clowes, who was moving to the brave new technology world of BBC Online as its first Creative Director.

It was to be - in Nick's own words - "the start of a new *Radio Times* era".

CHAPTER THIRTEEN
2000 ...

feel like a kid with the keys to the toy shop. It's my first week in the editor's chair and if I can't indulge myself now, when can I?"

Sue Robinson

Sue Robinson's first issue was not, of course, the self-indulgent fantasy of which she wrote in her first editorial. In fact, apart from her photograph atop the editorial letter, there were no signs of any upheaval. Since Sue had been responsible for much of the magazine anyway this was hardly surprising.

Robinson had trained as a reporter at a journalism college, and on local newspapers in Essex, graduating to sub-editor after a few years before moving to magazines. In 1979 she'd joined *Woman,* one of the IPC's best known titles. As she puts it,

Issue 3791   21 Sept 1996

"There are only so many suntan and diet stories one can stand, so I decided to follow my interest in television and apply for jobs on *Radio Times* and *TV Times*. I got interviews on both, but RT offered me the job first!"

Issue 3793
5 Oct 1996

Her first role with the paper (in 1980) was as a Features Sub-editor. She worked her way up - becoming Chief Sub, then Features Editor, then Deputy editor before taking on the top job.

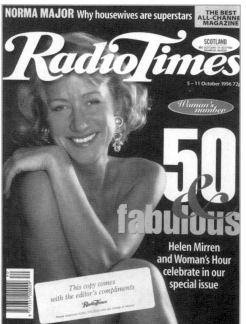

One tradition, which had vanished with the outbreak of war, was revived by Robinson - the Women's Number. With a startling nude photograph of actress Helen Mirren (by Sven Arnstein) and the caption "50 and Fabulous" this was truly groundbreaking. A nude on the cover of *RT*? And a 50-year old nude at that? And the decision of a woman editor?

The real hook for the celebration was the 50th anniversary of *Woman's Hour*, but inside Robinson pulled out all the stops. A list of 'First Ladies of Broadcasting' (First announcer, first TV producer, first soap star....) a flashback to the keep fit supplements with Eileen Fowler (now aged 90 and still as fit as ever); a handful of colourful 'Women's Number' covers from the '30s... and that was just the first two pages!

John Peel's column was handed over to his wife Sheila for the week. The 'Spotlight' feature looked at the highest paid woman in television - Oprah Winfrey. Andrew Duncan interviewed Norma Major, the Prime Minister's wife. Janet Street-Porter counted the number of famous women who had just reached their half-century. Along with Janet herself, the feature included photographs of 37 eminent ladies. Of course, there was a feature on *Woman's Hour*. And Alison Graham interviewed actor and sex-symbol Neil Pearson (it was a woman's number after all....).

BBC Television celebrated its sixtieth anniversary in November. The Special Issue (headed Shameless Nostalgia!) featured Jennifer Saunders and Joanna Lumley on the cover as Edina and Patsy from the comedy series *Absolutely Fabulous*. Inside nine striking specially commissioned photographs reunited the casts of classic programmes - *Z Cars*, *Nationwide*, *Dallas*, *Tiswas*, *Hill Street Blues*, *Man About the House*, *The Onedin Line* and *The Young Ones*. And there was even a special offer of a nostalgic CD of music from the BBC television test card! (Flyback records cat. no. FBCD 2000 from all good record shops, in case you're interested….)

by Matt Groening   Issue 3800   23 Nov 1996

* * * * *

In November, the creator of TV's most popular cartoon series of the '90s - Matt Groening - drew a special cover for *Radio Times* featuring his dysfunctional family, *The Simpsons*.

The commercial pressures that made the Christmas season last as long as possible had of course got to *Radio Times*, which for some time now had made the pre-Christmas number a festive one as well. Under Robinson this became a Special Issue in its own right. Her first featured Barry Humphries' terrifying creation Dame Edna Everage in the role of Good Fairy on the cover of the Christmas Preview issue.

Back page advertisement   Issue 3803

And on the back page a sign of things to come - one of a series of gaudily-coloured full-page advertisements for Britain's fifth terrestrial television channel, due to launch the following year.

Issue 3803   14 Dec 1996

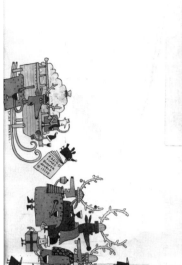

Envelope by Spike Gerrell

Cover by Mick Brownfield
Issue 3804
21 Dec 1996

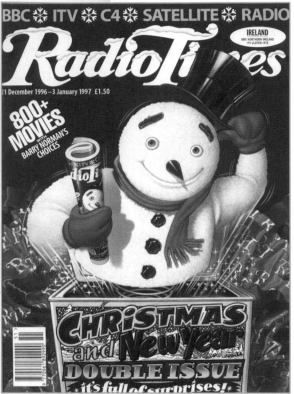

Robinson's first Christmas edition - with a cover, as usual, by Mick Brownfield - was labelled as 'full of surprises'. The first surprise was reserved for subscribers who received their copies in the post - they dropped through the letterbox in an envelope specially designed by Spike Gerrell.

The surprises included one of the new printing tricks - an HMV £1 record gift voucher stuck with removable gum to an advertisement page, an innovation of which *Radio Times* had already made considerable use. There were 18 pages of movie previews tied to an imaginative promotion for TDK Video cassettes which, under the tagline "Some Things Never Age", printed full-page portraits of Tina Turner, Raquel Welch and Britt Ekland on three consecutive right-hand pages.

Naturally there was a 24-page Holiday supplement, and all of the regular columnists including Alan Titchmarsh who had taken over the *Gardening* page from Geoff Hamilton. And of course there was the 124-clue Prize Crossword - with a complete computer system to be won.

Throughout 1997 much use was made of the 'half-cover' with a perforated removable half-page flap carrying promotional advertising covering the left-hand part of the cover. The first promotion of the year offered a free copy from a range of pre- recorded BBC videotapes in exchange for a number of tokens printed in *RT* over several weeks.

The film pages were amongst the most popular of *Radio Times* features. These were given more space in 1997. Usually occupying fourteen pages, they were always arranged to face as many full-page advertisements as was decently possible. A films front page was followed by a single page list of the week's TV films and a 'Ten things every fan ought to know' item on a leading star each week. The lead article by Barry Norman - now usually a film star interview - led into a series of previews no longer written by Derek Winnert, but now the work of half a dozen named reviewers. Movies were given star ratings that gave potential viewers a reasonable guide as to what was really good and those that were downright awful.

Where once the broadcasters had stoically refused to give any indication of a film's cinema certification, the advent of satellite movie channels had changed all that. One of the major arguments of the anti-monopoly lobby had been the lack of information about the content of movies on TV. *Cable Guide* had led the way by including in its film listings warnings of strong language, nudity, and violence. As a result *Radio Times* now did the same, and both in the film and billings pages gave the film's video classification (U, Uc, PG, 12, 15 or 18) where it was appropriate. Some films did not carry a certificate - those made especially for television, and some foreign movies.

Barry Norman concluded the feature each week with a page reviewing the week's new cinema releases followed by his daughter Emma's own column reviewing new video releases for sale and rental, with a list of the current top ten in each of these categories and a *My Favourite Videos* panel for a star to pick their own favourites.

All of the listings magazines directed significant resources into their film pages, since these were now the lifeblood of the listings industry, but *Radio Times* devoted more space than any of its rivals to films.

Channel 5 is launched
Issue 3817   29 March 1997

by Ian McKinnell   Issue 3817   1997

Sue Robinson's chance for a complete redesign came at Easter with the launch of Channel 5 making it necessary to revamp the programme pages anyway. On Ian McKinnell's cover a chick perches precariously on a chocolate egg.

Much of the new-look was purely cosmetic, with changes to the headings and layout. Robinson described it as "a good shake, tidied up the pages, polished our heirlooms (aren't John Peel and Polly Toynbee looking lovely?)". This pair was now brought forward to immediately follow the opening *This Week* feature. The last column of each of the opening pages was occupied by *News and Notes*, which was, of course, a sort of great grandniece of *Both Sides of the Microphone*.

LATE NIGHT

⑤ CHANNEL 5

9.00pm Beyond reason: Stephanie Slater (Gina McKee) was the victim of a ruthless kidnapper

6.00pm This Is 5!
A host of stars introduce Channel 5's programming.
Rptd at 5.30am Stereo 1855498
◆ The view on Channel 5: p 20

6.30 Family Affairs
New soap opera about three generations of the Hart family. The Harts gather for Easter.
Written by Keith Temple, Stuart Morris
Producer Morag Bain; Director Steve Goldie; For cast see Wed 12.30pm
Repeated tomorrow 12.30pm
Stereo Subtitled 1839450

7.00 Two Little Boys
A film revealing the childhood influences that shaped the lives of Labour leader Tony Blair and Prime Minister John Major.
Director Chris Jeans Stereo 7768081

8.00 Hospital!
A comedy special about a brilliant young brain surgeon set in an anarchic hospital.
Dr Jim Nightingale........GREG WISE
Harley Benson.....................BOB PECK
Dickie Beaumont......HYWEL BENNETT
Dr Ralph Crosby..............MARK HEAP
Victoria Barking.........HAYDN GWYNNE
Sister Muriel....................CELIA IMRIE
With Claire Rayner, Julian Clary, Alexei Sayle, Nicholas Parsons, Martin Clunes.
Written by Laurie Rowley; Director John Henderson; Producer Sue Vertue
Stereo Subtitled 7968289

9.00 Beyond Fear
Drama based on the true story of estate agent Stephanie Slater, who was kidnapped by Michael Sams.
Stephanie Slater.............GINA MCKEE
Michael Sams........ SYLVESTER MCCOY
Warren Slater...............JAMES GRANT
Betty Slater.............. JUDITH ANTHONY
Jo Fennimore........... KATE MCGEEVER
DS Anne Woolley.........SALLY ROGERS
Supt Clarke....................BOB MASON
DS Steve McBride...... IAIN ROGERSON
Written by Don Shaw; Producer Jenny Wilkes; Director Jill Green
Stereo Subtitled 9385740

10.30 The Jack Docherty Show
Late-night chat and comedy.
Stereo 2546059

11.10 The Comedy Store Special
Stand-up acts and interviews.
Stereo 9629295

11.40 Turnstyle
Analysis of the weekend's sport.
Stereo 7311059

12.10am Live and Dangerous
Including a preview of the new US major league baseball season. Stereo 27636306

5.30—6.00am This Is 5!
Shown at 6pm Stereo 4643851

Su
Sunday 30 March Easter Day

Robinson introduced a handful of new, very short featurettes which would be scattered around the pages, including *Buried Treasure* - 'a weekly gem unearthed from the TV schedules'; and *Out There - sci-fi news from the small screen*. Six pages of *People* dealt with the antics of sundry TV folk and included Andrew Duncan's detailed interviews as well as *Everybody's Talking About....* which was really an extended caption for a full-page photograph of a topical star. *Questionnaire* put a bundle of stock questions each week to another TV 'person'.

The regular columnists continued - minus antiques and sci-fi, and the 'children's' page was now restyled as a 'family' page. "We've put a few things away and placed a few new ones on display" was how Robinson described this.

The TV programme pages were redesigned to create an extra column for Channel 5. The evening pair of pages now had ten columns which were laid out in this way: Column 1 was devoted to 'Other Regions' - in some editions this included a bit of space each day, depending on how many regional variations there were; in other editions the space was used for billings for the complete programmes from a smaller ITV region or channels like S4C or RTÉ. BBC1 occupies columns 2 and 3; BBC2 got 4 and 5; ITV was on 6 and 7; Channel 4 on 8 and 9; and Channel 5 got the last column to itself.

On the satellite pages, besides the hour-by-hour movie guide, Sky 1 and 2, Bravo, UK Gold, Granada Plus, Discovery and four sports channels benefitted from detailed billings and VideoPlus+™ codes, whilst another dozen channels were listed with times and titles only. The gelignite-loaded radio pages, Sue Robinson wisely left well alone! The cover price was now increased to 75p - "our first increase in 15 months".

REVIEW

Alison Graham

And at the back a real innovation. After 74 years of previewing programmes, *Radio Times* had never reviewed them on a regular basis. Now Alison Graham was given a weekly page to give her (often very) frank opinions on the week's TV highlights, and Roland White the same for radio.

Free BBC books (collect more tokens) were on offer in April, the month of a General Election. This time instead of a 16-page booklet, a gatefold pull-out guide to the Election studio with the usual maps showing the marginals to watch out for.

In May, *Radio Times* joined the gathering band of publications that made themselves available electronically to users of the Internet. On Thursday 5th June 1997, *Radio Times* went online as the first television listings publication in the UK to launch its own site - http://www.radiotimes.beeb.com.

Readers could customise their own listings pages to give just their favourite channels, or display their favourite genre of programming. Choices could be highlighted and 'dumped' into an individual daily diary of 'must-see' programmes. Andrew Duncan's weekly interviews could be heard as well as seen. Readers could take part in instant voting on 'happening issues'.

But most exciting of all, the information could be constantly updated, so last-second programme changes could be accommodated. No pages to print or paper to distribute by train or vans. Just a click of the mouse and *RT* was on-screen!

One of the first occasions upon which the updated online *RT* came into its own was on the morning of Sunday 31st August 1997, when the world awoke to find that its favourite Princess - Diana, Princess of Wales - had been killed in a profoundly shocking road accident in Paris.

The resulting major changes to television and radio programming - not just on the BBC but all the UK's services - could only be accurately dealt with by an online *Radio Times*.

Diana's visit to Angola focused world attention on land mines

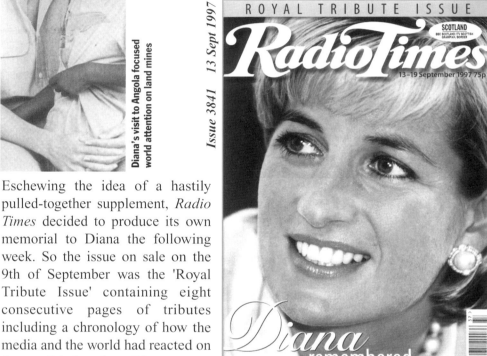

Issue 3841   13 Sept 1997

Eschewing the idea of a hastily pulled-together supplement, *Radio Times* decided to produce its own memorial to Diana the following week. So the issue on sale on the 9th of September was the 'Royal Tribute Issue' containing eight consecutive pages of tributes including a chronology of how the media and the world had reacted on that terrible last day of August.

Photograph by John Stillwell

The simple cover featured a close-up photograph of Diana by John Stillwell of the Press Association.

Issue 3840   6 Sept 1997   Scotland

The Princess of Wales made one more cover appearance in June the following year when her brother gave a television interview.

*   *   *   *   *

A different kind of election was held in September - the referenda to decide whether or not Scotland and Wales would have their own parliament. The Scottish referendum was held on 11th September, the Welsh a week later. Suitably devolved covers should have been the order of the day. But although the Scotland edition boasted a saltire on its cover, the Welsh edition the following week carried the tribute photograph of Diana, Princess of Wales.

Rewind

4–10 September 1938

That famous trio Will Hay, Moore Mariott and Graham Moffatt broadcast a radio adaptation of part of their forthcoming film *Old Bones of the River*...A reader wrote to *RT* enthusing about a recent broadcast of the Coronation train's journey: "It was so realistic that we instinctively drew back in our chairs as she thundered through the stations." ML

WHAT YOU WERE WATCHING . . .

5 YEARS AGO
1	Coronation Street
2	EastEnders
3	The Bill
4	Cocoon: the Return
5	Family Fortunes
6	Casualty
7	You Bet!
8	Neighbours
9	Birds of a Feather
10	Take Your Pick

10 YEARS AGO
1	EastEnders
2	Romancing the Stone
3	Coronation Street
4	Beyond the Bermuda Triangle
5	Blind Date
6	Taggart
6=	The Last Frontier
8	News (Sat ITN)
9	The Two of Us
10	Bread

20 YEARS AGO
1	Bruce Forsyth/Generation Game
2	Starsky and Hutch
3	Winner Takes All
4	The Benny Hill Show
5	Survival Special
6	The New Avengers
7	The World of Pam Ayres
8	Crossroads
8=	The Dick Emery Show
10	Van Der Valk

◆ For what you're watching now, turn to page 124

Issue 3840

In September, Sue Robinson tried another innovative idea. Perhaps for the first time in publishing a magazine was made available with a variety of different front covers for the same issue, allowing readers to choose the one they wanted.

The phenomenon celebrated in this very special way? *The Teletubbies* of course! These four furry creatures had, in a very short time, become the biggest children's programme on the box, so *RT* printed four different covers each containing a large picture of one of the tubbies. Tinky Winky, Laa-Laa, Dipsy and Po each had their own fans - and their own cover!

Radio Times - whose circulation evidently benefitted from this novel form of promotion - repeated the idea several times. In July 1999, to coincide with the release of the new *Star Wars* film, it offered four of the film's stars as alternative covers; in October 1999 it promoted the BBC Television series *Walking with Dinosaurs* with four fold-out covers, each featuring a different dino - and in June 2000 *The Simpsons* got the alternative-cover treatment with one each for Homer, Marge & Maggie, Bart and Lisa.

Tinky Winky
& Laa Laa
Issue 3843
27 Sept 1997

The Simpsons *by Matt Groening*   *Alternative covers*   **Page 3**   **Issue 3982   17 June 2000**

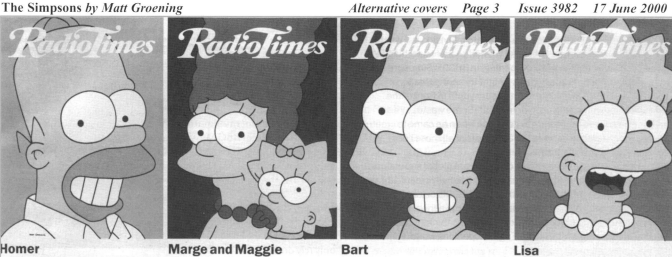

Homer   **Marge and Maggie**   **Bart**   **Lisa**

Issue 3850
15 Nov 1997

75 years of the BBC warranted a celebration - with the cast of TV's *Have I Got News For You* in evening dress, seated in front of a classic BBC microphone. A 16-page A4 pull-out naturally included some classic pictures from *RT*s past (including the *Teletubbies*).

The autumn offer was a free 3-hour videotape. (*More* Tokens. Gotta collect tokens.) And out came the gold ink for a special issue to celebrate the Wedding Anniversary of Her Majesty the Queen and HRH The Duke of Edinburgh. The 156-page *Radio Times* (somewhat over-stuffed by the inclusion of a 36-page British Home Stores Xmas Supplement) searched out four other couples who had married in the same year.

Devolution (both Scotland and Wales had voted in favour of their own elected assemblies) meant that Scotland, Wales and Northern Ireland more often followed a different path to the basic London version of BBC ONE and BBC TWO. A case in point was the *Big Night of Sport* - a themed night on BBC TWO Scotland with over six hours of special programmes, causing BBC TWO Scotland to deviate from the network programmes from 4.15pm until half past one the following morning.

This really begged its own cover, and *Radio Times* picked one of the programmes - *A Question of Scottish Sport* - for a front page that featured 'Sport' regulars Sue Barker and Aly McCoist along with Scotland skipper Rob Wainwright.

Issue 3854
13 Dec 1997
Scotland
edition

And for Christmas, a gold half-cover cut in a cracker shape that talked telephone numbers (**900** films, **230** pages, **200** TVs to be won, **5** Spice Girls interviewed by Andrew Duncan) and opened to reveal the whole of Kevin Hauff's unusual Father Christmas. Hauff also designed the 'page embellishments' for the Double Issue that came complete with its £1 HMV Gift Token and a reworking of the previous year's TDK advertisement featuring Raquel Welch.

Both the front cover and the next four pages were printed on very heavy paper, ensuring the rigidity of the 230 pages for the entire festive fortnight.

*   *   *   *   *

One of the major television awards ceremonies of each year was organised by the British Academy of Film and Television Arts - otherwise known as BAFTA. Members of the Academy normally voted for the recipients of these awards, but in 1998, *Radio Times* readers were given their chance to vote in a new category - The Lew Grade Audience Award.

The creation of this award, and *RT*'s association with it, meant that the BAFTAs would now enjoy substantial publicity in the high-circulation magazine, which could offer prizes of tickets to the awards ceremony for a handful of winning readers. *Radio Times* did all right out of the deal as well, with the publicity that it got from sponsoring television coverage of the ceremony.

London edition

In June, both England and Scotland qualified for the World Cup in Brazil. Naturally this meant two different covers - both of them gatefolds. The English version showed the BBC's commentary team seated on the bench in the players' dressing room, while for Scotland a saltire-adorned fan in a crowd of Scotland supporters posed the question, "Who's afraid of Brazil?"

Issue 3878
6 June 1998

Scotland edition

The rescheduling of network programmes in the Nations (as the BBC called them) frequently led to problems for *Radio Times,* especially when the carefully-chosen colour pictures for the billings pages turned out to be for programmes being shown on a different day in Scotland, Northern Ireland or Wales.

Sometimes a picture would appear atop the programme pages (or worse, the BBC CHOICE pages) with the cryptic caption 'Not Scotland'. But worst of all (fortunately very rarely) a programme chosen for the *RT* cover would not be shown in one of the Nations. This had happened occasionally in the '60s on the BBC, and more often on ITV. *TV Times* in its monochrome days often produced a variety of local covers and *RT* would - as we have seen - do the same.

The problem with colour was its 'lead time' and the substantial costs involved in changing colour pictures because of the more complex printing process.

A rare example of this happening in the '90s appeared in July 1998 when BBC ONE's comedy series *The Hello Girls* starring former *EastEnders* actress Letitia Dean was chosen for the cover, and tied to a feature article by Sue Arnold about life during the '60s, the period in which the series was set. (This feature included a revealing photograph of Sue Arnold herself aged 16!)

Then BBC Scotland 'timeshifted' *The Hello Girls* to make room for a local health series. Unfortunately it was rescheduled to begin the following week making a cover picture irrelevant.

So *RT* led the Scottish edition with photographs of the wedding of singer and star of the series *The Cruise*, Jane McDonald, who also featured in that issue. What was unusual about this arrangement was that the separate Scottish cover was not for a Scottish programme!

North West edition   **Issue 3882**
                 4 July 1998

Women's Special

Scotland edition

Sven Arnstein could always be relied upon to produce stunning cover portraits, and did so when asked to photograph Charlie Dimmock, who had unexpectedly found herself pin-up star of gardening series *Ground Force.* Arnstein's picture was different, if not quite original....

Photo by Sven Arnstein
Issue 3887   8 Aug 1998

Radio Times had never been quite sure what to do about children. Assorted attempts to cater for the younger readers had generally petered out, and the innovative *Junior Radio Times* had fallen foul of the 1960 revamp.

Assorted cartoon strips came and went, but in 1998 *RT* added the clay-modelled heroes *Wallace and Gromit* (from Nick Park's Oscar-winning animation) as 'columnists'. The *Family* feature was revamped to include a 44-part *Wallace & Gromit* strip cartoon, and the pair appeared in true August Bank Holiday (not Scotland) mood on the cover.

Alison Graham's witty and honest style of writing had not only endeared her to readers, but won her a second weekly feature - *Soap and Flannel* which, from September 1998, followed the goings-on in television's soap operas (and radio's *The Archers*) through Graham's cynical eyes. For many it became the first thing to turn to when opening up a new *Radio Times*.

Issue 3890 29 Aug 1998

Photographed together
(L to R)
John Thaw
Julie Goodyear,
Bruce Forsyth,
Desmond Lynam,
Michael Palin,
Amanda Burton,
David Jason,
Nicholas Lyndhurst,
Francesca Annis,
Robert Hardy,
Christopher Timothy
Peter Davidson,
Kate Adie,
Trevor Harrison and* Play School's *Jemima & Big Ted.
On the TV and radio sets:
Morecambe & Wise,
George Clooney,
the cast of **Cathy Come Home** *&* **Hancock's Half-Hour.**

Issue 3894
26 Sept 1998

In September 1998 The Official Organ of the BBC was 75 years old, and its celebratory gatefold cover featured the winners of the readers' *Poll of Honour* - representing the people and programmes that had been voted the greatest of all time.

Copiously illustrated with past covers, thirteen pages looked at the past and future of British Television, complete with a holiday competition to win 75,000 air miles. The *Letters* page was filled with various readers' fond recollections of *RT,* and included greetings from Her Majesty the Queen, who described the anniversary as "...a notable landmark in a publication which has become central to British broadcasting.". Prime Minister, Tony Blair, wrote: "*Radio Times* has willingly undergone modification without losing its essentially British character or its journalistic qualities.".

Various TV stars offered their observations: Helen Mirren (its only nude cover star) appropriately described it as "one of the sexiest of magazines"; Luciano Pavarotti wished everyone at *RT* "*buon compleanno*"; Joanna Lumley said that in her household it was always pronounced "...raddy-o-timmeez as if it were Greek - rather learned, rather fun, rather fab, just like you, dear *Radio Times*".

One reader recalled that writer and broadcaster, Malcolm Muggeridge, had described *RT* as "that compendium of ineptitude" - but comedian Lenny Henry advised the 75-year old to "Go out, paint the town red, find sailors, get arrested and go home happy with a headache."

And squeezed into a little corner of that issue was news of a new book on the work of long-time *RT* illustrator, Eric Fraser.

*   *   *   *   *

At Christmas time *Radio Times* published a unique special edition that wasn't for sale. It was produced for the benefit of staff, particularly those who had recently joined "Britain's Biggest Magazine" - and detailed the history of the magazine along with features on how it was produced, the role of the advertising department and a series of spoof *Letters* which asked a variety of questions about the paper. There was even *My Kind of Day* featuring Naz Flora, one of the Films sub-editors.

This special issue gave a detailed breakdown of the staff in each department necessary to produce the paper.

Special edition   NOT FOR SALE

Features (18) including two assistant editors, four commissioning editors, two researchers, a chief sub-editor and five 'subs' (sub-editors);

Listings (21) Listings editor, six chief subs, fourteen subs;

Films (6) chief sub, four subs and an assistant;

Copy Desk (6) copy assistants;

Art (9) Art Editor, creative editor, designers;

Pictures (9) Pictures Editor, six researchers, two assistants;

Secretaries (5) PAs and secretaries;

Advertising (25) Advertising Director, sales team;

Marketing (13) Marketing Director and team;

Systems (3) computer support team;

Production (9) print and paper liaison team;

...giving a total of 124 people - plus the Editor and Managing Editor.

The Galton and Simpson Radio Playhouse

Radio 4: 11.30am

by Clifford Harper
From issue 3906
19 Dec 1998

Once again 1998 benefitted from two Christmas issues - the pre-Xmas edition of 12th December, and a Double Issue covering the period up to New Year's Day, boasting 1000 film reviews. It featured a cowboy Santa from the pens of Mick Brownfield and lots of gold ink, both on the outside and inside pages (not to mention the now annual HMV voucher!).

*   *   *   *   *

COMIC RELIEF SPECIAL ISSUE

Radio Times

SCOTLAND
BBC SCOTLAND/ITV SCOTTISH
GRAMPIAN/BORDER

6-12 March 1999 79p

Edited by
Victoria Wood

with a littl
help from ..
Dawn French Nick Hanco
Emma Freud Ewan McGreg
Geri Halliwell Richard Curt
Alan Partridge Rowan Atkins
Julie Walters Jancis Robins
and (seriously) Gordon Bro

Issue 3916   6 March 1999

There was a "Guest Editor" for the Comic Relief Special Issue in March 1999 - comedienne Victoria Wood took over Sue Robinson's office for a week: none of the regular features were safe from her. Dawn French replaced John Peel. Richard Curtis seized Polly Toynbee's page. Victoria Wood and Emma Freud penned *Soap and Flannel*; Julie Walters was the subject of the 'Andrea Duncan Interview' (Wood again). Only the Normans (Barry and Emma) were safe.

In producing a newspaper or magazine there is, naturally, a small risk that something that appears in print is no longer appropriate by the time it reaches its readers. In the case of *Radio Times* this was most often a result of programmes being changed at the last minute, but of course sudden death could also render the paper out of date - the deaths of various senior members of the Royal family and Sir Winston Churchill had resulted in changes to the published magazine.

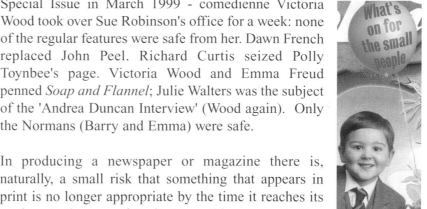

What's on for the small people

Photo by Sven Arnstein Illustration by Jenny Tilden-Wright   Issue 3920   3 April 1999

The deaths of contributors or performers occasionally led to their work unexpectedly appearing posthumously.

But the most horrifying of all possibilities happened in April 1999. Popular presenter Jill Dando - who had appeared on the cover several times - was kitted out in leather gear to promote her new BBC ONE series *The Antiques Inspectors*. Inside, she told *RT*'s William Greaves of her impending marriage and her pleasure at presenting this new series, as well as being asked to host the *Radio Times*-sponsored BAFTA awards two weeks ahead.

As the issue reached newsagents, so did the news of her murder.

Shot on the doorstep of her London flat, the violent and inexplicable nature of her death had a profound effect on her friends, colleagues and the British public at large. Here was a comfortably familiar figure and universally liked personality who, at 38, had read the BBC News and appeared in a whole variety of programmes. Viewers around the country felt they knew her and shared the sense of loss with those for whom that loss was more personal.

Radio Times especially felt the loss. And it dedicated its BAFTA Night feature to Dando. The main colour feature had clearly been prepared prior to her death, and new words from William Greaves fitted at the last minute over the poignant photograph of a smiling Dando.

THE BEST OF BRITISH TV WHO'S UP FOR A BAFTA?

Radio Times

SCOTLAND
BBC SCOTLAND/ITV SCOTTISH
GRAMPIAN/BORDER

24-30 April 1999 79p

VROOO OOOM!

The holiday's over as Dando changes gear

F 472

Jill Dando   Issue 3923   24 April 1999

The *Letters* page was given over to tributes to the star from both the famous and the ordinary reader, with reproductions of the five covers upon which she had appeared. Anna Ford, writing on the day of Dando's death, put what everyone was thinking into words.

> The awful word "murder" keeps swilling around in the mind like a tongue poking at a sore tooth. Why Jill? Why murder? The two are impossibly incongruous.

Sue Robinson recalled seeing Jill a week before she died.

> It was early on Monday morning and most of us weren't quite at our best. Jill, however, was immaculate, elegant and cheery as always. She gave me a hug and lit up the room with her smile.

As reader Peter Lewis put it:

> She was one of my favourite presenters and I shall miss her bright presence on our screens.

*   *   *   *   *

An altogether happier event was the Royal Wedding in June as Prince Edward and Miss Sophie Rhys-Jones were married in St George's Chapel, Windsor. A less formal, lower-profile Royal Wedding than hitherto and the mood was set with a cartoon-style cover by Janet Woolley.

RT devoted a mere four pages to the wedding, and that included a brief look at Royal weddings past. It was a very different approach to the reverential treatment meted out by the *RT* of the '40s and '50s.

by Janet Woolley

Issue 3931   19 June 1999

Photo by Bruce Coleman   Issue 3938   7 Aug 1999

The total eclipse of the sun on 11th August 1999 received extensive coverage on television. *Radio Times* got in on the act with an eclipse cover photographed by Bruce Coleman of Astrophoto, and five pages of features including a detailed timetable of when the eclipse would be seen in 32 towns and cities across the British Isles.

Columnist John Peel turned sixty in September, and BBC TWO devoted a whole night to the event - so *RT* had a legitimate excuse to present its long-running writer with a special cover.

Issue 3941
28 Aug 1999

*   *   *   *   *

It was time for a little redesign. In September 1999, Robinson's team indulged in the annual ritual of makeover. The *Letters* pages were brought to the very front of the paper.

Wrote The Editor:

> To make the magazine even easier to use, we've organised it into four sections - all the articles at the front, followed by films, television and radio listings - and signposted the days consistently and clearly. For the many of you who are light, selective viewers and listeners we've devoted more space to our choices of the day and created one-page snapshots of the week's best films, TV and radio.

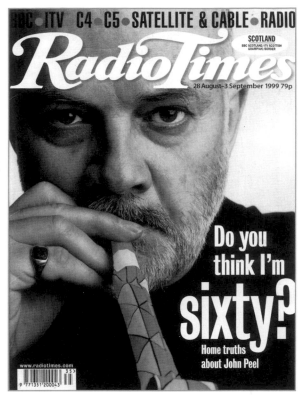

Pasted on to an advertisement page was a folded leaflet containing the BBC's *Promise to Viewers and Listeners* (why it couldn't have been printed as a simple page is not at all obvious). The regular contributors' photographs atop their pages were renewed, a weekly *Webwatch* feature checked out new websites, and Jonathan Ross (now presenting *Film '99* following Barry Norman's departure to Sky TV) was given his own *Movie Moment* column, although the Norman family (father and daughter) continued to write.

The programme pages (TV and radio) were restyled - smaller headings, smaller type and therefore more billing information, and a narrower column for the Channel 5 programme listings. The advent of digital television (both on satellite and terrestrially) meant more viewers for the additional channels, and more of these were now listed - including some new regional digital channels, such as BBC CHOICE which was available in versions to match each of the four nations, and ITV2 which appeared in Scotland as S2 and Northern Ireland as You 2. This meant *Radio Times* had to produce regional versions of the satellite pages as well.

The *This Week's TV* and *This Week's Radio* introductory pages were a return to the layout of the mid '50s, with the Puzzles and 'Next Week' panel separating the TV and radio pages.

A prize competition featured on the half-cover, and a full-page advertisement at the back featured the new tagline...

The best thing on tv.

The front-page oval that had identified the regional edition (with description of which local BBC & ITV areas it covered) was gone; the paper returned to a short bold-type descriptor in the top right-hand corner. The size of the barcode on the front was reduced, and the drop shadow eliminated from the masthead.

This was an issue that also contained a *Radio Times* advertising supplement. These features - generally 32 pages A4 - branded as 'The *Radio Times* Selection' were in fact produced by Selective Marketplace Ltd who provided this customised service to a variety of users.

Photograph by Lord Snowdon
Issue 3952   13 Nov 1999

Silver ink (probably every bit as expensive as the gold...) was used for a special cover signalling the return of *Doctor Who*. In fact it was a series of repeats being shown on BBC TWO, but it gave *Radio Times* the excuse it needed to put a picture of a Dalek on the cover. Well, not just any old picture. Lord Snowdon took this one for a commemorative postage stamp.

Christmas 1999 was the last of the decade, and as far as the broadcasters were concerned, the last of the century. Celebrations to mark the new millennium were unprecedented, and *RT* allowed itself no less than *three* special issues.

Soap and flannel

Alison Graham on romances, affairs of the heart and close encounters of an absurd kind

by Janet Woolley   Issue 3952

The pre-Christmas issue featured Nicholas Lyndhurst as Uriah Heep in *David Copperfield*. *Radio Times* risked revocation of its Artistic Licence by picturing Heep studying the following week's *Radio Times*, itself featuring an unusual design by Matilda Harrison of an angel gazing into a crystal ball. The first week of January continued the same design.

by Matilda Harrison

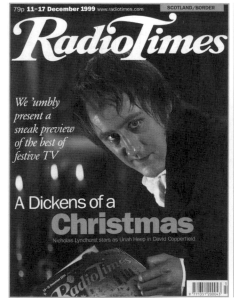

Issue 3956   11 Dec 1999

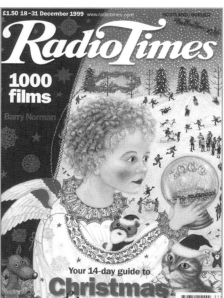

Issue 3957   18 Dec 1999

Issue 3958   31 Dec 1999

A new advertising trick in the first of these three issues was the insertion of an adhesive "Post-It®" note, promoting Universal Pictures home video releases. This was stuck to page 3, while the inevitable HMV voucher attached itself to page 35.

The Double Issue was 228 pages, with glossy covers of such heavy paper that it was almost card and (as if that wasn't big enough) a bound-in 12-page supplement for Renault cars. Regular columnists were pictured in festive attire, there were 24 pages of Holiday ads, and the TV listings ended with a summary of programmes for the first few hours of New Year's Day. The following issue duplicated quite a lot of information; repeating all the listings for Friday 31st December, covering BBC ONE's marathon 28-hour programme, *2000 today.*

Plate 12b

DRESS SHOE
ELTON JOHN *circa* 1974

* * * * *

Issue 3965
19 Feb 2000

EastEnders celebrated its 15th anniversary with a foldout cover of stars, present and past, and five pages of memories inside penned, naturally, by soap queen Alison Graham.

Photograph by
James Johnson
Issue 3987
22 July 2000

And yet another Royal Souvenir Issue for the 100th Birthday of Queen Elizabeth, the Queen Mother. A striking hand-coloured cover photograph from a 1907 issue of the *Illustrated London News* showed Elizabeth Bowes-Lyon as a little girl and a special 16-page A4 picture supplement, much of it written by BBC Royal correspondent Jennie Bond, was produced "in association with Royal Mail" who took advertising at the bottom of each page to illustrate Royal stamps of the past. An interesting collaboration.

Sue Robinson wrote of her return from a *Radio Times* cruise - another intriguing marketing idea which had taken 100 readers (who had paid dearly for the privilege) from New York to England on the QE2 in the company of Robinson, Barry Norman, Delia Smith, John Peel and Alan Hansen. Delia Smith described it as "the best and longest party ever."

Editing, and writing for *The Radio Times* has its rewards!

Elizabeth Bowes-Lyon, 1907
from the Illustrated London News: Camera Press
Issue 3988   29 July 2000

CHAPTER FOURTEEN
...And Beyond

Knowing when to leave is - according to some - the secret of success. Judging that twenty years with *Radio Times* was sufficient, and having for the third time been awarded the accolade of 'Editor of the Year' by the British Society of Magazine Editors, Robinson handed back the keys to the toy shop on 22nd December 2000.

An offer to work for her long-time friend Delia Smith on a variety of her publishing ventures - including Sainsbury's own magazine and a new range of books - was too tempting to refuse.

But with yet another makeover planned for the Spring of 2001 who was to lead *Radio Times* into the twenty-first century? Leaping back into the vacant editorial chair Nick Brett agreed to return - to fill the gap until a suitable successor could be found - to the role he had perhaps reluctantly handed over to Sue Robinson four years earlier.

There will be more chapters to write in this history, but my printers cannot wait for them. This is where - some 4,000 issues from its beginning - my version of the story will have to end.

IT'S OUR 4000th TODAY!

A right Royle 156-page edition, including an extended 17-page film special launching the *Radio Times Guide to Films*

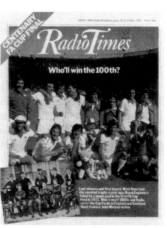

1st issue – 28 September 1923, 2d. Included an informative "What's in the air?" introductory column and "gossip about the artistes"

1000 – 29 November 1942, 2d. *RT* soldiers on, reflecting current events with a feature on the radio series *Transport Goes to War*

2000 – 10 March 1962, 5d. *The Six Proud Walkers*, a TV crime mystery starring Lana Morris and Tony Britton, made the front cover

3000 – 9 May 1981, 20p. A big football week as BBC TV and radio celebrated the centenary FA cup final year

Issue 4000
21 Oct 2000

With the rising number of competitors and the falling circulation, how much longer can there be *Radio Times*? A historian rarely rejects the opportunity to offer his opinion on the future. But few such predictions are of merit, since it is much easier to interpret the hard evidence of the past.

Some things are clear. In an age when new players are constantly entering all fields the value of a trusted brand name increases dramatically. *Radio Times* is without a doubt still the most trusted brand name in broadcast listings.

Indeed, Joyce Taylor, Managing Director of Discovery Networks Europe, giving the Royal Television Society's 2000 Campbell Swinton lecture, ventured that the proliferation of channels will almost certainly demand trusted guides to forage into the ether on our behalf. It may well be that *RT* with its established reputation will have an even bigger role to play.

A fall in the popularity of printed programme guides is balanced by an increase in the various forms of EPG - Electronic Programme Guide. The first form of EPG was teletext, and viewers have become accustomed to consulting Ceefax or Teletext for the most up-to-date programme listings.

When cable television began in the UK, most operators offered a channel devoted to updated listings as the most accurate way of telling their viewers what was happening on a multitude of channels.

Pundits predicted that the introduction of digital television would spawn a new generation of EPGs provided by the operators of the digital platforms - in other words the cable, satellite or digital terrestrial operators who not only determine who will and won't have a place on their systems but may chose to promote some channels more vigorously than others.

But as always the development of new technology is determined by its users , not its progenitors. Those who saw the platform-related EPG as the future reckoned without the Internet. The BBC's website is one of the most popular in the world, and **www.radiotimes.com** is now a familiar place for many to find not only the listings that can be adapted to suit the unique requirements of each reader, but also the place to listen to Andrew Duncan's weekly interviews, or to study the film previews in more detail than would be possible with a *Radio Times* even twice the size of the paper version.

The video recorder's quarter century of success is also now being challenged as tape-free hard disk-based recording systems enter the marketplace. One such system - *TiVo* - downloads accurate and updated programme listings daily via a telephone line, and also offers its subscribers the *Radio Times* 'Choice' programmes each day in a form that allows users to record those that interest them by merely clicking on the appropriate electronic *RT* page. New technology is wise to associate itself with such a trusted brand; *RT* understands the importance of expanding its outlets to include such innovations.

"It's *Radio Times*, Jim, but not as we know it!"

Future historians will probably have to rummage through old computer files and archaic hard disk formats to research their e-books. I wish them luck - but I suspect they will not have nearly as much fun as I have had sitting on my basement floor for weeks on end, surrounded by mountainous piles of dusty old newsprint.

Now you must please excuse me.

The Christmas 2000 issue of *Radio Times* has just popped through my letterbox. *Harry Potter* has ousted Santa to be on the cover of its 204 pages, and I can't wait to read it.....

by Mary Grandpré
Issue 2009
23 Dec 2000

241

RADIO TIMES CIRCULATION

Year	Circulation	Year	Circulation
1923	n/a	1960	6,784,487
1924	501,739	1961	n/a
1925	738,478	1962	5,461,320
1926	735,936	1963	5,254,774
1927	851,657	1964	4,646,315
1928	977,589	1965	4,359,978
1929	1,147,571	1966	4,343,595
1930	1,334,065	1967	4,265,640
1931	1,576,758	1968	3,955,996
1932	1,826,793	1969	3,883,815
1933	1,962,040	1970	3,595,767
1934	2,155,371	1971	3,406,466
1935	2,455,027	1972	3,674,932
1936	2,628,756	1973	3,997,061
1937	2,823,020	1974	3,727,021
1938	2,882,352	1975	3,479,856
1939	2,595,721	1976	3,552,527
1940	2,302,399	1977	3,698,095
1941	2,272,422	1978	3,777,874
1942	2,718,654	1979	3,666,774
1943	3,179,327	1980*	3,487,592
1944	3,679,859	1981*	3,469,741
1945	4,058,675	1982	3,385,354
1946	5,202,937	1983	3,288,984
1947	6,271,563	1984	3,254,836
1948	7,090,424	1985	3,143,103
1949	7,765,791	1986	3,150,253
1950	8,100,121	1987	3,127,188
1951	7,880,718	1988	3,122,634
1952	7,717,501	1989	2,999,374
1953	7,903,969	1990	2,831,771
1954	8,223,178	1991	1,761,668
1955	8,801,895	1992	1,577,755
1956	8,591,378	1993	1,494,087
1957	8,259,370	1994	1,452,611
1958	7,953,559	1995	1,448,807
1959	7,214,725	1996	1,406,139
		1997	1,403,211
		1998	1,400,213
		1999	1,363,772,

* The figures for 1980 and 1981 do not include the Christmas issue which was audited separately.
SOURCE:
1924-1934 BBC Publications
1935-1999 Audit Bureau of Circulations

Christmas issues

Year	Circulation
1980	9,314,775
1981	9,456,660
1982	n/a
1983	n/a
1984	10,050,834
1985	10,283,911
1986	10,617,421
1987	11,057,818
1988	11,220,666
1989	11,073,139
1990	10,601,244
1991	4,810,013
1992	4,146,396
1993	3,731,888
1994	3,458,767
1995	3,366,201
1996	3,064,643
1997	3,043,124
1998	3,045,413
1999**	2,870,000

**estimated

SOUTH WITH SHACKLETON
Unpublished issue 3100
9 April 1983

UNPUBLISHED EDITIONS
In its 78-year history there have been only 11 editions of *RADIO TIMES* which have failed to appear

Date	Reason
14 May 1926	General Strike
21 February 1947	Fuel crisis
28 February 1947	" "
8 September 1950	Printing dispute
13 October 1950	" "
20 October 1950	" "
27 October 1950	" "
1 August 1981	" "
2 April 1983	" "
9 April 1983	" "
3 December 1983	" "

EDITIONS IN VARIANT FORMAT
due to printing disputes or operational difficulties

1 July 1949 - LONDON edition printed by the *Daily Graphic*

15 September 1950 - NINE DAY ISSUE covering 15-23 September

3 November 1950 - NINE DAY ISSUE covering 3-11 November

1956: the following 6 issues were printed in broadsheet format in Paris:
24 February
2 March
9 March
16 March
23 March
30 March

1978: the following issues were issued with monochrome covers:
11 November
18 November
25 November

BIBLIOGRAPHY

The sources for quotes, etc - apart from the major use of back number of *Radio Times* itself - are as follows:

PREFACE:
Briggs (Professor Asa) **THE BIRTH OF BROADCASTING** - OUP, 1961

1
Briggs (Professor Asa) **THE BIRTH OF BROADCASTING** OUP, 1961
Eckersley (P. P.) **THE POWER BEHIND THE MICROPHONE** Jonathan Cape, 1941
McIntyre (Ian) **THE EXPENSE OF GLORY** Harper Collins, 1993
Twisk (Russell), ed. **RADIO TIMES 50th ANNIVERSARY SOUVENIR** BBC Publications, 1973

2
BBC HANDBOOK, 1965 BBC Publications, 1964
Burrows (Arthur R.) **THE STORY OF BROADCASTING** Cassell and Company Ltd, 1924
Driver (David), compiler **THE ART OF RADIO TIMES** BBC Publications, 1981
Gorham (Maurice) **SOUND AND FURY** Percival Marshall, 1948
Linklater (Andro) **THE CODE OF LOVE** Weidenfeld & Nicolson, 2000
Twisk (Russell), ed **RADIO TIMES 50th ANNIVERSARY SOUVENIR** BBC Publications, 1973

3
Briggs (Professor Asa) **THE GOLDEN AGE OF WIRELESS** OUP, 1965
Gorham (Maurice) **SOUND AND FURY** Percival Marshall, 1948
McArthur (Tom) and Peter Waddell **VISION WARRIOR** Scottish Falcon, 1990
McIntyre (Ian) **THE EXPENSE OF GLORY** Harper Collins, 1993
Twisk (Russell), ed. **RADIO TIMES 50th ANNIVERSARY SOUVENIR** BBC Publications, 1973
Viney (Kenneth R.) 'The History of the *Radio Times*' "World's Press News", 18 Dec 1947
Waterlow & Sons **THE PRINTING OF RADIO TIMES** 1936

4
Author's interviews with Hilary Cope Morgan and Grace Harbinson, MBE - 1st June 2000

5
Author's interview with Hilary Cope Morgan - 1st June 2000

6
BBC HANDBOOK 1957 BBC Publications, 1956
Driver (David), compiler **THE ART OF RADIO TIMES** BBC Publications, 1981

Usherwood (R. D.), ed. **DRAWING FOR RADIO TIMES** Bodley Head 1961
Twisk (Russell), ed. **RADIO TIMES 50th ANNIVERSARY SOUVENIR** BBC Publications, 1973
TV MIRROR - 29 Aug 1953
TV TIMES - 20 Sep 1955
THE INDEPENDENT - 26 Jan 2000
THE TIMES - 11 Feb 2000
Author's interviews with Hilary Cope Morgan and Grace Harbinson, MBE - 1st June 2000

7
Usherwood (R. D.), ed. **DRAWING FOR RADIO TIMES** Bodley Head 1961
TV TIMES - 20 Dec 1963
THE VIEWER - 21 Dec 1963

8
Twisk (Russell), ed. **RADIO TIMES 50TH ANNIVERSARY SOUVENIR** BBC Publications, 1973
THE SUNDAY TIMES 10 August 1969
Author's interview with Hilary Cope Morgan - 1st June 2000

9
Driver (David), compiler **THE ART OF RADIO TIMES** BBC Publications, 1981

10
Deayton (Angus) and Geoffrey Perkins *RADIO ACTIVE* Sphere Books, 1986
REPORT ON THE POLICIES AND PRACTICES OF THE BBC AND ITP LTD OF LIMITING THE PUBLICATION BY OTHERS OF ADVANCE PROGRAMME INFORMATION Monopolies and Mergers Commission, 1985
TV TIMES - 8 Nov 1980
SBEC - 1 Nov 1982
TV CHOICE - 5 Nov 1982
RESTRICTED VISION TV Listings Campaign, 1988
CABLE GUIDE **Advertising Dummy** - 1986

11
BROADCASTING ACT 1990 Chapter 42 HMSO 1989
RESTRICTED VISION TV Listings Campaign, 1988
THE RIMES - 14th Sep 1988
CLYDE GUIDE - 28th Sep 1978
RADIO GUIDE - 1st Apr 1976

12
Driver (David), compiler **THE ART OF RADIO TIMES** BBC Publications, 1981
TIME OUT - 27 Feb 1991
TV TIMES - various, from Feb 1991
WHAT'S ON TV - various from Feb 1991
TV PLUS - various, March 1991
TV QUICK - various, from April 1991
CTV TIMES - 15 Oct 1991

13, 14
no references

Tony Currie has held a  passionate interest in broadcasting since, aged eleven, setting up his attic radio station in 1963. Ten years later his was the first voice on Radio Clyde. Then, after twelve years as an announcer with STV, he joined the Cable Authority as Controller of Programmes, overseeing the rapid development of satellite and cable channels in the 80s.

He then went on to run a cable TV station for Asians living in Britain; set up Ireland's first satellite channel, TARA TV, as its first Director of Programmes; his consultancy work has included a variety of projects from the UK's first secondary school radio station to the launch of commercial broadcasting in Kiev; and on-air broadcasting for TV and radio stations from C-SPAN to Radio Northsea International, and most recently BBC Scotland.

As a journalist he has contributed to all the major braodcasting publications including *Broadcast, The Listener, Radio Times, TV Times, The Guardian, Times Educational Supplement* and *Television*.

His first book, *A Concise History of British Television 1930 - 2000,* was published in March 2000.

PRINTED AND BOUND IN GREAT BRITAIN BY MASLANDS LTD., TIVERTON, DEVON.